A POETRY PRECISE AND FREE

A Poetry
Precise and Free

Selected Madrigals of Guarini

Nicholas R. Jones

University of Michigan Press
Ann Arbor

Copyright © 2018 by Nicholas R. Jones

Published in the United States of America by the
University of Michigan Press
Manufactured in the United States of America
⊗ Printed on acid-free paper

2021   2020   2019   2018   4   3   2   1

A CIP catalog record for this book is available from the British Library.

Library of Congress Cataloging-in-Publication Data

Names: Guarini, Battista, 1538–1612 author. | Jones, Nicholas R., 1946– translator. |
    Guarini, Battista, 1538–1612. Poems. Selections. English. | Guarini, Battista,
    1538–1612. Poems. Selections.
Title: A poetry precise and free : selected madrigals of Guarini / Nicholas R. Jones
    [translator].
Description: Ann Arbor : University of Michigan Press, 2018. | Includes
    bibliographical references and index. |
Identifiers: LCCN 2017054859 (print) | LCCN 2017060300 (ebook) | ISBN
    9780472123612 (e-book) | ISBN 9780472130726 (hardcover : alk. paper)
Classification: LCC PQ4626 (ebook) | LCC PQ4626 .A2   2018 (print) |
    DDC 852/.5—dc23
LC record available at https://lccn.loc.gov/2017054859

Cover credit: Sebastiano Florigherio (1500–1543), *A Musical Entertainment*. Bavaria, Staatsgemäldesammlungen. Photo © Blauel Gnamm—ARTOTHEK.

ACKNOWLEDGMENTS

The impetus for *A Poetry Precise and Free* came from singing Monteverdi's settings of Guarini's madrigals in a small chorus some years ago. I realized that to perform them effectively, I and the other singers would benefit from a poetic translation in order to appreciate the meanings, forms, and affects of the texts. Gradually, the project got bigger. As I learned how rich and extensive Guarini's output was, I began to collect his madrigals more systematically and to develop protocols for translating them. Eventually, there were enough to make a book. The project began in 2001, when I lived in Berkeley, California, on sabbatical from Oberlin College, and was completed sixteen years later, also in Berkeley, where my wife and I moved after my retirement from Oberlin.

Oberlin students Tammela Platt and Chen Liang provided research assistance, insight, and enthusiasm at crucial stages in this project. Another Oberlin student, Christine Jay, sang three of these madrigals at Oberlin College, accompanied by my wife and my longtime friend Dan Hathaway. Professor Alison Cornish at the University of Michigan read and discussed with me some of Guarini's poems and my early translations of them. My colleagues at Oberlin have been extraordinary in their enthusiasm and advice; among the many whom I consulted about this project are Andaleeb Banta, David Breitman, Jed Deppman, Andria Derstine, John Hobbs, Wendy Hyman, Charles McGuire, Liliana Milkova, Stiliana Milkova, Steven Plank, Peter Swendsen, Thomas van Nortwick, and David Young. I would never have ventured upon these translations without having sung Monteverdi and other Renaissance masters with John Ferris at Harvard and Carol Longsworth and Marci Alegant at Oberlin.

Oberlin College has been generous in its support of this and other projects through the four decades I taught there: in particular, a sabbatical leave in 2001–2 allowed me to begin exploring and translating these madrigals, and an H. H. Powers Travel Grant in 2009 let me experience firsthand the court cities of northern Italy, where Guarini lived and worked. The staff of the Oberlin College Libraries and the Bancroft Library at the University of California at Berkeley provided much-needed help in locating editions of Guarini and of the composers who set his texts to music. Sue Elkevizth in Oberlin's English Department office was unfailingly cheerful and efficient with her administrative assistance. This book would not have come to light without the support of Ellen Bauerle at the University of Michigan Press, who believed in the idea and worked hard to help me craft and refine the manuscript for publication.

Finally, I am grateful to Sue Copeland Jones, who has accompanied me throughout this project, both as we delighted in the Baroque splendors of the courts of northern Italy and as I wrestled with my translations in our living rooms in Oberlin and Berkeley. From her I have gained wise advice and warm support through many years: *cara mia luce.*

CONTENTS

PREFACE

Sometime in the latter half of the sixteenth century, Giovanni Battista Guarini, a Ferrarese poet, professor, and diplomat, wrote a poem about the excitement of hearing another poem sung by a brilliant female singer. These poems—both the unknown poem she sang and the poem that Guarini wrote about it—were known to Italians as *madrigali* (madrigals), a category that at that time applied both to music and to poetry. This madrigal, *Mentre vaga Angioletta*, is a fitting text with which to introduce this collection; like his other madrigals—but more self-consciously and explicitly—it combines the exactness of poetic craft with the liberties of improvisation and livens the expectations of convention with the inventions of wit. It is at once both poetry and music, both precise and free.

Here is my translation of *Mentre vaga Angioletta*:

> *As Angie sings,*
> *delighting every listener,*
> *   I'm borne aloft,*
> *a glider carried by her song.*
> *   How does she seize*
> *   the music's soul,*
> *her voice making, remaking it,*
> *   summoning such*
> *delicious, fluent harmony?*
> *Her music's both precise and free:*
> *   it slides and thrusts*
> *with broken accents and with turns;*
> *   now slow, now quick;*
> *   now murmuring*
> *in moving bass lines, mixing runs*
> *with rests and cadences;*
> *   focused or loose,*
> *weighty, or broken, or subdued;*

it vibrates, turns
and pierces through;
pulls back; and once again it's firm
and resonant.
Inventing, reinventing, she
makes of my heart
a nightingale,
flying from sorrow into mystery.

As exciting as is this account of a virtuoso concert, the madrigal tells us little of the actual situation: yes, we learn that the lady is a very accomplished singer, a master of the most sophisticated musical ornaments ("mixing runs / with rests and cadences"); yes, we see that this is a successful public performance ("delighting every listener"); and, yes, we learn that the poet, listening to her song, finds that it echoes his own sorrow. The nightingale, classical emblem of sadness, appears at the end as a metaphor for the poet's unfulfilled desire—perhaps for this very singer.

Or perhaps not. As with all these madrigals, the poem gives us only the briefest glimpse of the situation, a teasing insight without details. Who is the singer? I've called her "Angie," but that is a translator's license. The Italian *Angioletta* might be her name, but equally well it might be an endearing description—"little angel." Who is listening to her? The audience is likely to have been other poets and musicians at the Ferrarese court, perhaps the duke himself, but we don't know.

Nor do we need to know. The madrigal is self-sufficient, full of its own pleasures—both the pleasure of hearing her sing and that other bittersweet pleasure of experiencing sadness. The translation describes Angie's virtuosic music as "precise and free," and that phrase also characterizes the poem itself. It is precise, particularly in its focused attention on the many specific delights of her performance. It is precisely concentrated on musical and emotional pleasure. It is precise, too, in its craft, constructed with metrical ingenuity and resonant with assonance that supports the expressiveness of the poem and the song it describes.

But the madrigal is free as well as precise, like Angie's singing. Its intricate arrangement of short and long lines is bound to no predetermined pattern, as if each line were drafted by the poet, in the moment, to imitate the singer's freedom of tempo and expression. The poem, like the song, is loose, deliberately unsettled and inventively playful. As the song comes to its final cadence, the poem seems to resolve as well, with a full stop at "firm / and resonant." But that turns out to be a false cadence, a liberating moment of surprise leading to a coda that reconnects the singer and the poet in a figurative ecstasy that goes well beyond cadence:

> *Inventing, reinventing, she*
> *makes of my heart*
> *a nightingale,*
> *flying from sorrow into mystery.*

I've chosen the phrase "precise and free" for this book's title because it captures the madrigals' combination of artfulness and spontaneity. Each of Guarini's madrigals is a highly crafted gem, but each also is manifestly, and self-consciously, imbued with an air of spontaneity. The poems' beginnings constantly surprise: they can be expository ("My life's become / love's fire-fight"), declamatory ("Cruel and beautiful"), or questioning ("To speak or not?"). In the middle, the poems often pivot, turning on a dime to surprise the reader with some new event or way of thinking: "But then you fled / and I dissolved." We never know in advance where the pivot will happen. We know only that with Guarini's love of poetic freedom, some kind of about-face is likely before we get to the end.

There is a kind of freedom, too, in the very number of these madrigals—so many, and so obviously diverse. In the edition of Guarini printed in Venice in 1598, the poems are arranged with an apparently deliberate heterogeneity: they adhere to no formal structure and tell no coherent story, but tumble in an improvised spiral of familiarity and surprise in both form and content.

For two centuries following the earliest editions, Guarini's poems were often reprinted in Italian—both the madrigals and his long verse drama, *Il pastor fido* (*The Faithful Shepherd*). In 1737 four volumes of an intended eight-volume edition of Guarini's complete works were published in Verona. But after that, until the latter part of the twentieth century, there was little interest in Guarini. In 1950 Luigi Fassò published a selection of Guarini's works in Italian, and in 1971 Marziano Guglielminetti compiled a more complete edition of the works in Italian, including the madrigals. However, there is still no scholarly critical edition of the madrigals in Italian. *Il pastor fido* has been translated into many languages, including Neapolitan, French, German, and English (the first and most influential English translation, by Sir Richard Fanshawe, was published in 1647). But to my knowledge no substantive collection of the madrigals in English translation has been published. The musical settings of these poems as vocal madrigals have fared rather better: in 1999 the musicologist Denis Stevens published a slim volume with texts and translations of the texts of Monteverdi's madrigal compositions, including many by Guarini. Occasional translations of individual madrigals continue to appear over the years as program notes for madrigal concerts or liner notes for recordings. But there has been no concerted attention to making these extraordinary poems accessible for their own sake to readers in English.

This collection presents 150 of Guarini's madrigals, both in their original Italian and in idiomatic English in my own poetic translations, with the hope that those who read and study Early Modern poetry, music, and culture will be encouraged to include Guarini in comparative discussions of late Petrarchanism and of the Baroque. In homage to the 1598 volume edited and printed by Giovanni Battista Ciotti, I have chosen to include 150 madrigals—the number assembled in that volume, though not precisely the same selections (Ciotti seems not to have had access to some of the best of the madrigals, and some of those that he does include I find less exciting than most).

In this collection, I have tried to retain that sense of freedom and variety that seems to have delighted Guarini's early readers. So, reading from poem to poem, one will find shifts of moods and affects. But because modern readers of lyric poetry are used to volumes with something more of a structure to them, I have grouped the poems into sections with some commonality of mood. The ten sections of this collection center, respectively, on the unpredictability of love, the cruelty of the beloved, the anguish of the lover, the fiery skirmishes of love, the faint possibility of bliss, the theatricality of love's interactions, the incursions of jealousy, the connection of love and song, the parting of lovers, and finally the hope for a calmer life free of love's skirmishes.

In recent years, scholarly ground has been laid for closer study of Guarini as a poet. Over the last several decades, increased attention has been paid to the cultural history of the vocal madrigal in the late sixteenth century, in which Guarini's madrigals figure heavily (for example, Anthony Newcomb's 1980 study *The Madrigal at Ferrara, 1579–1597*, and essays by Iain Fenlon on the madrigal in Mantua and other Italian courts). At the same time, two collections of scholarly essays, written largely in Italian, have focused explicitly on Guarini: a 1997 anthology of essays about his importance for musical studies (edited by Angelo Pompilio) and a 2008 anthology including more about his life and poetry (edited by Bianca Maria Da Rif). As Susan Hammond's useful 2011 research guide to the madrigal shows, some shorter musicological analyses of individual madrigal settings have appeared in recent years, as well. As far as I can tell, however, there is as yet little discussion of Guarini's poetry in the English language or in critical circles engaged with comparative studies across languages.

This collection comes, then, at a point of renewed interest in the madrigal and in Guarini. In preparing these translations and commentaries, I have also been conscious of the increasing attention to poetic texts and poetic rhetoric within the early music performance community. We are hearing more and more historically informed performances of early sixteenth-century text-based music, whether purely vocal madrigals, vocal pieces with instruments, or operas (the Boston Early Music Festival of 2015, for example, saw back-to-back staging of three Monteverdi operas). Studies such as Judy Tarling's *The Weapons of Rhetoric* (2004) and Susan McClary's *Desire and Pleasure in Seventeenth-Century Music* (2012) theorize and support a growing sense of the necessity to understand the texts behind the music and to acknowledge the ubiquity of rhetorical theory and practice in programming and performing the music of the sixteenth and seventeenth centuries.

Indeed, Guarini's madrigals themselves are central to this growing acknowledgment of poetic text as a key part of early music. As *Mentre vaga Angioletta* makes clear, these poems were not purely "verbal icons" in themselves (the phrase alludes to the way some mid-twentieth-century literary criticism—the "New Criticism," in particular—tried to get readers to think of a lyric poem as free from contextual ambiguities and interpretations). In their original courtly contexts, these madrigals were not so much texts for poetic close reading as "pretexts," scripts for public performance. The poems are highly performative, full of a declamatory rhetoric that some readers of English poetry will recognize from reading John Donne (I've borrowed from Donne on occasion in translating them). They are loaded with interjections and exclamations (the Italian *oimè*, for example—"alas!"), ample evidence that they were intended to be performed aloud, whether spoken or sung. Like their contemporaries, the sonnets of Shakespeare, Guarini's madrigals are little scripts that can be staged like miniature dramas.

These madrigals have an intricate relationship with actual music, and with the performance of music. Whatever song it was that "Angie" sang, its text was almost certainly itself a madrigal, perhaps one of Guarini's, and its composer may well have been present at the performance, perhaps accompanying the singer on a lute. Perhaps the singer herself was the poet or composer. Whatever occurred in that courtly palace in Ferrara where the performance most likely took place, that performance of a poem set to music engendered yet another poem, the one here translated. And that poem, in turn, became the occasion for another song in the hands of a composer—in this case, Claudio Monteverdi, who set Guarini's Angioletta poem to music in his *Eighth Book of Madrigals* (1638). Monteverdi's composition, then and now, depends on being performed, and the musician who performs it must embrace, as Angioletta had to, the dual responsibility of precision (remaining faithful to the song as written) and freedom (engaging the song through her own interpretation and embellishment).

The translator, too, needs to negotiate the two poles of precision and freedom, and that is what I have tried to do in this collection (a fuller discussion of the various protocols I have placed on my translation, and the liberties I have taken, will be found in the Introduction). As a teacher of poetry, I encouraged my students to acknowledge the precision of a poem—its craft—in formal, figurative, and rhetorical terms. At the same time, I encouraged them to remain free to interpret and perform it in ways that mattered to them. As a singer, too, I find in madrigal settings the exhilarating and paradoxical demand that all musical scores make on the performer—both to sing what is present, prescribed by the composer (the pitches, the rhythms, the rests, and the words), and to decide on the many aspects that are unspecified in early music—the dynamics and the tempo, for example. Above all, the performer has to engage the affect and the swing of the piece. As the translator, I have held these two other roles—the teacher and the singer—as touchstones in the challenging task of re-creating the precision of a poem from another culture long ago, and in the wonderful opportunity to remake it in a language and time very different from its original.

This collection is not primarily a book of literary history or analysis. Nonetheless, some historical and critical context may help the reader to enjoy these poems, written as they are in what may be an unfamiliar set of conventions. In the Introduction and to some degree in the commentary that follows each translation, I sketch out some of the contexts in which we might read the madrigals. The Introduction begins with an overview of the poet's life. Following that, I draw on Guarini's principal model, the fourteenth-century poet Petrarch, to lay out the tradition of love poetry in which Guarini and his contemporaries worked, and which must have seemed like second nature to his original readers. There follows a close reading of one madrigal, *Voi pur da me partite, anima dura*, to illuminate the craft that characterizes all of these madrigals. Since the genre of the madrigal cannot be seen as a purely poetic phenomenon, I go on to summarize the popularity and extent of the musical madrigal in the sixteenth and seventeenth centuries, focusing particularly on Monteverdi. The Introduction concludes with a fuller account of decisions I have made in translating these madrigals and in assembling this collection.

Fig. 1. Guarini at age sixty-three, in about 1601. Engraving by L. Kilian in Guarini, *Il pastor fido* (Venice: Ciotti, 1602). Harvard University Library.

Introduction

Giovanni Battista Guarini was born in the ducal court city of Ferrara in northern Italy in 1538, the descendent of a distinguished fifteenth-century humanist scholar, Guarino da Verona. Guarini studied in Padua and then returned to Ferrara to take up the post of professor of rhetoric and poetry at its distinguished university (see figure 1). He married into an important Ferrarese musical family—his wife's sisters were noted singers. He was the father of eight children, including an even more famous singer, Anna Guarini, who became one of a celebrated trio of women singers, the so-called *concerto delle donne*, known across Italy as one of the principal cultural assets of the court at Ferrara.

The latter years of the sixteenth century were a vital period for musical and artistic culture in Ferrara. The city and the ducal court flourished under the patronage of the d'Este family, who had transformed the old fortress in the center of the city into a Renaissance palace sumptuously decorated and lavishly furnished for entertainments. Even today, Ferrara shows much of its Renaissance splendor in the many early sixteenth-century palaces that grace the main street of the old section of the city. Guarini's own imposing residence, now a part of the university, gives evidence of the distinguished position he held in the city and the court.

Guarini's patron was Duke Alfonso II d'Este, who ruled Ferrara from 1559 until his death in 1597. Alfonso supported Guarini both for his contribution to the artistic splendors of Ferrara and for his diplomatic abilities as well. The poet traveled extensively on the duke's foreign missions—to Turin, Venice, Rome, and even (twice) to Crakow. In 1583 Guarini retired to the country, but two years later he returned to Ferrara to become private secretary to the duke. After only three years, however, he went back to his villa in the country again; apparently something had occurred to alienate him from the duke. In 1595 Guarini was reconciled with his patron, but when Alfonso died only two years later without a legitimate heir, the rule of Ferrara passed to the papacy and the golden period of Este patronage of the arts came to an end. Guarini transferred his allegiance to ducal courts in Florence, then in Mantua, and finally in Urbino. He died in Venice in 1612.

Along with diplomatic service, Guarini contributed to the splendor of the Ferrarese court with his poetry. Central to that were his poetic madrigals, which were widely read, extensively set to music, and frequently performed throughout Italy during his lifetime. He was himself aware of the musical uses of his poetry, revising his madrigals to make them more fitting for the new expressive styles of composers like Monteverdi. In addition, his pastoral drama *Il pastor fido* earned him international attention into the seventeenth and even the eighteenth centuries. Begun in the early 1580s, this verse drama about Arcadian shepherds went through multiple editions in Italian as well as translations into many languages, including an influential 1647 English version, *The Faithful Shepherd*, by Richard Fanshawe. It is probably best known today as the basis for George Frederick Handel's opera of the same name, composed in 1712 and significantly revised in 1734. By the 1590s, the appeal of *Il pastor fido* and of the madrigals and their musical settings made Guarini—with his fellow citizen of Ferrara, Torquato Tasso—"one of Italy's two most celebrated living poets."

The Petrarchan Tradition

Guarini's madrigals are inseparable from the long tradition of love poetry derived from the work of the great fourteenth-century humanist and poet Petrarch, whose enormously influential collection of 366 poems, known as *Il canzoniere* (simply, "the song book"), details his love for a woman named Laura; the first half of the collection praises her beauty, intelligence, and spirit, and the second half mourns her early death. The poems, centered on this love, also range far beyond, paying homage to Petrarch's fellow humanists, describing the seasons of nature and of the Christian calendar, and commenting on the turbulent politics of northern Italy and southern France.

In the *Canzoniere*, Petrarch could be said to have invented the "lyric poem"—that is, the poem that explores the emotional and spiritual life of the poet. Petrarch essentially created that language of compressed, expressive metaphor that we now expect in a lyric poem, by which things in the world—birds, flowers, landscapes, encounters—become markers of the poet's feelings. Unlike earlier medieval writers who tended to see the world as a fixed lectionary of meaning (a flower traditionally signified transience, for example), Petrarch opened up new, multiple, and flexible meanings. His poetry is full of excitement, the sense that at any moment a poem, or even just a single metaphor, might morph into something quite unexpected. For example, in these lines images of dawn and rainbow subtly become metaphors for his luminous revelation about Laura's beauty. Here, as elsewhere in this volume, Petrarch's poetry appears in translations by David Young:

> *I never saw the sun come up so fair*
> *when all the sky is free of mist and clouds,*
> *nor after rain the great celestial arc*
> *spread itself out through air with many colors,*
>
> *as on that day when I took on my burden*
> *and saw her lovely face transform itself*
> *blazing before me (and my words here fail me)*
> *as something that no mortal life could match.*

The sense of newness ("I never saw . . .") is accentuated by a poetic surprise as Petrarch suddenly thrusts himself in ("and my words here fail me")—he is not just the lover but also the poet, who struggles to manifest in language this transcendent experience. Petrarch's constant self-consciousness about the burden of matching words to intense experiences—"the poetry of ceaseless self-qualification," in the words of one reader—became an enduring feature of the Petrarchan lyric tradition, echoed much later in the work of Romantic and post-Romantic lyric poets. Centuries after Petrarch, Keats, in his "Ode to a Nightingale," sees himself carried upward "on the viewless wings of Poesy" and feels the Petrarchan contradiction between the poet's imagination and the reality of the body: "the dull brain perplexes and retards."

Before we turn to the related form of the madrigal, it will help to sketch out the workings of the sonnet, Petrarch's favorite form. The Italian sonnet comprises fourteen lines in two parts: an expository "octave" (eight lines, in two groups of four) followed by a "sestet" (six lines, in two groups of three). The octave allows the poet to set out the situation in depth, as in this exploration of emotional ambiguity:

> *If it's not love, what is it then I feel?*
> *But if it's love, by God, what sort of love?*
> *If good, why kill me with its bitterness?*
> *If bad, why is each torment then so sweet?*

If I burn willingly, why weep and howl?
And if against my will, what good's lament?
Oh living death, oh you delightful pain,
how can you rule me if I don't consent?

The themes of this octave are utterly characteristic of Petrarch—love's doubleness of affect, the lover's uncertainty of will, the ambiguity of moral judgment,
and the strange limbo of unconsciousness that desire brings. They have a
characteristic Petrarchan resonance as the questions swirl and the key words
echo.

But the sestet of the sonnet pivots sharply, collapsing into the impossibil-
ity of answering those questions:

And if I do consent, why then I'm wrong
thus to complain. Amid contending winds
I am at sea, and my frail boat is rudderless,

empty of wisdom, and so prone to error
that I myself do not know what I want,
burning in winter, shivering in summer.

"I'm wrong / thus to complain": that is, I'm not going to be able to change
this with mere rhetoric; I'm part of this paradoxical situation, and it is part of
me. So the poem turns from question to metaphor—"I am at sea." It ends by
emptying itself of any pretension to wisdom and clarity of intention, the lover
lost in a figure of antithesis ("burning in winter, shivering in summer") that
recurs throughout the Petrarchan canon.

Remarkably, this sonnet made its way into English while Petrarch was still
alive, translated by Geoffrey Chaucer in the 1380s as the "Song of Troilus."
Chaucer's use of Petrarch's lyrical and meditative metaphor allows the English
poet to deepen his protagonist, the lovesick and baffled young Troilus—
"Thus possed to and fro / Al stereless within a boot [boat] am I / Amidde the
see, betwixen windes two." In later years Petrarch's poems were widely read
and imitated in English, first by the poets of Henry VIII's court, such as Sir
Thomas Wyatt, and then in the Elizabethan flowering of Petrarchan sonnet
sequences by Sir Philip Sidney, Edmund Spenser, and William Shakespeare,
to cite only the most well-known of dozens of sonneteers in England.

As in English, the Petrarchan tradition in Italian reached a peak of popularity in the late fifteenth and sixteenth centuries. In 1501 the humanist Pietro

Bembo oversaw the first printing of *Il canzoniere* (it had previously circulated in manuscript copies), which reinforced the influence of Petrarch in the new century, on such different poets as Michelangelo, Tasso, and Guarini.

That extraordinary blooming of Petrarchanism in the sixteenth century—in English, Italian, and almost every language across Europe—came with an ambivalent attitude toward the very tradition that it drew on. On the one hand, the poets honored the power and inventiveness of the Petrarchan conventions. But along with homage eventually came exhaustion: the Petrarchan mine, however rich it once was, had yielded its best ore. At its worst the long tradition became a force of inertia, and the poetry merely a complacent reworking of clichés.

And yet the centuries-old mode of poetry could still inspire poets. Without Petrarch, for example, Shakespeare would likely not have written such a profound meditation on time and death as this:

> *Not marble, nor the gilded monuments*
> *Of princes shall outlive this pow'rful rhyme,*
> *But you shall shine more bright in these contents*
> *Than unswept stone, besmear'd with sluttish time.*
> *When wasteful war shall statues overturn,*
> *And broils root out the work of masonry,*
> *Nor Mars his sword nor war's quick fire shall burn*
> *The living record of your memory.*
> *'Gainst death and all-oblivious enmity*
> *Shall you pace forth; your praise shall still find room,*
> *Even in the eyes of all posterity*
> *That wear this world out to the ending doom.*
> > *So till the judgment that yourself arise,*
> > *You live in this, and dwell in lovers' eyes.*

Sidney and Shakespeare—and Spenser to a lesser degree—looked at their Petrarchan heritage with an amused, ironic, and sometimes exasperated eye. Probably the most famous of their critiques is Shakespeare's parody of unconditional and unthinking Petrarchan praise:

> *My mistress' eyes are nothing like the sun;*
> *Coral is far more red than her lips' red;*
> *If snow be white, why then her breasts are dun;*
> *If hairs be wires, black wires grow on her head.*

I have seen roses damask'd, red and white,
But no such roses see I in her cheeks,
And in some perfumes is there more delight
Than in the breath that from my mistress reeks.
I love to hear her speak, yet well I know
That music hath a far more pleasing sound;
I grant I never saw a goddess go,
My mistress when she walks treads on the ground.
    And yet, by heaven, I think my love as rare
    As any she belied with false compare.

Pointedly mocking, the sonnet nonetheless ends with surprising sincerity. After reducing his beloved, and his poem, to mere realism (she merely "treads on the ground"), Shakespeare ends by evoking a Petrarchan sense of wonder at his lady's "rare" distinctiveness: "as rare / As any she belied by false compare."

The Poetic Madrigal

By the mid-sixteenth century, the poetic madrigal began to challenge the dominance of the sonnet and to inject new life into the old conventions of Petrarchan love poetry. Though a sonnet is relatively short, it is long enough to demand considerable amplification: the poet has to keep finding new ways of saying things, and as any reader of sonnets knows, that can become mechanical. The sonnet is fixed in its length and rhyme scheme, but the madrigal offers a lithe responsiveness with its shorter lines, variable length, and looser rhyme scheme. In a madrigal, the poet can focus on one subject and still maintain a sense of inventiveness and surprise.

Among hundreds of sonnets, there are just four madrigals in Petrarch's *Canzoniere*, but they are notable for their brevity and focus. This is one:

Diana's form did not delight her lover,
when just by chance he got a look at her
bathing all naked in the cooling waters,

more than the cruel mountain shepherdess
delighted me while rinsing out the veil
that keeps her golden curls from the wind;

she made me then, despite the sun's hot rays,
shiver a little with the chill of love.

Much shorter than a sonnet, this madrigal compresses and intensifies the situation. The erotic thrill is introduced right away by a reference to the hunter Actaeon, who happened upon the goddess Diana bathing in the nude. This allusion sets the stakes high: the offended Diana transformed Actaeon to a stag, whereupon he was torn apart by his own hounds. But with a deft simplicity, the poem turns away from the mythical, as if saying, "I was talking of Diana, but really I want to show you this shepherdess . . ." And then, without delay or explanation, the poet moves on to how the sight of her affected him. He uses the familiar trope of burning and freezing, but, in typical madrigal understatement, the shivering is only "a little." The poem doesn't need to hype things up too much, nor to fuss about showing us everything from every possible perspective. What it shows us, though, is as clear as the sound of a plucked lute string, a more penetrating sound for not being embedded in the clutter of a sonnet.

Petrarch's madrigals were written with an unvarying eleven-syllable line, as were his sonnets. By the sixteenth century, though, the madrigal poets added a shorter line of seven syllables to the eleven-line poem, allowing them to complicate the meter and to write with more freedom, musicality, and charm. Anthony Oldcorn points out that it is the quality of charm that allows the madrigal to succeed, to seek, as he says, "the significant in the apparently insignificant." Oldcorn cites as an example this mid-sixteenth century madrigal by Ariosto. Here is the Italian (as with other madrigals in this volume, I have indicated the seven-syllable lines by indenting them):

> *Se mai cortese fusti,*
> *piangi, Amor, piangi meco i bei crin d'oro,*
> *ch'altri pianti sì iusti—unqua non fôro.*
> *Come vivace fronde*
> *tòl da robusti rami aspra tempesta,*
> *così le chiome bionde,*
> *di che più volte hai la tua rete intesta,*
> *tolt'ha necessità rigida e dura*
> *da la più bella testa*
> *che mai facessi o possa far Natura.*

Here is a literal, line-by-line translation of Ariosto's madrigal (the subject is the cutting of the beloved's hair):

> If ever you were kind,
> weep, Love, weep with me for the lovely golden curls,
> for never was there a juster cause for weeping.
>   As the living leaves
> are stripped from the strong branches by the fierce storm,
>   so the fair locks,
> from which you often used to weave your net,
> inflexible and grim necessity has stripped
>   from the loveliest head
> that ever Nature made or ever can make.

The short lines of the madrigal allow the rhyme words—for example, *fronde* (leaves) and *bionde* (blonde)—to resonate more closely than they would in a sonnet. That resonance accelerates the movement into the figure of cut hair as foliage stripped off by a storm. The short penultimate line lets the poet assert, simply and without fuss, his hyperbole about her head (*la più bella*—"the loveliest"). And the longer final line allows for a deft extension of that hyperbole, a riff on the forms of the verb *fare* (to make): she has *la più bella testa / che mai facessi o possa far Natura* ("the loveliest head / that ever Nature made or ever can make").

Guarini and the Poetic Madrigal

The poetic madrigal came into prominence in the later decades of the sixteenth century, both as a form in its own right and as a text for musical composition. Guarini was at the center of both of these explosions. Before appearing in print, Guarini's madrigal texts must have circulated widely in manuscript, since they appear as the texts of vocal madrigal publications well before their first printings as poetry. They are, for example, central to published volumes of music by Filippo de Monte (1585), Luca Marenzio (1586), and Claudio Monteverdi (1587). In 1587 a selection of Guarini's poems was published in Bergamo, as part of a handsome anthology, *Rime di diversi celebri poeti dell'età nostra* (Poems by various famous poets of our age). A decade later, 150 of Guarini's madrigals appeared with his sonnets and a few other poems in another volume, *Rime del molto illustre signor cavaliere Battista Gua-*

rini (Venice, 1598): the title page features a proud dedication to one of Italy's most powerful figures, Cardinal Pietro Aldobrandini, a nephew of the pope and ruler of Ferrara after the death of Alfonso d'Este (see figure 2).

The editor of the 1598 *Rime* was Giovanni Battista Ciotti, a Sienese printer working in Venice. In many of his publications, Ciotti presented himself not only as a printer but also as an editor in the modern sense, and he was evidently well-known to many of his authors. In the preface to his Guarini volume, Ciotti highlights his role in collecting Guarini's scattered oeuvre; his comments shed light on the fluid nature of poetic texts as they circulated in manuscript among friends and intellectual companions:

> Most humane readers, these are those poems of Signor Cavalier Guarini, so much requested and widely desired in the world, of which, wishing according to my custom to give satisfaction as much as possible, I set out a long time ago to make a good collection, not only from the hands of their own author, but from the poems of the Ethereals [a club called the *Accademia degli Eterei*] and from those of other writers to whom they had wrongly been ascribed, and from the hands of those who had them in manuscript, and from the musicians of Ferrara, and in sum from whatever other source where I could imagine obtaining them. And when I believed myself to be at the end of this labor, and to be able to send them out into the world, I was informed, that the author had for some time changed them in ways that made them more compact, that corrected them, so to speak. Thus I was constrained to change my plan and give myself over to seeing how I might obtain originals drawn from the author himself, who was now so well known. From the hands of those from whom I had first recovered them, and from the author himself, so that I might have no contestation, I expended the greatest effort and the greatest patience in the world.

Ciotti makes it evident that he has worked hard: the poems were gathered "with the greatest effort" from scattered sources—from earlier publications, from musicians (who would have had the poems as texts for vocal madrigals), and from Guarini himself, who apparently had revised the madrigals over a period of time, making them "more compact," "correct[ing] them, so to speak."

Ciotti also goes out of his way to make sure we know that his volume has passed the scrutiny of the Inquisition (necessary to permit its sale in Italian cities less tolerant than Venice). But he does so with a barely concealed scorn for church censorship:

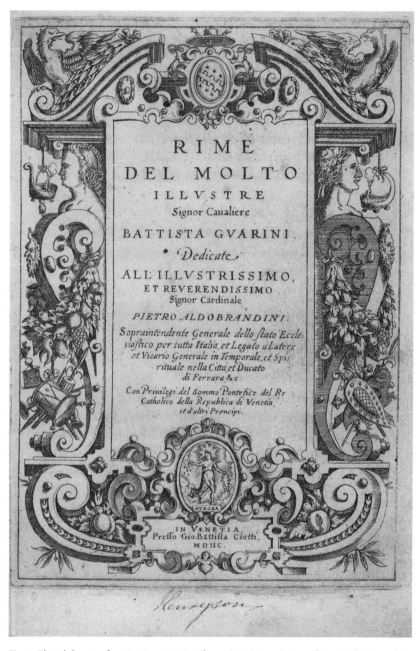

Fig. 2. The elaborate frontispiece to Ciotti's 1598 Venice edition of Guarini's *Rime del molto illustre signor cavaliere Battista Guarini*, with dedication to Cardinal Aldobrandini. Harvard University Library.

If, then, reading these, you should run across any gaps in the text, do not blame me, for I have been constrained to do thus to obey the office of the most holy Inquisition, who has excised the words "fortune," "destiny," "fate," and others of that sort, which you, with the discretion of your judgment, will recognize from the context, as they fit the clarity of the feeling.

Presumably, the censors objected to the presence of eschatological terms like *fate* in a collection of love poetry. Ciotti all but laughs at the absurdity of removing such words, when the context (often the rhyme) makes it patently clear exactly which word was originally intended. The danger, however, was not laughable: a year after this publication, the Inquisition arrested Ciotti for importing seditious material from Germany—not surprising, given his connection with the controversial philosopher Giordano Bruno, tried for heresy in 1593 and burned in Rome in 1600.

Like any editor, Ciotti praises the work he is printing: the poems are, he says, "sure to bring you the greatest joy of language, of ideas, of liveliness, of grace, and, that which matters most, of the most accomplished purity, sustained with meter and nobility, and, in a single word, a model of good sonnet and graceful madrigal, which good style would wish to emulate in this sort of writing."

Ciotti's repeated praise for the madrigals, in distinction from the sonnets, is to mark them as *leggiadro* (graceful), as he does here. It is an apt description: they are elegant and light, taking no more room than they need to, gesturing stylishly like a courtly dancer. They are focused and unified, but nuanced and varied as well. In their gracefulness, they share with other High Renaissance works of art the untranslatable quality of *sprezzatura*—roughly, nonchalance, the ability to accomplish difficult things without any visible effort. Baldassare Castiglione's well-known *Book of the Courtier* (1528) speaks of it as the ability "to do his feats with a sleight, as though they were rather naturally in him, than learned with study: and use a recklessness to cover art, without minding greatly what he hath in hand, to a man's seeming."

The horseman managing a difficult stallion, the painter catching the translucence of a veil, the musician improvising an ornament, the diplomat delivering a compliment without seeming to flatter—all were demonstrating this courtly ability. The madrigalist, as well, needed to be able to create a poem that disguised its verbal and rhetorical intricacy beneath a calm surface of ease.

A Madrigal of Guarini

One of the most popular of Guarini's madrigals among contemporary vocal composers was *Voi pur da me partite, anima dura* (#126 in this volume). As with all the madrigals in Ciotti's 1598 *Rime*, the poem occupied a full page, set off by an elaborate initial letter and convoluted baroque ornaments (see figure 3). In the original, the shorter lines were not typographically distinguished from the longer lines, but here, as later in this collection, I have added indentations to distinguish seven-syllable lines from those with eleven.

> *Voi pur da me partite, anima dura,*
>   *né vi duole il partire,*
>   *oimè quest'è morire*
>   *crudele, e voi gioite?*
> *Quest'è vicino aver l'ora suprema,*
>   *e voi non la sentite?*
> *O meraviglia di durezza estrema.*
>   *Esser alma d'un core,*
> *e separarsi, e non sentir dolore.*

Following is a literal prose translation, arranged line-by-line to correspond with the Italian (my poetic translation, taking more liberties, can be found in #126):

> So you are leaving me, hard soul,
>   nor does leaving sadden you.
>   Alas, this it is to die,
>   cruel one, and you enjoy it?
> This it is to come close to the last hour,
>   and you don't feel it?
> Oh, the wonder of such extreme hardness,
>   to be the soul of a heart,
> and to pull oneself away, and not feel pain!

The poem treats the departure of his beloved with a gracefully ambivalent rhetoric. It is both hyperbolically insistent on showing his pain and at the same time casually nonchalant about it, congratulating her on her "cruelty." Although packed with an implicit bitterness, the poem deflects that emotion by concentrating on what the lady *doesn't* feel (*non . . . sentite, non sentir*), as if the best way to express his own emotions were to show their absence in the beloved.

The madrigal begins with apparent casualness. *Pur* (in the first line) is a barely translatable linking word implying that the poem begins in midstream, perhaps as part of some ongoing discussion; here it means, roughly, "so," or "and yet," or "OK. . . ." The isolated *né* in the second line strengthens the sense of a discussion that has begun without a firm beginning (*né* usually means "neither," but here there is no second *né* to provide a "nor," so the word remains strangely indeterminate: I have used "nor" as a fallback). After this noncommittal opening, the next four lines intensify the rhetoric with a metaphor that characterizes parting as dying—not once, but twice. In a longer poem, the poet might have gone on to further amplify the lover's suffering, but here the hyperbole is contained by the poem's brevity and focus: this is a poem not about "me" but about "you," and each mention of the lover's pain is balanced with a baffled question about how the beloved could witness his pain and not feel sympathy.

The pivot near the end is meant to surprise. The rhetoric seemed focused on blame ("hard soul," "cruel one"), but it swings over to ironic congratulation ("Oh, the wonder . . . !"). By veering away from recrimination, Guarini prepares the way for another, final surprise: he reprises the earlier image of the deathbed of the lover ("to die . . . to come close to the last hour"). But now, with a powerfully compressed and questionable logic, it turns out that it is not the lover but the beloved who is on the deathbed. Death entails the soul leaving the body: so, since *she* is his soul, she must be dying if she leaves his body. The wonder that ends the poem emphasizes her indifference, her "cruelty": it constructs her as so tough that she doesn't even feel her *own* death! As the poem ends, the rhetoric has shifted from blame to congratulation and then on to sadness, as he ascribes to her a pain that she doesn't even recognize.

Guarini's madrigals gain resonance by their compactness. The rhyme words come swiftly upon each other, and they echo with similar sounds within the lines as well as at the end of the lines. Here, for example, *dura* (hard) in the first line is echoed almost immediately by *duole* (sorrow) in the second. *Partire* (to leave) is followed in the very next line by its rhyme word, *morire* (to die), linking departure with death. The final rhyme words, *core* and *dolore*, place the sadness exactly where the lover wants it. Integral to this resonance is the rhetorical figure of antithesis (opposition): *dura* and *duole* are echoes both in the sense of being similar and in being different: the beloved's cruelty is the opposite of the lover's sadness, though the two are causally linked. The antitheses work both on the local level, within a phrase or line, and across the

Partita della amata.

LXXXVIIII.

VOI pur da me partite, anima
    dura,
Ne vi duole il partire,
Oimè quest'è morire
Crudele, e voi gioite?
Quest'è vicina hauer l'hora fu-
prema,
E voi non la fentite?
O'merauiglia di durezza eftrema.
Effer alma d'un core,
E fepararfi, e non fentir dolore.

Di-

Fig. 3. Guarini's *Voi pur da me partite, anime dura* as printed in Ciotti's 1598 edition of *Rime del molto illustre signor cavaliere Battista Guarini*. Harvard University Library.

poem itself: the beautiful pivot line, *O meraviglia di durezza estrema*, with its liquid consonants and words of three and four syllables, helps to move the poem from its harsher opening to an ending of tender lyricism. *Separarsi, e non sentir dolore* at the end has a liquid affect distinctly contrasting with the jagged and plosive monosyllabic opening, *Voi pur da me partite.*

Unspoken but implicit in this madrigal, as in almost all of Guarini's, are assumptions about gender and power that his courtly world—or at least its poems—lived by. The lover is virtually inseparable from his masculinity. His command of language—speaking, writing, and poeticizing—enables him to occupy the center of the poem and privileges his feelings, even the negative feelings of rejection and suffering. I said above that the poem is not about "me"—the lover; but of course it really *is* all about him. The lover is the only real subject, the only viable source of identification in the poem. By contrast, the beloved—the lady, that is (these being exclusively heterosexual relationships)—is a being seen only through the eyes of the lover; she is primarily a means of justifying the lover's pain and expressing the complexity of his responses to it.

The Vocal Madrigal

The vogue of the vocal madrigal—the musical setting of a madrigal poem, most often for unaccompanied singers, but sometimes including instruments— grew directly alongside the popularity of the poetic madrigal. In its most common form, the sixteenth-century vocal madrigal is a setting for five un- accompanied voices ranging from soprano to bass, though the number could vary. In later years (generally, after the turn of the seventeenth century), some madrigal composers began to write with fewer voice lines, sometimes even using only a single voice. With the decrease in voice parts came the addition of instrumental accompaniment—continuo parts for lute, keyboard, and vio- la da gamba, or even treble lines for other instruments such as violins.

Some composers wrote their own poetic texts, but many kept a sharp lookout for the best new poets and their poetic madrigals. Poets—Tasso and Guarini prominent among them, but no means the only ones—wrote with an eye to their verses being picked up by the composers. The high point of this synergy between poetry and music was in the latter sixteenth and early sev- enteenth centuries. Emil Vogel's bibliography of secular Italian vocal music lists more than three thousand published volumes of vocal compositions in the sixteenth and seventeenth centuries. Given that each of these volumes contains one or two dozen individual madrigals, one comes to realize the madrigal fever that seems to have gripped Italy in that period, a fever felt by both poets and composers—not to mention those who purchased and sang the madrigals. Lorenzo Bianconi provides data about the publication of vocal madrigals over the century between 1550 and 1650 (see figure 4).

As is apparent in the chart, there was an enormous boom in printed madrigal compositions through the latter half of the sixteenth century, peaking near the end of the century. By Bianconi's count the decade 1581–90—when Guarini was at perhaps his most active—saw an astonishing output of printed madrigal books: 271 published volumes of new madrigals and 96 subsequent editions of madrigals that had been published earlier.

The vogue for buying madrigals in print continued for about two decades after the turn of the century, but as figure 4 shows, the interest declined sharply after about 1620. Likely causes for this drop include a growing interest in instrumental chamber music, the increasing complexity and difficulty of new vocal compositions, and the enormous disruptions of the Thirty Years' War across the continent.

Guarini's poems were at the forefront of the madrigal explosion. More than nineteen hundred separate madrigals set to Guarini texts were published in the sixteenth and seventeenth centuries, the work of more than three hundred composers. The chronology of these publications is indicated in figure 5. Published texts of Guarini's stand-alone madrigals, especially those in 1587 and 1598, facilitated the swell of compositions using these texts, which peaked about 1615. Composers were not content merely to set Guarini's individual madrigals, and turned to *Il pastor fido* for more material shortly after its publication in 1590. The chart shows the popularity of vocal madrigals "mined" from that text, which reached its peak about 1620. Some of Guarini's madrigals were set dozens of times, much as today's popular songs appear and reappear as "covers" in different arrangements and performances; *Ardo sì, ma non t'amo* (#103) is the text for settings by thirty-nine different composers.

The Italian-language madrigal was not limited to Italy: it was a European phenomenon. Known settings for each of the madrigals in this volume are listed in Appendix 2, where one can note the poems that were particularly attractive to composers and observe the geographical spread of publications—the majority in Venice, but southward to Florence, Rome, Naples, and Palermo and northward to Augsburg and Antwerp.

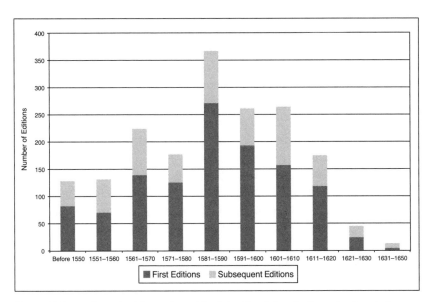

Fig. 4. Editions of vocal settings of madrigals by Guarini and others, by decade from 1550–1650, including both first editions and subsequent editions. Chart by author, based on data from Bianconi, *Music in the Seventeenth Century*, 2.

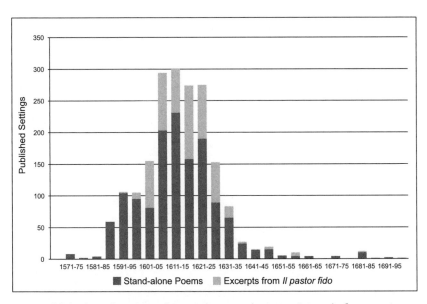

Fig. 5. Published vocal settings of Guarini's poetry, by 5-year intervals, from 1571 to 1695. "Stand-alone" poems are those published as Guarini's in the *Rime* of 1598 and other editions, in contrast to the poems that were excerpted by composers from *Il pastor fido*. Chart by author, compiled from data in Vassalli and Pompilio, "Indice delle rime di Battista Guarini poste in musica" and Chater, "*Il pastor fido* and Music."

Madrigals were printed as part-books: that is, the music for a single voice part (soprano, for example) was printed and bound separately from that for the other voices (the modern concept of a score—all the parts lined up with each other—did not exist until much later). In most madrigals, the voices sang in polyphony—that is, the parts were equally melodic and largely independent, entering at different times and, while sometimes imitating each other, usually moving in different directions. The great musical contribution of the madrigal was its expressivity: the rhythms, melodic lines, and harmonies could turn on a dime to match the swiftly varying affects of the text. Thus the complex poetry of the madrigal, often pivoting, often full of ironies, almost always deeply resonant, could find in the music a fitting performance.

Madrigals were generally performed in chamber settings by one singer to a part. Sebastiano Florigherio's painting (figure 6) suggests such a gathering, although only one line is shown as being performed (the *altus* part, in the hand of the woman in the center); the picture seems to concentrate more on

Fig. 6. Reading music from a part-book in the sixteenth century. Sebastiano Florigherio, *A Musical Entertainment*. Credit: Florigherio, Sebastiano, 1500–1543. Bavaria, Staatsgemäldesammlungen. Photo: © Blauel Gnamm—ARTOTHEK.

the complicated social and sexual interactions around madrigals than on an actual performance. In the courts of Ferrara and Mantua where Guarini was working, these performances were often held in the ducal palaces: the madrigal was a genre that supported the intimate gatherings of aristocratic and elite coteries. But with the boom in printing and distribution of madrigals across Europe, bourgeois households certainly had access to them, and madrigals became essential for amateur musicians.

Monteverdi and the Madrigal

Today, the best-known composer of madrigals is Claudio Monteverdi, though many more were active in the period. Between 1587 and 1638 Monteverdi published eight books totaling about two hundred madrigals, nearly fifty of which were based on Guarini's poems. Guarini was by far Monteverdi's most favored poet, followed next by Torquato Tasso (sixteen madrigals), and the younger Neapolitan Giambattista Marino (twelve madrigals). Whether Guarini and Monteverdi were friends or rivals—or both—we do not know. There is no evidence that poet and composer had a personal or epistolary connection. But they frequented the same court circles in northern Italy at the same time, and it is highly likely that they met. To take only one possibility, in 1608 both were closely involved with festivities in Mantua celebrating the wedding of Francesco Gonzaga to Margherita of Savoy. One performance at the wedding was of Guarini's comedy *L'idropico*, and another was of Monteverdi's opera *L'Arianna* (the music of which survives only in one great recitative, "Ariadne's Lament"). In the close-knit environment of such a ducal court, the two surely interacted, if only to argue about which of them was most favored by the duke at the moment. Given how central Guarini's emotionally laden poems were to the expressive revolution in music that Monteverdi was leading, there can be no doubt that Guarini must have been well aware of Monteverdi's work.

Born in Cremona in 1567, Monteverdi was a generation younger than Guarini. In his early twenties, Monteverdi moved to Mantua to work under the patronage of Duke Vincenzo Gonzaga; it was in Mantua that *L'Orfeo*, the so-called first opera, was premiered. On Vincenzo's death, Monteverdi found a new position as *maestro di cappella* at the basilica of San Marco in Venice, one of the most important musical posts in northern Italy. Venice was to be Monteverdi's home until his death in 1643.

Like Guarini, Monteverdi served his patrons in diplomacy as well as art. Between the publication of Monteverdi's third book of madrigals (1592, with nine poems by Guarini) and the fourth book (1603, with ten Guarini texts), Monteverdi accompanied Duke Vincenzo on an extended military expedition against the Turks and a diplomatic trip to Flanders. Monteverdi complained that the Flemish trip forced him to leave Italy just a few weeks after his marriage to a young singer—and that for these trips, he was very badly paid.

During one of these absences, a heated controversy arose about Monteverdi's innovative style of text setting; a little-known critic named Artusi published an attack on composers who were introducing "new rules, new modes, and new turns of phrase . . . harsh and little pleasing to the ear . . . deformations of the nature and propriety of true harmony." While Artusi does not mention Monteverdi by name, his examples are drawn from several Monteverdi madrigals (in particular, *Cruda Amarilli* and *O Mirtillo*), and it was widely assumed by his readers that Monteverdi was his target. In a series of highly technical objections to Monteverdi's practice, Artusi makes clear that he believes the craft of music is going to the dogs, what with Monteverdi's liberal use of dissonance, hyperbolic word painting, and exciting musical contrast—all qualities we tend to value highly in Monteverdi's writing today.

The new style associated with Monteverdi was quickly dubbed *seconda pratica*, the "second way" of writing. In defense of *seconda pratica*, a critic writing under the pseudonym "L'Ottuso" ("the obtuse one") asserted that expressive musical style was justified by the madrigal's expressive poetic texts, citing in particular poems by Tasso and Guarini. His argument gives us a vivid picture of the dynamic way in which these madrigals must have been performed at the time, a description that corroborates Guarini's own account in *Mentre vaga Angioletta* (see earlier in this introduction). Another report details the florid style of the performance of madrigals in Guarini's time:

> [The Dukes of Mantua and Ferrara] took the greatest delight in the art [of music], especially in having many noble ladies and gentlemen learn to sing and play superbly, so that they spent entire days in some rooms designed especially for this purpose and beautifully decorated with paintings. The ladies of Mantua and Ferrara [this must have included Guarini's daughter Anna] were highly competent, and vied with each other not only in regard to the timbre and training of their voices but also in the design of exquisite passages delivered at opportune points, but not in excess. . . . Furthermore, they

moderated or increased their voices, loud or soft, heavy or light, according to the demands of the piece they were singing; now slow, breaking off with sometimes a gentle sigh, now singing long passages legato or detached, now groups, now leaps, now with long trills, now with short, and again with sweet running passages sung softly, to which sometimes one heard an echo answer unexpectedly. They accompanied the music and the sentiment with appropriate facial expressions, glances and gestures, with no awkward movements of the mouth or hands or body which might not express the feeling of the song. They made the words clear in such a way that one could hear even the last syllable of every word, which was never interrupted or suppressed by passages [that is, ornaments] and other embellishments.

The description gives us a glimpse of the excitement and vitality of contemporary performances of these madrigals. The writer's focus on dramatic representation through appropriate gesture and on clear diction makes it clear that the text and the music were of equal importance to this learned and discriminating coterie of composers, poets, musicians, and nobles.

Translating Guarini

To translate is to make a leap of faith, in this case hoping that one can provide a reasonable English equivalent of a four-hundred-year-old poem written in Italian. My goal has been to produce a set of readable, understandable poems in contemporary English. Thus at times I have sacrificed the syntax of the original in pursuit of other goals, such as brevity, clarity, and distinctiveness of voice. Sometimes I have kept the conventional Petrarchan vocabulary ("heart," "soul," "pity," and "mercy"); at other times, depending on context, I have chosen more modern equivalents. I have treated each madrigal as a separate challenge, just as the composers seem to have created an individualized musical language for each madrigal they set to music. As a consequence the reader will experience significant differences in tone and diction among these translations.

I have held it essential to retain, or at least provide an equivalent for, aspects of poetic form, in part because it was Guarini's combination of mastery of form with expressive flexibility that first attracted me to these poems. So these translations strive to be poems and employ formal poetic qualities in so doing.

Meter and, correspondingly, line length are the principal tools of form in these translations. The madrigals in Italian use lines of seven or eleven syllables, which occur in irregular patterns, different in each madrigal. In translating, I have maintained each original poem's distinctive pattern of short and long lines. Italian verse is syllabic (that is, the number of syllables determines the length of the line), but English verse is primarily accentual (that is, based on patterns of stressed and unstressed syllables). Therefore, rather than working with a set number of syllables, I have used an accentual pattern, the iambic foot, which is a unit consisting of two syllables, the first unstressed and the second stressed ("dah DAH"). In my translations, short lines in the Italian get fewer iambs in my translation and longer lines get more. But just what constitutes "fewer" and "more" varies from one translated madrigal to another: the seven-syllable line sometimes gets two iambs (the verse is called dimeter) and sometimes three (trimeter). The eleven-syllable line can have three iambs, four (tetrameter), or occasionally five (pentameter).

I have reluctantly decided not to use rhyme in these translations. English, lacking the resonant inflections of Italian, does not rhyme as gracefully or as flexibly: the often-repeated rhymes in these madrigals would sound boring in English. In Italian, we often encounter rhymes like *core* (heart) and *amore* (love), and their assonance is pleasing. But not many English words rhyme with "love" (as Benedick discovers in *Much Ado about Nothing*). In abandoning rhyme, as in almost every translator's decision, something is lost. The Italian texts space out their rhymes irregularly, and the unpredictability of just when rhyme occurs (or whether it occurs at all) is an important part of their expressive form; it would have been nice to be able to keep that quality, but readability seemed more important to me than fidelity.

The madrigals in Italian are here transcribed from early editions whenever possible, primarily from the 1598 Venice edition and occasionally from other early editions (the source for each is listed in the Notes). In a few cases, I have used a version that a composer drew from *Il pastor fido*. I have regularly dropped the capitalization of the letters that immediately follow a decorative initial letter as well as the capitalization of the first letter of each line. I have regularized the texts by silently adopting modern Italian conventions of spelling and diacritics and correcting a few printing inconsistencies. I have chosen not to modernize punctuation except in a very few places. The original Italian madrigals had all lines justified along the left margin (see figure 3). In my transcriptions of them, the metrically shorter lines (seven syllables) are indented to indicate their difference from the longer lines.

In the commentary that accompanies each madrigal, I point out aspects of form, language, rhetoric, and context that may illuminate the reading of the poem. Citations and sources for this introduction, the headnotes, and the commentaries, as well as the source of texts for the Italian originals, are to be found in the Notes near the back of this volume. Also at the end are two appendices: an index of first lines in Italian and a list of the vocal madrigal settings of the poems included in this volume.

Sometimes translations of vocal texts are made to allow singers to perform in another language. I do not intend these translations for that purpose. While I hope fervently that the musical settings of these poems will continue to be performed by amateurs and professionals, I believe they should be sung in Italian, not in English. In Italian, the intricate sound effects of the musical text setting can be preserved; in English translations, inevitably, they must be diminished. Nonetheless, I do intend these translations for singers and their audiences, as well as for all readers of poetry in English and in Italian, as guides to the intricate poetics and expressive range of these trenchant and flexible madrigals, this "poetry precise and free."

The Madrigals

Fig. 7. Raphael's mischievous Cupid on the ceiling of the Villa Farnesina. Raphael (Raffaello Sanzio), 1483–1520. *Cupid and the Three Graces*. 1518. From the series of scenes from the story of Cupid and Psyche. Rome, Villa Farnesina. Photo: © Angeli Alessandro—Alinari—ARTOTHEK.

SECTION 1   Cupid's Mischief

All you who want a quiet life
   beware of Love!

Cupid—deceptively cute but full of mischief—is the poster boy of Renaissance love poetry. Cupid's sensually attractive and unpredictable power fills the ceiling in the beautiful Villa Farnesina in Rome, where Agostino Chigi, banker to the pope, held parties and negotiated deals (see figure 7). Here, in Raphael's lovely ceiling frescoes telling the story of Cupid and Psyche, we can sense the appeal of a figure like Cupid to Guarini's audience, the elite, well-educated Italian courtiers of the sixteenth century. In one of the spandrels, a teenage Cupid hovers at the edge of heaven, wings poised for flight. Though he is in the company of the three Graces, he is not content merely to hang around with these lovely women: he's off on an escapade. Bow at the ready, he is about to plunge some poor mortal into a love affair (in this case, his victim is Psyche; as the story proceeds, Cupid himself will be implicated in the complications of his own love arrows). The image shows us how Cupid both thrives on beauty and opts for mischief. These contradictions are what we are going to see in Guarini as he rings changes on the teenage boy who is also the god of Love.

Translating Italian poems of the sixteenth century into English inevitably leads us to the English Petrarchans who were Guarini's contemporaries. Edmund Spenser delved deep into the paradoxes of Cupid, composing a series of almost a hundred sonnets that he called *Amoretti*—"little Loves." Spenser's Cupid is both a powerful tyrant, against whose wrongs the lover loftily complains, and also a mischievous boy who simply delights in the suffering he has inflicted on lovers. Here's one of Spenser's Cupid sonnets:

One day as I unwarily did gaze
   on those fair eyes, my love's immortal light,
   the whiles my astonished heart stood in amaze,
   through sweet illusion of her looks' delight;
I might perceive how in her glancing sight,

legions of loves with little wings did fly,
  darting their deadly arrows fiery bright,
  at every rash beholder passing by.
One of those archers closely I did spy,
  aiming his arrow at my very heart:
  when suddenly with twinkle of her eye,
  the damsel broke his misintended dart.
Had she not so done, sure I had been slain;
  yet as it was, I hardly 'scaped with pain.

Beware of Cupid, indeed! His arrows bring pain, and unrequited love, and death. As Puck notes in *A Midsummer Night's Dream*, "Cupid is a knavish lad, / Thus to make poor females mad." On the other hand, as Spenser's arch sonnet shows, the power of Cupid is secondary to that of the beloved lady, the "damsel" who can laugh both at her lover and at the God of Love.

Did Spenser and Guarini believe in Cupid as a god? Almost certainly not: they were both Christians and would never have formally acknowledged such a pagan idea. But for each of them, the winged god is a potent symbol for the multiple and unpredictable ways in which love can act on the heart.

1

Chi vuol aver felice, e lieto il core,
  non segua il crudo Amore.
  Quel lusinghier, ch'ancide
  quando più scherza, e ride,
ma tema di beltà di leggiadria
  l'aura fallace, e ria.
Al pregar non risponda; a la promessa
  non creda; e se s'appressa
fugga pur, che baleno è quel ch'alletta,
né mai balena Amor se non saetta.

All you who want a quiet life
    beware of Love!
    He smiles and laughs
    while shooting you;
he seems so beautiful, but that
    is all a fake.

He never satisfies; he breaks
   all promises.
Keep clear! He's like a powder flash . . .
brilliant—and very dangerous!

Love is both brilliant and dangerous: this is the central contradiction of the Petrarchan tradition. Love is endlessly attractive, and endlessly painful. Guarini's Cupid is a trickster spirit, Olympian in his amorality, totally unconcerned for human well-being.

Guarini writes of Cupid as a "flash" (*balena*); I have used gunpowder to intensify that metaphor of sudden illumination, thinking of how dangerous guns and gunpowder must have been in the sixteenth century. Those early flintlocks and blunderbusses emitted bright and terrifying flashes, sometimes killing the enemy, but other times exploding in the shooter's face.

2

   O miseria d'amante,
     fuggir quel, che si brama,
e paventar quella beltà che s'ama.
   Io moro: e se cercando
     vo pietà del mio male,
più de la morte, è la pietà mortale.
   Così vo trapassando
di pena in pena, e d'una in altra sorte;
né scampo ho dal morire altro, che morte.

   Love is a wretchedness,
     running from what it seeks,
fearing the beauty it desires.
   Love's terminally ill,
     longing for sympathy,
but pity hurts far more than death.
   Love never rests, but flies
from pain to pain, from fate to fate.
No cure for dying but to die.

The restless energy of unrequited love is an asset for the poet: the suffering of a lover serves as the catalyst for a recurring and almost inexhaustible poetic creativity. Naturally, these poems are "all about me": in the Italian, almost every one of them is built on the first-person pronoun. "*Io moro*": I'm dying, the lover cries. But who is the "I" here? A fiction, of course: the poet's created avatar, a rhetorical figure rather than a subject of autobiography. The poet is happy to dwell for a while in the Petrarchan paradoxes of the invented lover. So in translating this madrigal, I have removed the first-person pronoun and concentrated on the poet who looks at Love with fear and (I think) considerable awe.

3

> *Che dura legge hai nel tuo regno, Amore.*
>   *L'amare, e non gioire*
> *è troppo insoportabile martire.*
> *Che non provedi tu, se vuoi che s'ami,*
>   *o che quel non si brami,*
>   *che non si può fruire;*
> *o che dietro al desio volin le piante,*
> *e dove giugni tu, giunga l'amante.*

> Love, there's a bitter law in your domain,
>   enforcing our desire
> and yet sequestering fulfillment.
> If we're to love, let's try a new approach:
>   exempt all those who love
>   and never will find bliss;
> or else give joy to all your followers,
> and let them join Love in your promised land.

Cupid is here not only a god, but also a head of state and a lawmaker. But is he a tyrant or a statesman? As tyrant, he has imposed a harsh law: "Be it hereby known that lovers shall never succeed in love." But might this tyrant hear the lover's plea? Might he feel sympathy with the suffering of his subjects? The poet appeals to his "lord" for reform, as Guarini might have appealed to the Gonzagas of Mantua or the Estes of Ferrara, despots who nonetheless wanted to be seen as enlightened rulers. The lover has a reasonable point: why would Love keep lovers in subjection, if he needs a polity of willing and faithful followers?

4

   Dov'hai tu nido, Amore,
nel viso di Madonna, o nel mio core?
    S'io miro come splendi,
    se' tutto in quel bel volto;
ma se poi come impiaghi, e come accendi,
    se' tutto in me raccolto.
Deh, se mostrar le meraviglie vuoi
    del tuo poter in noi,
    talor cangia ricetto;
ed entra a me nel viso, a lei nel petto.

   Love, where's your home?
In her? or in my heart?
    When you are sweet,
    you shine in her.
But when you fire things up,
    I take the heat!
It's time to show your power,
    change things around.
    Be like a god:
shine out in me, and burn in her!

In Petrarchan tradition, Love is a fire. Here the poet imagines Love as a bird that makes its nest (*nido*) in two very different places: in the radiant face (*bel volto*) of the beloved and in the suffering heart (*core*) of the unrequited lover. This symmetrical poem turns on the asymmetry of the situation: Love shines in her face but nurtures suffering in his heart. So the lover throws out a challenge to Love: if you would live in the lover's face instead, things would turn around. She would take one look at the lover and finally return his passion. The lover would be radiant and the beloved would suffer.

5

   Amor, poiché non giova
l'amar un cor fugace, un cor ingrato,
    poiché l'esser amato
    lui non fa più costante,

né me fa men amante
l'aver dura mercede,
fammi giustizia. O cresci in lui la fede,
   se'n me cresci il desio;
o spegni co'l suo foco il foco mio.

Listen up, Love!
It's useless, going after her:
   my promises
   won't make her love,
   but I can't stop
   promising love.
So, give me justice! Melt her heart;
   or let disdain
incinerate my futile love.

If Love is a god, he should mete out justice to his followers. The lover boldly—brashly, even—complains to his god about the intolerable condition of his life: his beloved is faithless. Yet he loves her in spite of that. He knows that loving her won't make her love him; he also knows that her unfaithfulness won't make him stop loving her. So he petitions Love: either make her love, or let him off the hook by letting him stop loving her!

As often in these poems, the ostensibly reasonable rhetoric (in this case, an appeal to justice) hides a darker purpose: to label the beloved's indifference as cruelty. Blame takes many guises in these madrigals.

6

Deh ferma, ferma il tuo rubella, Amore
   che fugge dal tuo Regno,
   et ha seco il mio core.
Fa che mi renda il mio fidato pegno.
Ma non tardar ch'io mor, s'ei s'allontana,
   vola veloce, in fretta,
   prima che giunga a tana;
che se non fai di me, Signor, vendetta,
   ecco di te si gloria
con la sua crudeltade aver Vittoria.

Cupid, arrest that fugitive!
    She's on the move,
        my heart in hand!
Make her give back the heart she stole!
Hurry! I'll die if she escapes!
    Move now, before
        she goes to ground!
If you don't catch her soon, you'll see:
    "Victoria"
will tell the world she's beaten you!

Love is a feudal lord, and the lover is Love's vassal. The subject has lost his heart to his beloved, so he petitions his lord for redress, or perhaps revenge (*vendetta*). As he figures it, the situation is urgent: if she leaves Love's domain with his stolen heart, he'll never get it back. He reminds Love that if a vassal is dishonored, so is the lord.

The beloved's name—as in a few other poems in this collection—suggests a real-life situation, apparently referring to a recognizable woman named Vittoria. Her name then becomes the punning occasion for the poem.

7

Troppo ben può questo tiranno Amore,
    poiché non val fuggire
    a chi no'l può soffrire.
Quand'i' penso talor com'arde, e punge.
    I' dico ah core stolto
    non l'aspettar. Che fai?
Fuggilo sì, che non ti prenda mai.
Ma poi sì dolce lusinghier mi giunge,
    ch'i' dico ah core sciolto
    perché fuggito l'hai?
Prendilo sì, che non ti fugga mai.

Kidnapper Love's too tough by half—
    I can't escape,
        only endure.
Sometimes I see how cruel he is,

and tell myself,
 "Don't wait around,
escape! Don't let him keep you here!"
But then he treats me tenderly;
 I say, "Crazy!
 Why should I run?
I should make sure *he* never runs!"

Love is a dangerous predator, the one who hurts you while he makes you think he loves you. As in the Stockholm syndrome, Love's prisoner recognizes two contrasting impulses: "Run! Get away from Love!" / "Stay! Don't let Love get away from *you!*"

8

Dice la mia bellissima Licori
 quando talor favello
seco d'Amor, ch'Amor è spiritello,
che vaga, e vola, e non si può tenere,
 né toccar, né vedere.
 E pur se gli occhi giro
 ne' suoi begli occhi, il miro:
ma no 'l posso toccar, che sol si tocca
 in quella bella bocca.

Once in a while we talk of Love,
 just she and I.
She says that Love's a little sprite
that wanders where it will, and can't
 be touched or seen.
 And then I see
 Love in her eyes!
But I can't touch it there—only
 on her soft lips.

The tension around Love in so many of the other poems is diffused in this simple lyric. Not an accusation but a chat, it ends in a delicately imagined kiss. The lover archly asserts that he knows where to *see* this airy spirit of Love (in her eyes) and where to *touch* it (on her lips). Those lips are, not coincidentally, the very lips that are conversing with him about Love. Slyly, he thus introduces what he hopes for, a shift from chatting to kissing.

Love as a sprite (*spiritello*) appears throughout the sonnets and madrigals of the Renaissance, often in little poems called "anacreontics." The name Licori in the original is a stock female name in pastoral poetry.

9

> *Punto da un' ape, a cui*
> *rubava il mele il pargoletto Amore,*
>   *quel rubato licore*
> *tutto pien d'ira, e di vendetta pose*
>   *su le labra di rose*
> *a la mia Donna, e disse, in voi si serbe*
>   *memoria non mai spenta*
> *de le soavi mie rapine acerbe;*
>   *e chi vi bacia senta*
> *de l'ape ch'io provai dolce, e crudele*
> *l'ago nel core, e nella bocca il mele.*

> Stung by the bees from whom
> he'd filched a honeycomb, the God
>   was eager for revenge.
> He daubed the stolen sweet
>   right on my lady's lips,
> and said: "Now and forever more,
>   here's a reminder
> of Love's two-sided destiny.
>   Whoever kisses you
> will learn that Love is sweet and cruel—
> a honeyed lip, a lasting sting."

A breezy, comic frolic about stolen favors. The mischievous Cupid steals honey from a bee and gets stung in the process. In revenge, he decrees that the lady's lips will be a permanent reminder of the double nature of the theft (stolen honey, stolen kiss): the sweetness of the kiss will be accompanied by the sting of her indifference.

10

Amor, non ha il tuo regno
più perfido del mio, più lieve amante;
né donna più di me fida, e costante.
  Qual ti dirò, Signore,
mobil fanciullo, o deità possente?
  Se tanto hai di valore
  sovra l'umana gente,
perché del Idol mio non fermi il core?
O, s'hai pur forza di cangiar desio,
  perché non cangi il mio?

Your kingdom, Love,
has no subject more loyal than I,
and none more treacherous than he.
  Are you divine,
Cupid, or just a little brat?
  If you're in charge
  of love, then why
not use some force: make *him* behave!
And if you legislate desire,
  can't you change *mine*?

Another challenge to Cupid, this time (unusually) in the woman's voice.
She is fed up with being in love with a man who sleeps around (he is treacherous and flighty—*perfido* and *lieve*). She appeals to Love's supposed power:
if you really rule, then use your power on my behalf, either to make him constant or to let me stop loving him.

Is there any hope in this appeal? It's doubtful. She's no happier than any
of the men whose voices we hear in the other madrigals. Love is not really
mighty, merely meddlesome.

SECTION 2   Love and Indifference

Only your cruel heart,
like toxic waste, poisons and corrupts.

Beauty and cruelty—a paradoxical combination, in the lover's mind, at least. The lover longs for beauty: gazes at it and nurtures it in his heart. But he "can't get no satisfaction." His beloved seems to him indifferent, evasive, tantalizing, or downright hostile. The Petrarchan beloved (almost always the woman) flirts with others and refuses to let him woo her—or even, sometimes, to look at her.

The poems in this section revel in the contradiction between beauty that invites and cruelty that rejects. The contradiction, of course, lies not only in the beloved, but in the lover as well. His "heart" is similarly bifurcated by love: desire battles with dejection, hope with fear, joy with pain. These poems look through the eyes of the frustrated lover, eyes that frame a self-consciously "male gaze." Appropriately, then, the eyes of the beloved are what the lover concentrates on. Those eyes are often imagined as stars, astrologically potent bodies that attract, control, or thwart the fortunes of the lover.

Sir Philip Sidney, a contemporary of Guarini in the court of Elizabeth of England, also explores the contradictions of desire. Sidney's sonnet sequence *Astrophil and Stella* reimagines Sidney's love for Penelope Rich, once his fiancée but now unhappily married to another man. Their affair was patently recognizable to early readers: Stella ("star") is Penelope Rich, and Astrophil ("star lover") is Sidney.

In this sonnet, Sidney, with tongue only partly in cheek, lays out his frustrations as Stella's lover (she has black eyes, hence the "black beams" of the second line):

What, have I thus betrayed my liberty?
Can those black beams such burning marks engrave
In my free side? Or am I born a slave,
Whose neck becomes such yoke of tyranny?
Or want I sense to feel my misery?

37

> *Or sprite, disdain of such disdain to have?*
> *Who for long faith, though daily help I crave,*
> *May get no alms but scorn of beggary.*
>   *Virtue awake! Beauty but beauty is;*
> *I may, I must, I can, I will, I do*
> *Leave following that which it is gain to miss.*
> *Let her go. Soft, but here she comes. Go to,*
>   *Unkind, I love you not. O me, that eye*
>   *Doth make my heart give to my tongue the lie.*

Sidney's restless questioning in the first eight lines gives way to an obviously self-contradictory set of assertions. It's clear that, for Sidney as for Guarini, the indifferent, "cruel" mistress controls the lover's reason and will. She tortures her lover with her beauty and power. The lover is unable—and indeed unwilling—to escape his destiny. The sonnet's rhetorical vitality dramatizes the obvious fact: he thrives on cruelty even as it tears him apart.

11

> *Se 'n voi pose natura*
> *bellezze, onde fra l'altre il pregio avete;*
> *perché nemica a le sue leggi sète?*
> *Ciò che fa il mondo adorno, herbe, fior, fronde;*
>   *e ciò che nutre, e pasce*
>   *l'aria, la terra, e l'onde,*
> *simile al seme suo fecondo nasce:*
>   *sol crudele il cor vostro,*
> *quasi ingrato terren produce un mostro,*
>   *ah, di voi troppo indegno;*
> *che se'n lui spargo amor, ne mieto sdegno.*

> Nature has given you
> beauty, the measure of all graceful things,
> but you ungraciously resist Her laws.
> All that live on earth or sea
>   or air—flowers and plants,
>   animals, fish and birds—
> grow by the patterns of their genes.

Only your cruel heart,
like toxic waste, poisons and corrupts.
    Be it a shame to you,
that I sow love in you, and harvest hate.

Neo-Platonic thought underlies much of Petrarchan poetry. In that ide-
alizing ideology, nature tends toward what is beautiful, and the beautiful in
turn leads toward the divine. So, in a beneficent nature, sexuality should be
good, and should lead to a higher good. In Milton's Eden, Adam and Eve
enjoy each other's beauty and participate in the pleasures of physical love. But
in a fallen world—the world where Guarini's encounters take place—Platonic
ideals do not often hold sway, and desire does not necessarily lead to a higher
good. The fields in which love is sown produce thorns. Here I've described
this as "toxic waste": the poet calls it *ingrato terren*—"thankless ground."

12

Ama, ben dice Amore,
    gli occhi, il viso, le chiome
di questa Dea; ch'angelica beltate
    non sta senza pietate.
    Ma, lasso, il fero nome
    par che nel cor mi dica,
fuggi d'Amor, e di pietà nemica
Barbara Donna, che gli amanti ancide;
    poi li burla, e sen' ride.

Love commands: "Love
    those eyes, that face,
that goddess. Such angelic beauty
    will love you back."
    But oh! my heart
    knows what she is:
the terror of the world, a real
"Barbarian"! I run away,
    and she just laughs.

The god of Love proposes that beauty will necessarily, always, be associated with goodness. But in this case, Love is unable to make his promise good.

This beloved woman may be beautiful, but everyone, including Love, runs away from her, terrified of her cruelty.

As in other madrigals, Guarini apparently puns on a name from among his circles, in this case, "Barbara"—a lady he denounces as "barbarous." She mocks her fearful lovers with that expressive Italian verb *burlare*—the root of our word *burlesque*: in my translation, "and she just laughs."

13

Perfidissimo volto,
ben l'usata bellezza in te si vede,
che mi consuma il core,
ma non l'usata fede.
Ah, se tu perdi amore,
perché seco non perdi ancor vaghezza,
o non hai pari a la beltà fermezza?

Like what you see?
Of course: you see beauty in her;
it sears your heart;
you trust in her;
but she walks out.
You think she looks so beautiful:
it's beauty, not fidelity.

The poem begins harshly in the Italian (*perfidissimo*—"utterly treacherous"). To keep something of the shock value of the disjunction between beauty and faithlessness that so angers the lover, I have invented a third party ("you") to whom the lover speaks bitterly about his beloved's treachery.

This poem was shortened by Guarini from fifteen lines to seven, sharpening the thrust of the poem's antithesis between beauty and inconstancy.

14

Sì voglio, e vorrò sempre
più tosto solo, e misero morire,
che di quel ben gioire,
che non è tutto mio.
Fingi, prega, e lusinga,

traditrice beltà; già non tem'io,
che, s'ardi, o leghi altrui, me scaldi, o stringa.
Fa pur vezzi, se sai,
se tutta mia non sei, nulla sarai.

I'd rather have
a life of woe, a lonely death,
than love where I'm
not sure of love.
Flirt where you want,
you Siren! Give it all away,
wherever! I am not afraid
of being burned.
You're nothing, if you can't be mine.

Caught in a tormented and frustrated love, the lover pretends to reimagine his wretchedness as a condition of free choice. However badly his beloved behaves with other lovers, he is—or claims to be—immune to her wiles. His convoluted assertions diminish her to a state of nothingness (*nulla*). Obviously in pain himself—despite his claims to the contrary—he lashes back with this rhetoric of bravado.

15

Poiché non mi credete,
quand'io vi giuro che voi sola adoro,
crederetel s'io moro?
Ahi ch'ogni Donna incredula è infedele;
e s'è tale e crudele.
Che chi non prova amore, amor non crede,
e fede non può dar chi non ha fede.

You won't believe
I love you. So will you believe
me if I die?
No; none of you believe in love,
so you give none—
knowing no love, believing none,
incapable of loving back.

Faith, vows, belief . . . love assimilates the language of religion. Those who cannot believe in love, who have no faith, cannot give love back. The lover generalizes from rejection by his beloved to all—all women, all beloved ones, must be the same: resistant to hearing love and unwilling to give love in return.

16

Lauro, oimè, lauro ingrato,
alcun de' pregi tuoi non hai smarrito.
  Più che mai odorato;
  più che mai colorito;
  e pur non sei quel lauro,
  ch'eri già del mio core
con la fid'ombra, e co'l soave odore
  dolcissimo ristauro.
O pianta insidiosa; in cui si vede
con fiorita bellezza arida fede.

  Ingrateful Laurel,
laden with empty promises!
  So beautiful,
    sweeter than ever!
    Yet not the one
    that used to shade
me from the heat, restoring me
    with cool breezes.
Now your Edenic greenery
rattles, like dry autumnal leaves.

The laurel (*laura*) gives a welcome dark green shade in the hot Italian sunshine; it also has a long poetic history. In Ovid, the maiden Daphne, pursued by Apollo, was saved from him only by being transformed into a laurel tree. "Laura" was the woman about whom Petrarch wrote his love poems and who, dying young, became the object of his grief and the symbol of hope. Guarini's "Laurel" may be a pun on the name of a contemporary, like Vittoria and Barbara (see *Ama, ben dice amore*, #12, and *Deh ferma, ferma*, #6).

The more Guarini plunges us into the disorders of love, the more we come to realize that the disease lies in the lover rather than in the beloved. To be sure, she is indifferent to him and pleasant with others, but it is the obsessive lover who constructs her indifference as cruelty and her friendliness as treachery.

17

> Cura gelata, e ria,
> che turbi, ed aveleni
> gli usati del mio cor dolci conforti:
> se falso è quel che porti,
> deh perché teco meni
> larve sì belle, e sì ben finti mostri?
> Crudel, ma se tu mostri
> il vero agli occhi miei,
> anco più falsa, e più mentita sei;
> che sembri gelosia,
> e se' la morte mia.

> You poison me
> with medicines
> that used to comfort me.
> You offer frauds
> wrapped in sweet words
> and well-concocted tales.
> To see the truth
> would be much worse:
> your lies too obvious.
> The certainty
> would do me in.

What seems sweet is bitter at the core. The beloved shows him some attentions, but the lover sees these overtures as mere fantasies, illusions that disguise a basic indifference. Her soothing words are only lovely specters (*larve sì belle*). Even so, the lover clings to his fantasies, for the bare truth would be too hard to accept. To *know* that she loves someone else would kill him.

18

A che tanto prezzar porpora, ed oro,
  chè dono di ventura,
se l'un nel crin, l'altro nel volto avete,
  chè dono di natura?
  Deh, se pur vaga sète
d'amar cosa mirabile in altrui,
amate amor in me, che non è in vui.

Why do you covet Fortune's rewards,
  rubies and gold?
Nature already gave you these—
  your cheeks, your hair.
  If you want things
that others have, and you do not,
then covet love; there's none in you.

In this tiny madrigal, the poet takes the moral high road, contemptuous of his beloved, who longs for the riches of the world but is indifferent to gifts of real value—beauty and love. At the end, the lover throws what he intends to be a knockout punch.

19

AMA[NTE]. *Deh dimmi Amor se gli occhi di Camilla*
          son occhi, o pur due stelle?
AMO[RE].   *Sciocco, non ha possanza*
          natura, a cui virtute il ciel prescrisse,
          di far luci sì belle.
AMA[NTE]. *Son elle erranti o fisse?*
AMO[RE].   *Fisse, ma de gli amanti*
          fan gir (no'l provi tu) l'anime erranti.

"Tell me whether Camilla's eyes
  are eyes or stars."
  "Nothing on earth,
nothing natural, could hope
  to shine like them."

"They're planets, then?"
"Fixed stars, that hurtle
lovers to outer space. Don't look!"

This dialogue between the lover and Love hangs on two astronomical distinctions from this period. The first is the difference between the natural and the celestial realms: the natural (or "sublunar," under the sphere of the moon in the old cosmology) is transitory and imperfect, but the higher celestial bodies are unchanging and perfect. The second distinction is between the fixed stars and the planets: the fixed stars do not alter in relation to each other, whereas the planets—especially in the days before Copernican theories—wander eccentrically. In astrological thought, the planets—not the fixed stars—determine our destinies.

20

Occhi, stelle mortali,
ministre de' miei mali,
che'n sogno anco mostrate
che'l mio morir bramate;
se chiusi m'uccidete,
aperti che farete?

Even in sleep, your eyes
are bright death stars; they shoot
me with their deadly rays,
the messengers of pain.
Closed, they're the death of me;
but open . . . worse disaster!

This concentrated madrigal is simple in form—three rhyming couplets, each line just seven syllables in Italian. The lover, bound to the wheel of torment, revels in the clear inevitability of his pain. When they are closed, the beloved's eyes give pain, but when open, they become agents of an even darker fate. The *stelle mortali* are malevolent signs, planets of astrological "disaster"—etymologically, the condition of being "star-crossed," as Shakespeare puts it in *Romeo and Juliet*.

21

Ite amari sospiri
a la bella cagion del morir mio,
e dite. O troppo di pietate ignuda;
     s'avete pur desio
di lungamente conservarvi cruda,
     allentate il rigore,
     che quel meschin si more:
e darà tosto fin col suo morire
a la durezza vostra, al suo languire.

Go, bitter sighs,
go find my torturer!
Tell her that she's too cruel
     for her own good;
that if she wants a life,
     she should relent
     and let me die;
then she'd be rid of me
and I could be at peace.

The poem purports to be a messenger to the beloved; in Renaissance terms, it is an "envoi," an ambassador, carried by the lover's sighs. The message itself is a harsh one, blaming his beloved for not loving in return. The envoi, though, suggests a possible compromise: if the beloved would lighten up, the lover could go ahead and die. Then the beloved could live without the cruelty that is killing both of them.

Is the offer made lovingly? I don't think so: in an especially bitter phrase, the poet describes the beloved as *troppo di pietate ignuda*—literally, naked of mercy.

22

Lasso, perché mi fuggi,
s'hai de la morte mia tanto desio?
     Tu se' pur il cor mio;
     credi tu per fuggire,
     crudel, farmi morire?

Ah, non si può morir senza dolore;
e doler non si può chi non ha core.

Why do you run?
Because you want me dead?
You think I'll die
if you take off?
No way: my heart
belongs to you. Without a heart,
no one feels pain, no one can die.

This madrigal is based on a favorite Petrarchan trope: the beloved possesses the lover's heart but places no value on that heart, scorns the love it
brings, and avoids the lover's presence. She even makes love to someone else.
It's a predicament: the beloved wants the lover to die; however, without a
heart (which, remember, has been given away to the beloved), no one can
live or die. So nothing can happen, nothing can change. In a way, the lover's
chopped logic wins the day (of course it does—the lover is the poet, the only
one speaking). But the victory is Pyrrhic, since the lover wins only by wearing
his suffering on the sleeve—he becomes a sort of zombie of love.

In the *Opere Omnia* of Monteverdi, this poem is attributed to Guarini's
contemporary Torquato Tasso, but its later inclusion in the 1598 edition of
Guarini's poems contradicts that attribution. With its combination of direct-
ness, melancholy, and expressiveness, it was a favorite of composers.

23

Ma tu più che mai dura
favilla di pietà non senti ancora,
anzi t'innaspri più, quanto più prego,
così senza parlar, dunque m'ascolti?
A chi parlo infelice, a un muto marmo?
S'altro non mi vuoi dir, dimmi almen muori
e morir mi vedrai.
Questa è ben'empio Amor miseria estrema
che sì rigida Ninfa
non mi risponda, e l'armi
d'una sola sdegnosa, e cruda voce

sdegni di proferire
al mio morire.

You are so hard,
no pity troubles you—
harder, the more I beg.
I speak; you say nothing—
like talking to a rock.
Want me dead? Just say, "Die!"
    You'll see me dead.
You are Love's poker face:
    a girl of stone
    who grudges me
that little clue, that word
    releasing me
    to blissful death.

Guarini's madrigals are little echo chambers. Here the imperative *mori* (die!) is echoed almost immediately by the same root word in the infinitive *morir* (to die). Similarly, *sdegnosa* (scornful) is followed by the same word in the next line—*sdegni* (you scorn). This varied repetition (polyptoton, in rhetorical terminology) provides resonance, a connective tissue that contributes to the coherence and intensity of this compressed poem.

24

Donna, lasciate i boschi;
che fu ben Cintia cacciatrice anch'ella,
ma non fu come voi leggiadra, e bella.
    Voi avete beltate
da far preda di cori, e non di belve.
    Venere in fra le selve
star non conviene, e se convien, deh siate
fera solo a le fiere, a me benigna:
Cintia ne boschi, e nel mio sen Ciprigna.

Put down that bow!
Goddess Diana rules the hunt,
but you're more beautiful than she;
    your arrows hit

the hearts of men, not animals.
    Venus should stay
out of the forest! If you must
shoot, aim at those too proud to love;
leave me to live and worship you.

Diana (Cynthia) is the fierce goddess of the hunt—beautiful, stern, and virginal. Venus (the Cypriot) is loving and sexy, not a hunter. In the often-recounted story, Venus tragically watches her lover Adonis die, wounded by a boar. Hunts were part of Renaissance courtly life, but this hunt and these arrows seem more figurative than realistic.

25

Udite lagrimosi
    spirti d'Averno, udite
nova sorte di pena, e di tormento:
    mirate crudo affetto
    in sembiante pietoso.
La mia Donna crudel più de l'inferno,
    perch'una sola morte
non può far sazia sua ingordo voglia,
    e la mia vita è quasi
    una perpetua morte,
    mi comanda, ch'i' viva,
    perché la vita mia
di mille morti il dì ricetto sia.

    Unhappy souls, weeping
    in Stygian darkness, hear
of even more excruciating pains,
    as cruelty puts on
    the cloak of tenderness.
My lady's more implacable than Dante's fiends.
    A single death—my death—
won't satisfy her appetite for blood
    (and anyway, my life
    is simply one long death).
    She orders me to live—

and thus my life, each day,
supplies her slaughterhouse a thousand deaths.

In the lover's gothic imagination, the beloved is both angelic and infernal. The lover feeds her with his repeated deaths. In a recurring Renaissance pun, "death" also means orgasm. When he refers at the end of the madrigal to those *mille morti* (thousand deaths), it is broadly unsettling: a thousand kisses might be desirable, but a thousand orgasms, each day?

SECTION 3   Lovers' Anxieties

> *In that fierce heat, I know,*
> *I may lose wings, and so my life—*
> *but may find joy as well.*

The lover is tossed by the conflicting winds of love: doubt, affirmation; fear, courage; silence, assertion. He shares the ambition of Icarus, to dare to fly toward the heights that he imagines his beloved to inhabit. But he also shares the fate of Icarus: he flies too close to the sun, the wax that holds his wings melts, and he falls. The essential condition is oxymoronic: flying and falling at the same time.

The ceilings of the palaces of northern Italy often depict men or gods in flight—Apollo, Phaeton, Daedalus, and Icarus—aviators who hover on the arched vaults, defying gravity. Seeing Daedalus in flight and Icarus falling from the skies must have astonished the pre-flight imaginations of those in the sixteenth century.

In a famous sonnet, Petrarch lays out the lover's storm-tossed existence:

> *I find no peace, and yet I am not warlike;*
> *I fear and hope, I burn and turn to ice;*
> *I fly beyond the sky, stretch out on earth;*
> *my hands are empty, yet I hold the world.*
>
> *One holds me prisoner, not locked up, not free;*
> *won't keep me for her own but won't release me;*
> *Love does not kill me, does not loose my chains,*
> *he'd like me dead, he'd like me still ensnared.*
>
> *I see without my eyes, cry with no tongue,*
> *I want to die and yet I call for help,*
> *hating myself but loving someone else.*
>
> *I feed on pain, I laugh while shedding tears,*
> *both death and life displease me equally;*
> *and this state, Lady, is because of you.*

The ambiguity of Petrarch's lover (who can't pin down what he feels) directly reflects that of the beloved (who can't decide what to do with the lover) and that of Love himself (who can't determine what his votary deserves—life or death; freedom or imprisonment).

The Italian sonnet, with its division into two groups of lines, was perfect for expressing Petrarch's dichotomies. The poet could develop one condition in the first eight lines, and then contradict it in the next six. Exploiting the resonance of the Italian language and the richness of its rhymes, an Italian sonnet becomes an echo chamber. The Italian word *stanza*—a short poem or section of a poem—means, literally, "room." With his sonnet rooms, Petrarch built for his lovers an oddly claustrophobic habitation—an exquisitely furnished palace that is nonetheless a hodgepodge of contradictory emotions. He walls off for the lover a private chamber for intimate thoughts and feelings, to which, paradoxically, every reader has unhindered access.

Shorter, freer, and more flexible than the sonnet, the madrigal was Guarini's preferred form for the expression of love's contradictions. The multiplicity of love's experiences and the oxymoronic anxieties of the lover manifest themselves in Guarini not so much in the variety contained in a single poem, but in the breadth of experience contained in the collection itself. The madrigals, taken in almost any grouping, propel us through a bewildering variety of affects and emotions. Reading through a series of Guarini's madrigals, we can watch from safe ground as the lover flies and falls like Icarus, or—to pick another Baroque aeronaut—like Milton's Satan, buffeted by the contrary winds of Chaos, in book 2 of *Paradise Lost* ("vans" = wings; "pennons" = feathers; "rebuff" = counterblast; "instinct" = filled; "niter" = saltpeter):

> At last his sail-broad vans
> He spreads for flight, and in the surging smoke
> Uplifted spurns the ground, thence many a league
> As in a cloudy chair ascending rides
> Audacious, but that seat soon failing, meets
> A vast vacuity: all unawares
> Flutt'ring his pennons vain plumb down he drops
> Ten thousand fathom deep, and to this hour
> Down had been falling, had not by ill chance
> The strong rebuff of some tumultuous cloud
> Instinct with fire and niter hurried him
> As many miles aloft. . . .

26

> *A voi, Donna, volando*
> *l'amoroso mio cor da me si parte,*
> *vago di riveder gli amati soli;*
> *   ma non so con qual'arte*
> *o d'Icaro, o di Dedalo se'n voli:*
> *   so ben ch'al caldo lume*
> *poria perder le piume, e poi la vita,*
> *   ma segua ove l'invita*
> *   suo destino o sua gioia,*
> *pur che Dedalo giunga, Icaro moia.*

> My heart launches itself
> into the air, to see the sun
> yet one more time. I cannot tell
>   whose artifice directs
> me—Daedalus or Icarus?
>   In that fierce heat, I know,
> I may lose wings, and so my life—
>   but may find joy as well.
>   Like Daedalus, I'll reach
> my goal . . . or drown like Icarus!

Guarini captures the wonder of moving precariously through the cloudy heavens. The lover evinces a knowingness, fully aware of the dangers ("I may lose wings . . ."). But underneath that collected awareness, there's a deep anxiety driving him, as he veers blindly toward the perilous object of desire.

Giovanni Battista Ciotti, the printer of the 1598 Venice edition, had to excise certain words in Guarini's poems, words that ran against Catholic orthodoxy. In this poem, it is the word *destino*—destiny—that he cautiously replaced with an ellipsis: destiny—as opposed to Providence—was too pagan a concept for the Inquisition. The word was restored in the 1731 edition of Guarini's collected works. Further ellipses of this type are indicated in the Notes.

27

> *Come non cangia stile*
> *il mio destino ingiurioso, e fero;*
> *così non cangerò voglia, o pensiero.*

Saetti pur fortuna
indarno ogni sua forza incontra'l core
di fede armato adduna;
che dove spinse Amore
suo dolce aurato dardo
ogni altro strale è rintuzzato, e tardo.

Fortune attacks
relentlessly, but I
won't yield an inch of ground.
Spears fly in vain,
useless against my shield
of constancy.
Love's arrow pierced
me long ago:
all others are too dull, too late.

Fate—*destino, fortuna*—hurls sharp weapons at the lover, assaulting him, trying to force him to give up his aspirations to love. What are these weapons? They may be the things of the world, the matters of business and day-to-day life—his relationship with the duke, his acceptance at court, or the problems that his irascible temper may have caused. "Whatever they are," the poem seems to say, "bring them on!" How can he say this so confidently? Because he has been wounded by Love's golden arrow (*aurato dardo*); with its all-consuming pain, the wound apparently inoculated him against further pain.

28

Cor mio tu ti nascondi
a l'apparir del nostro amato sole?
E inanzi a sì bel foco
mi lasci freddo, e fioco?
Quando a formar parole
per domandar mercede
l'anima tormentata ardir ti chiede?
Che paventi codardo?
Fuggi tu forse il folgorar del guardo,
per fuggir il tuo fato?
Non sai morir beato.

My heart in hiding shrinks
when she appears, bright as the noontime sun.
   Caught in that radiance,
   I'm frozen, dumb, inept.
   I'm desperate to ask
   for grace, but when and how
to screw my courage to the sticking point?
   —You foolish, coward heart!
You think if you escape those flashing eyes,
   you can avoid your fate?
   Die and be glad of it!

These tiny poems make bold flights, lofted by the ardent desire that is their constant theme. Here, the lover realizes how the beauty of his beloved conveys her cruelty. In his hyperbolic imagination, her eyes become the terrifying weapons of a mythical creature, the beacons of a goddess, the intense light of the Italian sun. Not surprisingly, the lover, a mere mortal, takes cover.

Macbeth, from which I've borrowed a famous phrase (Shakespeare was a contemporary of Guarini), shares this poem's interest in the conflict between intention and action, though rather more bloodily.

29

   Parlo, misero, o taccio?
S'io taccio, che soccorso avrà il morire?
S'io parlo, che perdono avrà l'ardire?
   Taci: che ben s'intende
chiusa fiamma talor da chi l'accende.
   Parla in me la pietate,
   parla in lei la beltate;
e dice quel bel volto al crudo core,
chi può mirarmi, e non languir d'amore?

   To speak or not?
Silence would be like death,
but speaking is too brash.
   —No words! Keep love
hidden, cover the embers!
   Pain speaks for me

and beauty speaks
to her: "He looks at you;
and so of course he loves!"

In the feast of words, the poet-lover suddenly leaves the table, abandons language. Confronted by uncertainty, he takes the easy way out, remaining silent. Can anything come of that? It's hard to know "what to make of a diminished thing," as Frost knew. For his part, the lover hopes that his silence, like a fire banked for the night, will be of more use than the open flame of his desire. In the morning, the fire will be brought back to life; she may notice it and perhaps understand how her beauty must enthrall anyone who looks at her.

30

Piangea Donna crudele
un fuggitivo suo caro Augellino;
e co'l Ciel ne garriva, e co'l destino.
Quand'il mio cor amante,
sperando di sua frode aver diletto,
preso de l'Augellin tosto sembiante,
volò nel suo bel petto.
Ahi, che l'empia il conobbe, ahi, che l'ancise,
e per vaghezza asciugò il pianto, e rise.

Her parakeet escaped,
and then—though hard of heart—she wept,
and railed at destiny and God.
    Meanwhile, my hungry heart,
thinking to cheat its way to joy,
disguised itself as that lost bird
    and flew straight back to her.
She glanced at it, then wrung its neck;
and then she dried her tears, and smiled.

The little bird-poet-lover reminds me of the ubiquitous, hovering, mischievous *putti* in Italian palaces—the little winged Cupids that flutter about the corners of the ceilings, getting into trouble.

Sorrow, sentimentality, fraud, and ghastly indifference . . . all in a little room. The lady weeps for her lost bird; the lover takes her tears as a welcome glimmer of tenderness in a heart that has shown him nothing but scorn. He thinks he can take advantage of the moment by transforming himself into an avatar of the bird and flying back to her. But his ploy leads only to more cruelty.

31

> Voi volete ch'io mora,
> ne mi togliete ancora
> questa misera vita;
> e non mi date incontra morte aita.
> Moro, o non moro? Omai non mi negate
> mercede, o feritate.
> Che'n sì dubiosa sorte
> assai più fero è il non morir, che morte.

> She wants me dead
> but I'm alive . . .
> barely. I see
> no possibility of life or death.
> To be or not to be? She's cut me off
> from pain and hope.
> A zombie knows
> undeath's the most unkindest state of all.

The lover lives in a purgatory, an aimless wandering between death and life—*dubiosa sorte*, a doubtful fate. The beloved refuses to do anything to help to move him from this state of uncertainty—neither welcoming him to love, nor finally dismissing him. As far as he can tell, she is simply indifferent. Her negligence so clouds his life that, by the end, his life is merely the minimalist condition of not being dead—*il non morir*.

My translation draws on Shakespeare, of course, for Hamlet's famous statement of ambivalence and Mark Antony's bitter accusation of Brutus.

32

> La bella man vi stringo,
> e voi le ciglia per dolor stringete,
> e mi chiamate ingiusto, ed inhumano,

come tutto il gioire
sia mio, vostro il martire: e non vedete
   che se questa è la mano,
che tien stretto il cor mio, giusto è'l dolore,
perché stringendo lei stringo il mio core.

   I seize your hand;
your eyes squeeze shut in pain.
You say I'm cruel, that I enjoy
   this victory.
You're not the only victim here.
   My heart is clamped
in that strong grasp; gripping your hand,
I squeeze my own poor heart.

Finally, the lover does something: he takes his beloved's hand in his. She winces and blames him for hurting her (and more than likely, he does). He defends himself by turning the tables—because she holds his *heart* in her hand, the pain is his, more than hers. This taut madrigal is severe: after a tender moment at the beginning, where he praises her "lovely hand," it is a hurtful justification for hurting her. It all hangs on the verb *stringere* (to tighten, to squeeze), used twice in the first two lines and three times in the last two (*stretto* is its past participle).

33

O Donna troppo cruda, e troppo bella,
   da voi vien la mia stella.
Voi sète la mia vita, e la mia morte.
   Ma se la morte sète,
perché la vita ne' begli occhi avete?
   E se sète la vita,
   che non mi date aita?

Cruel and beautiful,
   my fatal star,
are you my life or death?
   If you're my death . . .
why do your eyes beam life?

If you're my life . . .
then rescue me!

To the lover, the beloved is fate—in the Italian, *stella* (another of the dangerously pagan words omitted by the 1598 editor). The stars may dictate our destiny, but they are difficult to read. This madrigal plays with the ambiguity of the stars: in them, the lover can read two opposite destinies: death and life. Alone, neither is consistent with the beloved. Her vital beauty contradicts her mortal power, but her cruelty makes it impossible to celebrate her as life. There seems no choice but to live within the oxymoron.

34

Io mi sento morir quando non miro
  colei ch'è la mia vita.
Poi se la miro anco morir mi sento,
  perché del mio tormento
non ha pietà la cruda, e non m'aita,
  e sa pur s'i' l'adoro,
così mirando, e non mirando, i' moro.

When I can't look at her, I'm dead:
  she is my life.
But if I look at her, I die
  again; my pain
leaves her unmoved. She gives no help;
  she knows I love.
Looking at her—or not—I'm hooked.

The lover is wound up so tight that he dies—both when he cannot see the beloved and when he can. As often, Guarini fashions a heartless beloved: beautiful, but lacking the generosity of spirit (*pietà*, "mercy") that should accompany beauty. In contrast, the lover is all heart, constructed of sentiment (twice he refers to himself with a form of the verb *sentire*, "to feel").

The poem ends with a mournful resonance—*così mirando, e non mirando, i'moro*; the melancholy verbs echo each other—*mirare*, "to look," and *morire*, "to die."

35

Occhi, un tempo mia vita,
occhi, di questo cor dolci sostegni,
    voi mi negate aita?
Questi son ben della mia morte, i segni.
    Non più speme, o conforto,
tempo è sol di morire, a che più tardo?
    Occhi, ch'a sì gran torto
morir mi fate, à che torcete il guardo?
Forse per non mirar come v'adoro?
    Mirate almen ch'io moro.

Eyes that were once my life,
my sweetness, my heart's only food—
    why have you cut me off?
You are the harbingers of death,
    the omens of my grief,
the heralds of my play's last scene.
    My executioners,
will you not even look at me?
If you won't see how much I love,
    still, you should watch me die.

In the world of Petrarchan poetry, ordinary events take on a life-and-death significance. When the beloved turns her eyes away, the lover dies. Those eyes were once his life; now they are his death. Perhaps they look at someone else? Perhaps they just don't want to look at him at all? The poem employs a desperate rhetoric in a last-ditch effort to get her to look at him—even if it's only to watch him die.

36

Un cibo di fuor dolce, e dentro amaro,
    Donna, voi mi porgeste;
    quasi dir mi voleste,
gusta, e impara a saper che tale i' sono.
    Ma se la donatrice
si de' gustar, come si gusta il dono;
    deh perché non mi lice

prima assaggiar quel chè di dolce in voi:
che dolce mi saria l'amaro poi.

You handed me a sugared nut—
   sweet, with a bitter core—
    as if you meant to say,
"O taste and see what's in my heart."
   The giver and the gift
should taste alike; so why not give
   me first a taste of what
is sweet in you? Then, afterward,
the bitter part won't taste so bad!

The almond, in Guarini's time, seems to have had a bitter taste and to have been served coated with sugar. As often in Petrarchan poetry, the poet finds significance in an apparently trivial event—here, the lady's offering of a nut. The gift—if we could call it that (perhaps a mere gesture of politeness?)—enables the lover's recurring complaint about the cruelty of the beloved. The poem is like a little pinprick that one-ups her indifference.

Although Guarini's madrigal itself calls it merely a snack (*cibo*), the poem's title in the 1598 edition of *Rime* specifies a sugared almond (*mandorla inzuccherata*).

37

Baciai, ma che mi valse attender frutto
   d'amorosa dolcezza,
se sparsi il seme in arida bellezza?
Son dolcissimi i baci a chi ne prende
   quel fin, che se n'attende.
   Ma s'altro non se'n coglie
tormenti son de l'amorose voglie.

I kissed—but, after that, what more?
   Nothing at all—
like planting seeds in desert sand.
Kisses are sweet if they can grow
   and bring forth fruit.
   If not, they sting
like little scorpions of desire.

This madrigal is terse and bitter in its erotic frustration. A momentary reward—a kiss—is shown to be empty, even painful. The torment is sharply contrasted with the beauty of the barren land (*arida bellezza*), the potential fruitfulness of love (*frutto / d'amorosa dolcezza*), and the desire that constantly regenerates in the will (*amorose voglie*)—all despite the pains that accompany love.

38

> *Un bacio solo, a tante pene? Cruda.*
> > *Un bacio a tanta fede?*
> > *La promessa mercede*
> *non si paga baciando: il bacio è segno*
> > *di futuro diletto,*
> *e par che dica anch'egli, i' ti prometto*
> > *con sì soave pegno.*
> > *Intanto or godi, e taci,*
> *che son d'amor mute promesse, i baci.*

> One kiss? Just one for all I've done,
> > for all I've given you?
> > One kiss can't pay your debt!
> But maybe it's an IOU—
> > redeemable, sometime?
> Maybe it reads, "I guarantee
> > returns upon this pledge;
> > enjoy it now, and wait:
> kisses are silent promises of love."

Another madrigal contemplating the lover's meager reward. The register of this poem is financial, not romantic: perhaps scarcity ("just one kiss") can be transformed into plenty ("more kisses!")? If the kiss can be interpreted as a promissory note, it will guarantee future returns on a present investment.

The banking image is more than a little devious, to say the least. Did Guarini learn these tricks from wheeler-dealers like the Medici, his Florentine banking contemporaries?

39

Oimè, se tanto amate
di sentir dir oimè, deh, perché fate
chi dice oimè morire?
S'i' moro, un sol potrete
languido, e doloroso oimè sentire;
ma se cor mio vorrete
che vita abb'io da voi, e voi da me,
avrete mille, e mille dolci oimè.

Oh, God! If you so want
to hear me say, "Oh, God," why kill
the one who groans, "Oh, God"?
For if I were to die
you'd hear just one last moan—"Oh, God!"
Darling, if you'd give in
and let me live and love, you'd hear
a thousand thousand times, "Oh, God!"

Oimè is usually translated as "alas!" But in this gem of a madrigal, there are so many meanings packed into that throwaway word that "alas" seems inadequate. I rendered it instead as "Oh, God!"—combining despair and sexual ecstasy in one potent phrase.

With his "thousand thousand" groans, the lover is echoing the famous numerological request in Catullus's fifth ode, *da mi basia mille . . .* ("give me a thousand kisses, then a hundred, then another thousand, a second hundred, then another thousand and a hundred").

Like Guarini's poem, Monteverdi's setting of it in his *Fourth Book of Madrigals* obsessively repeats and varies the *oimè*. Both poem and vocal madrigal are elegant mannerist indulgences, playfully pivoting from the conventional to the erotic on this one repeated moan.

SECTION 4   Fire and Eyes

I thought her blazing eyes,
in sympathy with love,
told me, "Your passion has ignited mine."
But when the flame died down,
and all that joy was smothered up in ash,
I knew the difference of eyes and heart.

"I burn and turn to ice": Petrarch's famous oxymoron, which I quoted at the opening of Section 3, is central to the Petrarchan poets' elaboration of love's contradictory and perilous conditions. The lover burns with desire, but the beloved freezes him out with her indifference. Or, inversely, the beloved heats the air with the fire of her beauty, and the lover, in cowardice, self-protection, or disdain, shrinks away from those searing flames and retreats into the icy caves of melancholy.

The Petrarchan lover often finds himself in a landscape of great danger: opening up to the emotional turbulence of unrequited love, he lives in a constant state of skirmish, if not open war. The eyes of the beloved can dart like lightning flashes or explode like cannon fire; their beauty strikes the lover with both desire and terror. Inside, his heart, stricken with love, burns constantly—sometimes smoldering, sometimes bursting forth in flames, sometimes sending a fever through the rest of his body.

And so it is no wonder that the lover feels lost. He seems often to live in darkness, clouded by imagination, oppressed by inactivity. The shadows that often envelop the lover arise from his own desire, like the smoke from his burning heart. They curb his own will, so that he reacts to the beloved almost at random, as one might in a maze: Do I turn here? Or here? Or keep on straight? Without perspective, caught in the narrowness of the heart's topography, how could he know what to do?

A sonnet by Lady Mary Wroth (a niece of Sir Philip Sidney) develops this maze-like uncertainty:

In this strange labyrinth how shall I turn?
Ways are on all sides, while the way I miss:
If to the right hand, there in love I burn;
Let me go forward, therein danger is.
If to the left, suspicion hinders bliss;
Let me turn back, shame cries I ought return,
Nor faint, though crosses with my fortune kiss;
Stand still is harder, although sure to mourn.
Thus let me take the right, or left hand way,
Go forward, or stand still, or back retire:
I must these doubts endure without allay
Or help, but travail find for my best hire.
Yet that which most my troubled sense doth move,
Is to leave all, and take the thread of Love.

Despite a near paralysis of will, the flame of hope leaps up at the end: "take the thread of love." That thread is what saved Theseus as he negotiated the labyrinth of the Minotaur. But poor Ariadne, who gave Theseus both the thread and the idea to use it, ended up abandoned on Naxos. In Wroth's claustrophobic labyrinth there seems no lasting hope of happiness—only the momentary flame of passion.

Guarini's madrigals explore these dangerous mazes of desire within the smaller and tighter enclosure of the heart. In his poems, the lover's heart is often figured as a hearth or a forge where a fire smolders fitfully, damped down for the night, perhaps in hiding from the cold of the beloved's scorn. On occasion, the fire, stirred and opened to the air, leaps up and burns bright. But the flame never lasts long. And in the beloved (at least as the lover imagines her) there is a heart closed so tightly that it can never burn; she will never love, he believes. And yet she keeps sending that "blazing fire" from her eyes! Hence the inevitable "difference of eyes and heart"—the contrast between the heat of her beauty and the coldness of her heart, between the lover's fiery desire and his icy despair.

40

Ardemmo insieme bella Donna, ed io
di sì subito ardore,
al lampeggiar dell'uno, e l'altro sguardo,
che se fosse tra noi pari il desio,

o che soave amore.
Parean dir gli occhi suoi
verso me scintillando, ardi, ch'i' ardo.
Lasso m'avvidi poi,
quando il mio ben mi fu celato, e tolto,
che l'un ardea nel cor, l'altra nel volto.

Together we caught fire, my love and I,
    sparked by a moment's glance:
a flash from one, caught in the other's eyes,
as if desire were really mutual.
    I thought her blazing eyes,
        in sympathy with love,
told me, "Your passion has ignited mine."
    But when the flame died down,
and all that joy was smothered up in ash,
I knew the difference of eyes and heart.

Despite the struggles, partings, betrayals, and indifference that drive many of these madrigals, these two protagonists momentarily seem to love each other. It is a hot love: the key word is *ardire* (to burn, to be passionate): the verb appears five times in this short poem, in various forms. But the insidious word *parire* (seem) also shows up, lurking like a salamander in the crucible of love (salamanders were thought to live in fire). The beloved *seems* to love, but seeming, as Hamlet knows, is not the same as being.

41

Una Farfalla cupida, e vagante
    fatt'è il mio cor amante;
        che va, quasi per gioco,
        scherzando intorno al foco
di due begli occhi, e tante volte, e tante
vola, e rivola, e fugge, e torna, e gira;
        che ne l'amato lume
lascierà con la vita al fin le piume.
        Ma chi di ciò sospira,
sospira a torto. Ardor caro, e felice
morrà Farfalla, e sorgerà fenice.

My loving heart flits like a moth;
   careless, it plays
   without concern
   around her eyes,
among the flames; it turns and whirls,
it runs away, then circles back.
   Seeking for light,
it will beguile itself of life.
   But what of that?
Blessed by desire, the moth will die,
and like a phoenix, rise again.

This *Liebestod* depends upon two conventional Renaissance emblems, the moth that flies toward the light and the phoenix that immolates itself and rises, reborn, from the ashes of its own pyre. As so often in these poems, a further convention applies—the barely concealed denotation of death as sexual climax.

The madrigal has an intense sequence of six action verbs at its center, describing the back-and-forth of the moth: *volte* (turns), *vola* (flies), *rivola* (flies again), *fugge* (flees), *torna* (returns), and *gira* (whirls).

42

   E così a poco a poco
torno Farfalla semplicetta al foco,
   e nel fallace sguardo
un'altra volta mi nudrico, ed ardo:
   ahi che piaga d'amore
quanto si cura più tanto men sana:
   ch'ogni fatica è vana,
quando fu punto un giovinetto core
   dal primo, e dolce strale:
chi spegne antico incendio il fa immortale.

   The silly moth
turns to the flame again;
   and I too feed
on beauty and on fire.
   Love's scars hurt more,

the more I bandage them.
　　No doctor's art
can cure that primal wound
　　of love in youth,
which aches relentlessly.

The moth returns (see #41). The emblem is pushed here almost to the point of the grotesque. Just as a moth inevitably burns itself in the flame, so the lover, "wounded" long ago in love, returns to the fatal fires of beauty. He may have felt healed, but his wound still festers under the scar. He thought he could resist the flame, ignore the pain: but he flies back to it again and again, as a patient scratches a scab. By end of the madrigal, we've come full circle: the fire, it turns out, is not only in the beloved's beauty but also in the lover himself. The fire that burns him is his own smoldering ember, the remains of his first scarring fire of love, lit long ago and never fully extinguished.

43

Morto mi vede la mia Morte in sogno,
poi desta anco si duol ch'i' viva, e spiri;
　　e co' turbati giri
di due luci sdegnose, ed omicide
　　mi saetta, e m'ancide.
Occhi ministri del mio fato amaro,
　　qual fuga, o qual riparo
　　avrò da voi, se fate
aperti il mio morir, chiusi il mirate?

She dreams that she has seen me dead,
then wakes, and finds me still alive.
　　She turns on me,
stabbing with scornful looks, and I
　　give up the ghost.
Those deadly eyes!—there's no escape,
　　no remedy.
　　Awake, they cause
my death; asleep, they watch me die.

The beloved dreams that her lover is dead. When she wakes, she finds him still alive—that is, still bothering her with his unwelcome desire. She's angry, and she lets her anger show. The paradox of love is that even her harshest looks are dear to the lover. Her eyes control his strange destiny: to feed on her indifference, and to long for even the most painful of attentions from her. He can't escape those eyes, but does he want to?

He is a brother to Keats's haunted knight-at-arms, who dreams that he kisses the eyes of his "belle dame sans merci," yet wakes to finds himself "alone and palely loitering" on the cold hillside.

44

Può dunque un sogno temerario, e vile
        privo di vita farmi
        negli occhi di mia vita?
        Né porai tu portarmi,
Amor, tu che pur vinci uomini, e Dei,
        vivo nel sen di lei?
Vendica tu con la tua dolce aita
        questo presagio amaro.
        O fortunato, e caro,
morir in sogno ne' begli occhi suoi,
per tornar vivo in quel bel seno poi.

How could she—in whom I live—
        have dreamed a dream
        in which I die?
        Love, you control
all destinies: give me a chance
        to live in her!
Sweeten this bitter omen, Love,
        and rescue me—
        happy the man
who dies in her fair dreaming eyes,
and comes to life in her embrace.

Another dream of death: here, the beloved's dream nurtures the poet even as it haunts the lover. As Shakespeare's Theseus says, "The lunatic, the lover and the poet / Are of imagination all compact." Imagination allows the lover—indistinguishable here from the poet, and perhaps from the madman as well—to draw sustenance from the strangest of places. If Love wills it, her dream may lead to a happier fantasy of fulfilled love: perhaps the intimacy of such a murderous dream requites the pain that accompanies it.

45

Rideva (ahi crudo affetto)
la mia fera bellissima, perch'io
lagrimando sfogava il dolor mio:
      quando per mia vendetta
da l'una, e l'altra sua ridente stella
      cadde una lagrimetta,
che cristallo parea d'alba novella.
      O dispietato core,
dissi alor, che non senti il fier dolore,
che può, mal grado tuo, nel suo bel viso,
far lo scherno pietà, lagrime il riso.

   Lovely and wild,
you laughed at me because
I fell apart in tears.
   But as you laughed,
there fell from each fair eye
   a single tear,
clear as the light of dawn.
   In scorning love,
you thought you were immune,
but love knows how to turn
your mockery to tears.

Like many Petrarchan poems, this madrigal pays close attention to the smallest of effects—here, the tears that result from laughing too hard. In the lover's dubious alchemy, these tears become gold: they represent her remorse, her shame at mocking her lover. The fiction of these penitential tears gives him hope that she might someday feel love.

46

Dunque vapor mal nato
a te lice cotanto? e tu quel fai,
ch'amorosa pietà non poté mai?
    Conosco or le tue frodi,
perfido: amante sei: tu ardi, e godi
solo quel bel, ch'a tutti gli altri è tolto:
    tu baci quel bel volto
cagion di sdegno, e poi di pianto in lei.
Ah, che fumo parevi, e foco sei.

You bastard, smoke!
How do you get away with it?
No honest man could act like this!
    You sneak! I know
your game: you fall in love with her,
you want her; and you get to her,
    you kiss her face,
you make her angry, and she cries!
You look like smoke, but you are hot!

Does the smoke in this madrigal arise from an open wood fire? Or from a poorly ventilated fireplace in a side room of a palace? Or from someone's tobacco pipe (then a fashionable novelty)? Guarini calls the smoke "badly born" (*mal nato*); righteous indignation at the presumption of this lower-class upstart fuels this comic rant. The smoke becomes an inanimate, intangible rival that gets in where no faithful, courteous lover could possibly go. This bumptious smoke succeeds in part because it lacks courtly manners—it doesn't mind upsetting the beloved. Smoke gets in her eyes.

47

Quanto per voi sofferse,
e quanto sospirò, Donna, il cor mio,
tutto al girar de' be' vostri occhi oblio.
    E se quella è pietate,
che nel sereno sfavillar si vede
    de la vostra beltate,

amorosa mercede
forse n'avrò: che ratto in gentil core
con l'esca di pietà s'accende amore.

> Sorrow's my life.
> But when you turn to look at me,
> my suffering is all forgotten.
>   If that's for real—
> that glance, that spark of love,
>   so beautiful—
>   I'll live in hope.
> Somewhere I've read: "In gentle hearts,
> mercy's a spark that kindles love."

Three stages of love's complicated narrative are here: the long history of rejection and suffering; the redemptive epiphany of lightning from the eyes of the lady; and the hope that her glance foretells something better. Hope hangs on a slender thread, the assumption that she looks at him with pity, which might lead to love.

I've imagined in my translation that the lover dimly remembers an adage about mercy increasing love. It might have been from Dante, when Francesca speaks of her love: "*Amor, ch'al cor gentil ratto s'apprende*" (Love, that suddenly seizes the merciful heart). Or perhaps from Petrarch: "*per la pietà, cresce 'l desio*" (desire grows by mercy).

48

Ardo, mia vita, ancor com'io solia,
*   e sento a poco a poco*
rinovarsi nel cor la fiamma mia.
*   Né per arder beato*
chiedo dal vostro cor foco per foco;
*   però che smisurato*
è ben l'ardor in me, ma non l'ardire.
*   Chiedo sol che morire*
non mi lasciate, e che quel nobil core
non mi neghi pietà se nega amore.

> My life begins to warm again.
>   The old desire

freshens my being, spark by spark.
   Meet me halfway!
Kindle this sacred flame in you,
   or else my love
will ignite, out of all control.
   Don't let me die!
In common human decency,
show me some mercy, if not love.

The fire of the previous madrigal is now a sacred altar fire, ready to consume a sacrifice that may please his godlike beloved. But this flame is secular as well: it is passionate and intemperate (*smisurato*); it will burn too fiercely unless she meets it with her more controlled flame.

49

Donna, mentre i' vi miro,
visibilmente i' mi trasformo in voi;
   e trasformato poi
in un solo sospir l'anima spiro.
   O bellezza vitale,
   o bellezza mortale,
   poi che sì tosto un core
per te rinasce, e per te nato more.

   Looking at you,
I find myself becoming you.
   All that I was,
melting away like wax in fire.
   Beauty's the haunt
   of love and death.
   I am reborn
in you; and then, in you, I die.

Gazing at his beloved, the lover himself is transformed, *visibilmente*—that is, *in* sight (his transformation is visible to others) and also *through* sight (it is accomplished through vision, through looking at the beloved). His soul moves toward the beloved through the connection of their eyes. But once with her, his soul is separated from his body and cannot live. He expires in one last sigh (*sospir*): *spirare* means both "to breathe," and "to breathe one's last."

In Petrarchan poetry, the terms *heart*, *sigh*, and *soul* are conventional metaphors for the lover's emotions, suffering, and identity. In our time, these words lack the force they had when the soul was a matter of intense concern and the heart was an emotional mystery rather than a physical organ of the circulation system. In their place, I had in mind the Romantic notion of the appeal, and danger, of assuming another person's image—as in *The Tales of Hoffmann* or *The Picture of Dorian Gray*.

50

> *Negatemi pur cruda*
> *de be' vostr' occhi il sole;*
> *negatemi l'angeliche parole;*
> *negatemi pietà, mercede, aita,*
> *negatemi la vita:*
> *ma non mi promettete*
> *quel, che negar volete.*

> Deny me the sun
> that lights your eyes;
> deny me your angelic voice;
> deny me pity, mercy, love,
> deny me life!
> But don't promise
> what you'll deny.

In this compact madrigal, the eyes of the beloved are the first in an escalating series of gifts that she holds in her power: eyes, voice, pity, mercy, love, life. The insistent repetition of "deny me" (*negatemi*) allows the poet to catalog her praises while reinforcing his sense of her cruelty. The first occurrences of denial are hypothetical, almost invitational: "go ahead and deny me, if you are that cruel." But the final occurrence is accusatory: "don't promise me what you intend to deny." The lover is tired of being jerked around.

51

> *A un giro sol de' belli occhi lucenti*
>> *ride l'aria d'intorno,*
>> *e'l mar s'acqueta, e i venti,*
> *e si fà il Ciel d'un altro lume adorno;*
> *sol io le luci o lagrimose, e meste.*
>> *Certo quando nasceste,*
>> *così crudel, e ria*
>> *nacque la morte mia.*

A single glance of sparkling eyes—
> the breezes laugh,
> the sea grows calm,
and in the sky, new radiance.
Mine are the only eyes that weep.
> When you were born
> so cruel, that's when
> my death began.

Guarini's madrigals often turn on a verbal pivot, a sharp contrast. Here, the first four lines are joyous: the eyes of his beloved looking at him create new beauty in the beautiful world. It is the most splendid day one could imagine, and yet, as the poem swings around, the lover is consumed with tears, obsessed with pain, morbid in the extreme. The poem's balance of beauty and sadness makes it clear that both are present and real. He cannot deny the life-giving power of her eyes, but for him they only mark another birthday of sorrow.

52

> *Lumi miei cari lumi,*
> *che lampeggiate un sì veloce sguardo,*
>> *che appena mira, e fugge,*
>> *e poi torna sì tardo,*
>> *che'l mio cor se ne strugge;*
>> *volgete a me, volgete,*
>> *quei fuggitivi rai,*
>> *che oggetto non vedrete*
>> *in altra parte mai*

con sì giusto desio,
che tanto vostro sia, quanto son io.

You look at me.
Suddenly, lightning strikes my eyes—
Flash! and then gone.
Waiting for more,
my heart dissolves.
Turn to me, turn
your eyes again!
You'll never look
at anyone
so deep in love
as me, so ready to be yours.

The difference of eyes and heart, again: a glance ought to promise more, but that's not going to happen. The beloved looks away—out of indifference? Or shame? Or flightiness? What matters to the lover is the experience of that momentary glance, so much better than nothing. Though lightning supposedly never strikes in the same place, he offers himself for more, a lightning rod seeking another electric jolt.

53

Ahi, come a un vago sol cortese giro
*   di duo belli occhi, ond'io*
soffersi il primo, e dolce stral d'Amore,
*   pien d'un novo desio,*
sì pronto a sospirar torna il mio core.
Lasso non val ascondersi. Ch'omai
conosco i segni, che'l mio cor m'addita
*   de l'antica ferita;*
ed è gran tempo pur ch'io la saldai:
ah, che piaga d'Amor non sana mai.

That single random glance
   pierced me with love
as it did long ago,

when I first fell.
There's no mistaking it.
I'm due for pain once more.
I thought I'd gotten well—
    but now again
that old infection aches.
The years can't heal love's wounds!

The lover finds himself in love once more. Although Love had wounded him once before, he thought he had healed. But the wound still remains, and so a single glance, the lightest of touches, brings back love's pain. Now he is a veteran; he bears the scars and feels the pain of previous encounters. Even so, the second fall will be harder: he goes into it this time with eyes wide open.

54

Non più guerra, pietate,
    pietate occhi miei belli:
occhi miei trionfanti, a che v'armate
contr'un cor, ch'è già preso, e vi si rende?
    Ancidete i rubelli,
ancidete chi s'arma, e si difende;
    non chi vinto v'adora.
    Volete voi, ch'io mora?
Morrò pur vostro; e del morir l'affanno
sentirò sì, ma vostro sarà il danno.

Hold your fire, love!
    Those eyes have won,
and I surrendered long ago.
Why do you keep attacking me?
    Fight rebels,
enemies, terrorists—not me!
    I worship you.
    —Want me to die?
I'll face the firing squad with joy,
but you will have to bear the blame.

The poem begins abruptly in the midst of a figurative skirmish, the lover caught in the onslaught of beauty. The lover calls for an end to conflict, not because it is painful—which it is, apparently—but because it is dishonorable: it is shameful to wage war on one who has surrendered. Mercy (*pietate*) opens the poem; damage (*danno*) ends it. If he can get her to feel the shame in her position, he might hope for more—attention, mercy, or love.

55

> *Sì presso a voi, mio foco,*
> *che fate forza a le vitali tempre,*
> *qual meraviglia, oimè, che d'Amorosa*
> *febre il cor si distempre?*
> *Meraviglia è di me, che resti in vita,*
> *meraviglia è di voi, ch'aura pietosa*
> *di sospir non movete a darmi aita:*
> *né sentite il dolore,*
> *e pur, questo che langue, è vostro core.*

> So close to you,
> I feel your flames heating my blood.
> An inflammation grips my heart;
> my fever's high.
> The wonder is, I'm still alive.
> The other wonder is, you hear
> my groans and still don't give a damn.
> You don't catch on—
> my fevered heart is really yours.

This fever is metaphorical—the lover's self-destructive desire. It may also be real, for as with any sickbed scene, the affect is intense, stifling, claustrophobic. The poem begins with the physical proximity of the beloved (*Sì presso à voi*), a closeness that induces fever in the lover. At the end, the old metaphor of "your heart is mine" becomes literal: he possesses her heart; therefore, if he has a fever, so does she. How can she ignore the suffering that she must surely feel?

The repeated evocation of wonder (*meraviglia*) draws attention to the lover's (fever-induced?) imaginings, a state of astonishment at the marvel that she is, burning and indifferent at once.

56

Splende la fredda luna,
e si raggira agli infiammati rai
sempre del Sole, e non s'accende mai.
Così questa fatal mia fredda stella
    si fa lucente, e bella
a l'amoroso sol, che 'n lei resplende;
né però mai foco d'amor l'accende.

The chilly moon
shines bright, resplendent with the borrowed rays
of the hot sun, but never catches fire.
So too, that frigid planet I adore
    draws both light
and beauty from Love's sun, which shines in her,
but never kindles any sparks of love.

The astronomical metaphor, mixed with the emotions of adoration and distant love, echoes the intricate planetary cycles that fill *The Divine Comedy*. Dante's Beatrice was an intermediary of the grace of God, reflecting God's light to her lover. Guarini's beloved is an orb with a very different aspect, beautiful but cold as the moon.

57

Crudel, perch'io non v'ami
m'avete il sol de be' vostr'occhi tolto;
    quasi nel vostro volto
tutto s'annidi, e non nel petto mio,
e sia bellezza Amor più, che desio.
    Ma, lasso, nel mio core
    tanto Amore è più amore,
quanto il foco è più foco ov'arde, e 'ncende,
    che dove alluma, e splende.

You turn away from me,
hoping that I will then stop loving you—
    as if love only grew
by what we see, and not by what we feel!

You think love lives on beauty, not desire?
—No, in my heart I have
a love greater than that:
a fire is hotter when the coals burn dark
than when it merely flames.

Another lover might have been content simply to praise her beauty. But this lover gives his praise an unexpected turn: he berates the beloved for how she misuses that beauty. Gifted with extraordinary beauty, she thinks too much of what she can do with that power. If she turns that beauty off, she thinks, he will stop bothering her with his love. His hidden, smoldering desire, however, is like a blacksmith's forge—rough, hot, burning despite anything she can do.

58

E così pur languendo
me 'n vo tra queste piume, e 'n doppio ardore
quinci morte m'assale, e quindi Amore.
    Né voi cruda il sentite;
ed è pur vostra colpa, e vostra cura,
    via più che di natura:
che sprezzando l'un mal, l'altro nudrite.
    Legge proterva, e ria,
se vostro è il cor perché la pena, è mia?

    Lying in bed,
I'm burning twice over—
with fever and with love.
    You are both cause
and cure, but you don't care;
    you feed the fever
and scorn the medicine.
    I've lost my heart,
and yet I feel its pain!

Even on his sickbed (a featherbed, by the way: *tra queste piume*, "among these feathers"), the lover obsesses about love. The fever is a double one, a sickness of the body and a sickness of love. His beloved ignores both fevers, especially the one that she could cure. The poem is hardly pleasant, full of self-pity and blame. But its taut intensity exemplifies the concentrated—one might say claustrophobic—quality of the madrigal form, taking a single situation and not letting it go.

59

> *Soavissimo ardore,*
> *che da la vista mia calda, e bramosa*
> *ti parti, e 'n fra i ligustri*
> *di quel bel viso avampi, e sì t'illustri,*
> *che l'alba vinci, e la vermiglia rosa,*
> *che fai là dentro accolto?*
> *Purtroppo è fiamma il volto:*
> *scendi nel petto, e fa ch'arda d'amore,*
> *quella fiamma gentil, ch'arse il mio core.*

> My fever leaps
> beyond my flushed and lustful face,
> infecting her.
> There, in her face, it burns so hot
> it reddens all her whites and pinks.
> —Why in her face
> alone? The flames
> that burn in me should ignite her heart
> and there become a crucible for love.

The poem hinges on the Petrarchan idea of love as a fire in the heart, but it intensifies the trope by giving it a material reality. Fire in the lover bursts out as a visible inflammation in the poet's face; from there it spreads to the beloved, whose usually subtle coloration now flushes red. The poet tries (with what success?) to redirect this heat, to set the beloved's heart on fire with love.

60

> *Langue al vostro languir l'anima mia:*
> *e dico, ah, forse a sì cocente pena*

sua ferità la mena.
O anima d'Amor troppo rubella,
    quanto meglio vi fora
provar quel caro ardor, che vi fa bella,
    che quel che vi scolora?
Perché non piace a la mia stella ch'io
arda del vostro foco, e voi del mio.

Your fever makes me burn as well:
I turn on you—"Your cruelty
    has made you sick."
And then I hold a mirror up:
    "This fever's good,
transforming your cold elegance
    to a rich glow."
Lastly, I cry: "I am on fire
because of you; you should be, too!"

Fever attacks the beloved, but the lover, as he catches the infection, cruelly makes it clear that he prefers the beloved that way. The rhymes lead from
rubella (fever) to *bella* (beauty) and *stella* (star): the glow of her illness makes
her more beautiful to him than the pallor of her normal state. The poem is
a strange apologia for the lover's perverse dream of feverish consummation.

61

Sì, mi dicesti, e io
quel dolcissimo sì mandai nel core
    subitamente, e arsi
di quel foco bellissimo d'amore,
che per altr'esca non potea destarsi.
Or che voi vi pentite, anch'io mi pento,
e come un sì m'accese, un no m'ha spento.

You told me, "yes,"
and that one word seized me at once;
    I caught on fire,
and burned with that delicious flame,

that heat that's only sparked by love.
Now you repent. And so do I:
kindled by "yes," snuffed out by "no."

The madrigal plays with the sound of *sì* (yes)—echoed in the rhymes by *arsi* (I burned) and *destarsi* (to be awakened). But the bleak little narrative ends bluntly with the word *nò*, its dark implications echoed by the final rhymes—*pento* (I repent) and *spento* (I have been extinguished).

62

O come è gran martire
a celar suo desire,
quando con pura fede
s'ama chi non se 'l crede.
O mio soave ardore,
o mio dolce desio,
s'ogn'un ama il suo core,
e voi sète il core mio,
alor fia ch'io non v'ami,
che viver più non brami.

I'm burning at the stake,
hiding my love like this,
faithful in love to one
who can't believe in love.
And yet I live by love—
the passion, the longing.
They say we love *ourselves*,
but *you're* the self I love.
If I did not love you,
I would not want to live.

The lover lives by loyalty, but the beloved refuses to share his belief in constancy. So the lover has to hide his commitment and suffers not only the pangs of desire but also the pain of concealment.

More than two dozen composers set this poem, including Carlo Gesualdo, prince, masochist, murderer, and maker of brilliantly radical works of music.

SECTION 5   Mutual Love

Remake your double selves as one—
twin souls that live in unity.
Ask Love for nothing else than love.

Guarini's lover is usually starved in his love. Living with constant delay and frustration, he nonetheless hopes for something more—a glance from the beloved's eyes, a sweet word from her mouth. Like Romeo, he might cry to his lover, "O, wilt thou leave me so unsatisfied?"

In the world of Guarini's madrigals, there is little "satisfaction": the poems relentlessly explore suffering, not bliss. But here and there, we find hints of happiness—the radiance of her glance, the beauty of her voice, and the delicious feeling of being in love. These pleasures, though, are often tiny and transient.

The brevity of the madrigal form conspires with the dynamics of Petrarchan love to minimize fulfillment: no madrigal tells of more than one episode, and none of them last long enough to imply a durable satisfaction. The poems are short and tight, denying any significant satisfaction: there just isn't time.

There certainly isn't time for sex. Juliet answers Romeo's question with her own: "What satisfaction canst thou have tonight?" There is no opportunity, not tonight, not in this scene (later, Shakespeare's lovers do find a moment for satisfaction, but the call of the morning lark and the pressures of Verona's feud cut it short). In the Petrarchan canon, sex—that is, consummated sex—rarely occurs, and if it does, it is almost never happy. Shakespeare, in a bitter sonnet, bluntly calls sex "lust in action"—an "expense of spirit in a waste of shame."

Sir Thomas Wyatt, however, softens the bitterness of unrequited, frustrated love with his memory of a time when things were better:

Thanked be fortune it hath been otherwise
Twenty times better; but once in special,
In thin array, after a pleasant guise,

When her loose gown from her shoulders did fall,
And she me caught in her arms long and small,
Therewithal sweetly did me kiss
And softly said, "Dear heart, how like you this?"

Among the English Petrarchans, it is Spenser who most believes in the possibility of mutual love. His sonnet sequence *Amoretti* moves to fulfillment—not in lascivious or abandoned sexuality but in marriage, figured as a sacramental union. Capping the sonnet sequence is Spenser's "Epithalamion," an extended hymn in celebration of the wedding day, ending with the two lovers married and in bed together:

Now welcome night, thou night so long expected,
That long day's labor dost at last defray,
And all my cares, which cruel love collected,
Hast summed in one, and cancelled for aye:
Spread thy broad wing over my love and me,
That no man may us see,
And in thy sable mantle us enwrap,
From fear of peril and foul horror free.
Let no false treason seek us to entrap,
Nor any dread disquiet once annoy
The safety of our joy:
But let the night be calm and quietsome,
Without tempestuous storms or sad affray:
Like as when Jove with fair Alcmena lay,
When he begot the great Tirynthian groom:
Or like as when he with thyself did lie,
And begot Majesty.
And let the maids and young men cease to sing:
Ne let the woods them answer, nor their echo ring.

In its tender evocation of stillness and contentment, Spenser's marriage hymn catches an aspect of Petrarch's love poems for Laura. Despite delay and frustration, Petrarch's sonnets are also full of gestures toward transcendence, as if they understood sexual pleasure as a figure of spiritual fulfillment:

Love, let us pause to contemplate our glory
and see things high and strange, past Nature.
See sweetness that rains down upon her here,
see light that shows us Heaven come to earth;

see how much skill has gilded and made pearly
and ruddy-hued that body, surely matchless,
which moves sweet feet and lively eyes throughout
the shady cloister of these lovely hills!

Green grass and flowers of a thousand colors
scattered beneath that black and ancient oak
entreat her lovely foot to step on them;

the sky's aswarm with sparks, with shining fire,
and seems to be rejoicing everywhere
at being made so clear by eyes so fair.

In a similar vein of tenderness, this section of Guarini's madrigals celebrates—or at least hints at—mutual love. Here, still accompanied by the
recurring strains of doubt, indecision, passion, anger, and revenge, are also
glimpses of satisfaction: a kiss, the gift of a rose, an expression of tenderness,
a word of caring.

63

Anime pellegrine, che bramate
    amando esser amate,
se volete gioir, morendo in vui
    rinascete in altrui.
Non vi divida mai né tuo, né mio.
    Sian confusi i voleri,
    le speranze, i pensieri.
Faccia una sola fede un sol desio
di due alme, e due cori, un'alma, un core,
né sia premio d'amore altro, che amore.

You faithful souls who love, and hope
    to know love in return,
this is the way: die to yourself
    and live another's life.
Never divide—no yours, no mine.
    Mingle it all: your will,
    your desire, your thought.
Remake your double selves as one—
twin souls that live in unity.
Ask Love for nothing else than love.

This is one of the few of Guarini's madrigals that does not speak directly to the beloved. Reaching beyond earthbound lovers in their often fraught relationships, it engages a celestial realm of "pilgrim souls." Consequently, it has a more lofty tone than many, abandoning the lover's often petty reproaches. Like Donne in "Valediction: Forbidding Mourning" ("Our two souls . . . which are one"), Guarini describes a union of lover and beloved, transcending the ontological distinction of separate bodies.

64

    Felice chi vi mira,
ma più felice chi per voi sospira.
    Felicissimo poi
chi sospirando fa sospirar voi.
    Ben ebbe amica stella
    chi per Donna sì bella
può far contento in un l'occhio, e 'l desio,
e sicuro può dir quel core è mio.

    Happy who sees,
happier still who sighs for you,
    and happiest
who sighs, and hears you sigh for him.
    If only I
    could look at you,
and sigh for you, and by some grace,
could tell myself, "Her heart is mine."

The elegant symmetry of this madrigal attracted the attention of many composers: neatly framed in two sections of four lines each, each section moves through three phases of love—looking, feeling, and enjoying. Playing against that resonant parallelism are the polyrhythmic contrasts between the two quatrains: the first has alternating line lengths (seven, eleven, seven, and eleven syllables), the second has pairs of equal line lengths (seven and seven syllables, then eleven and eleven syllables). The first quatrain speaks in high-minded generalization ("Happy [the one] . . ."), and the second descends into the personal, the speculative, and the subjunctive ("If only I . . .").

The composers must also have loved the warm, affirmative ending of the madrigal: *quel core è mio* ([her] heart is mine). This pretext for music is too good to pass up, as Schubert knew when he wrote a song with a similar exultation, *Mein ist dein Herz!*

65

Baciai per aver vita,
ch'ov' è bellezza è vita, ed ebbi morte;
ma morte sì gradita,
che più beata sorte
vivendo non avrei:
ne più bramar potrei.
Di sì soave bocca in un bel volto
baciando, il cor mi fu rapito, e tolto.

Since beauty's the seat of life,
I kissed her, seeking life . . . but I found there
a blessed death, an end
so sweet—impossible
while I still lived—that I
hope for no other end.
Kissing those tender lips, touching that face,
so beautiful, I simply lost my heart.

"I lost my heart" is the oldest staple of romantic poetry. Here Guarini gives the cliché more than usual intensity: *il cor me fu rapito, e tolto*—my heart is taken (*rapito*), seized (*tolto*) in this kiss. And yet he feels no grief, no violence, no loss. His "blessed death" is a metonymy for a deeper, more passionate state of life.

66

O che soave bacio
da la mia Donna ebb'io;
non so se don di lei, se furto mio.
Ma se questo è pur furto, alcun non sia
  che brami Cortesia.
Fatti pur ladro Amor, ch'io ti perdono;
e ceda in tutto a la rapina il dono.

What an amazing kiss
I had from her just now!
Was it a gift of hers, or theft of mine?
Well, if it was a theft, that's not a crime
  under the rule of Love.
Love, *you're* the thief, for which I pardon you:
giving is always topped by robbery.

The lover's ambivalence about this kiss (gift or theft?) is worked out by appealing to *cortesia* (courtliness), an ideology in which "Love," not the lover himself, is responsible for the lover's actions. So this kiss, though stolen, can't be the *lover's* theft: "I'm not to blame!"

The strange last line feels as if it may be quoting a truism or common saying from the poet's era; the best I can make of it is that, having ascribed the theft to Love and having "forgiven" Love for it, he can assert this outrageously specious axiom: a gift is worth less than (*ceda a*) a theft.

67

Non fu senza vendetta
il mio furto soave;
però non vi sia grave
dolci labra amorose,
ch'a le vostre vermiglie, e fresche rose
caro cibo involassi ai desir miei:
se per pena del furto il cor perdei.

I stole that kiss.
I bear the blame,

> but, lovely lips,
>   don't scold too much.
> I know, I snatched a taste
> of your vermilion rose . . .
> but then I lost my heart.

Like honey on a lemon, the madrigal remakes the lover's sour theft into a sweet declaration of love. He has kissed her, with more than a touch of blame. But he asserts that it was sweet (*soave*)—sweet, of course, to *him*. How can he make his lady also taste the sweetness? By pretending he's just doing what comes naturally: he is a bee buzzing around the roses of her lips, harvesting the sweet nectar that he finds there, finding the sweets that she holds in that flower. If there's any punishment to be had, it will thus be a (bitter-)sweet one—to lose his heart to her. Which he has already done a hundred times.

68

> *Non sospirar cor mio non sospirare,*
>   *non son come a te pare,*
>   *questi sospiri ardenti*
>   *refrigerio del core,*
> *ma son più tosto impetuosi venti,*
> *che spiran ne l'incendio, e'l fan maggiore,*
>   *con turbini d'Amore,*
> *ch'apportan sempre a miserelli amanti.*
> *Foschi nembi di duol, pioggie di pianti.*

> Don't grieve, don't moan.
>   Those sighs
>   that give
>   relief
> are hurricanes
> that fan love's fire
>   and bring
> clouds of despair,
> monsoons of tears.

Here the suffering of deferred love returns, but this time with a tender tone of concern. Both of the parties seem to be sighing, sad that they cannot seem to enjoy their love. The sighing just makes things worse. But because the sighing is mutual, it adds to the love that each feels for the other. And yet neither of them can act upon that love.

The madrigal was excerpted by composers from Guarini's drama *Il pastor fido*. The first line was added some time before 1588 when it appeared in *Il secondo libro di madrigali* by the Mantuan composer Annibale Coma.

69

Cor mio, deh non piangete,
ch'altro mal io non provo, altro martire,
che 'l veder voi del mio languir languire,
       dunque non vi dolete,
       se sanar mi volete.
Che quell'affetto, che pietà chiamate,
s'è dispietato à voi, non è pietate.

My love, don't cry:
the only pain I feel
is that you grieve for me.
       For my sake, don't
       give in to sorrow:
your care for me hurts you
and multiplies my grief.

This compressed madrigal implies more than it says. The backstory is unclear—is he sick? Or hurt? Physically or emotionally? What is clear, though, is the tone—caring, affectionate. The beloved is made sad by the lover's discomfort, and the lover grows even sadder because of her sadness for him.

Pietà (pity, mercy, compassion, care) is at the center of this circle of mutual lamentation: the word recurs three times in the final couplet of the madrigal.

70

Cor mio, deh, non languire,
che fai teco languir l'anima mia.
Odi i caldi sospiri: a te gli invia
    la pietate, e 'l desire.
S'i' ti potessi dar morendo aita,
    morrei per darti vita.
Ma vivi, oimè, che 'ngiustamente more
chi vivo tien ne l'altrui petto il core.

Don't waste away!
I'm suffering along with you.
Listen! My sighs are messengers
    of sympathy;
if I could help by dying, I
    would die for you.
Live on! How can you die
while you hold fast my living heart?

In the Italian, this madrigal has an opening almost identical to the previous one (#69). It is no wonder this elegiac poem was set to music so often
in the seventeenth century: what composer could resist the cue of *odi i caldi
sospiri* (hear my fervent sighs)? The tone of sorrow is maintained so beauti-
fully throughout by a sequence of sad sounds and feelings—*languir* (griev-
ing), *sospiri* (sighing), *morendo* (dying).

71

Non miri il mio bel sole
    chi lui sol non adora,
com'io, ch'altro non bramo, altro non miro
    da l'una a l'altra Aurora.
A gran ragion sospiro,
e cheggio per giustissima mercede
    d'un amor, d'una fede,
d'un languir per bellezze al mondo sole
    sola solo il mio sole.

No one can see
my sun without
worshipping, as I do,
    day after day,
    sighing in hope,
begging a ray of love
    from her, who is
the world's beauty, and still
    my only sun.

If this poem is idolatrous in its sun worship, it pursues its idolatry with admirably unchanging vigor. The sun (*sole*) floods this poem with light. There is no half measure in the lover's worship of his sun, his beloved; he is constant in his devotion, and that constancy may—just barely may—occasion a tender reward, a sign of hope. The ending is especially resonant and intricate in Italian: *sole / sola solo il mio sole*—verbally entwining uniqueness, constancy, and brilliance.

Does the capitalization of "Aurora" signal a specific lady of Guarini's acquaintance as the subject—so named or identified to those in the know?

72

Donò Licori a Batto
una rosa, cred'io, di paradiso;
    e sì vermiglia in viso
donandola si fece, e sì vezzosa,
che parea rosa, che donasse rosa.
    Alor disse il pastore,
con un sospir dolcissimo d'Amore,
    perché degno non sono
d'aver la rosa donatrice in dono?

She gave a rose
that might have come from paradise.
    Giving it, she blushed
vermilion, so beautiful,
as if she were the rose she gave.
    So in response

I gave a sigh that might have said,
   "Why can't I have
the blossom and the blusher, too?"

This is one of the simplest and most direct of the madrigals. The beloved gives a rose; she blushes in giving it, and in consequence she looks as beautiful as the rose. He notes the imbalance of the situation: he gets the rose, but he doesn't get the giver. One might guess that if the relationship goes on in this vein, sooner or later he will get the giver, too.

As in several other madrigals of Guarini (including #74), the names in the Italian ("Licori" and "Batto") allude to the poems of Theocritus.

73

   Voi, dissi, e sospirando
violenza d'Amor ruppe il mio core;
   da sì breve scintilla
sorse la fiamma del mio chiuso ardore;
   di cui s'una favilla
   sola scaldasse VOI,
o felice quel dì, ch'i' dissi VOI.

   I whispered, "You!"
And though I'd tried to hold love down,
   with that short sigh
my heart became a raging fire.
   Someday a spark
   may kindle you
and make me glad I whispered, "You!"

This compressed and straightforward madrigal has a great energy at its core, fusing present pain with future joy. Here the lover finds himself astounded at the power of his whispered word, *VOI*—"you." Uttering this one word has cracked the lid he's put on his passion—with it, he says, love's violence broke open his heart (*ruppe il mio core*). The fire suppressed at the center of his being now surges out in flames of passion and hope. Maybe, someday, some word, some unpredictable event, will also set his beloved on fire. The strength of the verb he uses there—*scaldare* (to scald or ignite)—reminds us that in these little poems he's playing with fire.

74

> *La tenera Licori*
> *caduta in braccio al suo focoso amante*
> *dicea vinta, e ferita,*
> *e con lo sguardo languido, e tremante,*
> *che mi darai pastore*
> *in guiderdon del mio rapito onore?*
> *E l'aver, e la vita,*
> *rispos'egli morendo. Oimè ben mio,*
> *l'anima saettar ti potess'io.*

> A tender girl,
> she found herself in bed with him.
> Dazed, overcome,
> shaking with sobs, she stammered out,
> "What can you give
> me back for my lost innocence?"
> "All that I have,"
> he answered her. "My life is yours,
> if only I could pierce your heart."

She is young and naïve (*tenera*—"tender"); he is hot and insistent (*focoso*—"fiery"). Afterward, she has second thoughts. Her honor has been stolen, she says. When she complains to him by asking for recompense (*guiderdon*, a feudal term), he responds in courtly language: "I will give you all that I have, and all that I am." But, he adds with an echo of his fiery love, he wishes he could "give" her something even more lasting, that he could wound (*saettare*) her soul. Under the tone of tenderness and the veneer of mutuality lies violence, reminding us of the way these madrigals hover on the brink of an intense and painful sexual politics.

In the Italian, the woman is named Licori (as in #72), an allusion to the work of Theocritus. The allusion is made explicit by the title given this madrigal in the 1598 Venice edition, *Amoroso furore di Teocrito*—"Loving Frenzy, from Theocritus."

75

Dolce spir'to d'Amore
in un sospir accolto,
mentre i' miro il bel volto
spira vita al mio core.
Tal acquista valore
da quella bella bocca,
che sospirando tocca.

Sighing, she gave
a breath of love.
I watched her mouth
send life to me.
So powerful
are the fair lips
that shaped that sigh!

Breath is at the core of this madrigal. The lady's sigh passes her lips, gaining power from the beauty of her mouth, breathing life into his heart as he watches her. It is a resonant, echoing, song-like madrigal, playing changes on the verb *spirare* (to breathe): *spir'to* (spirit); *sospiro* (sigh); *spira* (breathes); *sospirando* (breathing). Just as the mood is undisturbed by surprise or irony, the meter is undisturbed by longer (eleven-syllable) lines. A simple corporeal moment becomes a compact, heightened epiphany of love.

76

Oggi nacqui, Ben mio,
per morir vostro. Ecco la bella Aurora,
che produsse colui
che 'l vostro Sole adora.
O fortunato il mio natal, se vui
direte con la lingua, e co'l desio,
oggi nacque il Ben mio.

Born on this day,
I live only to worship you.
Blessed be the dawn

of life and love!
Happy the day, if only you
would say (and mean it, too): "My love
    was born today."

The poet celebrates his birthday, giving thanks for the life he leads as lover. The madrigal hangs on the ambiguity of the congratulations he hopes for from his lady. She may say, "My love was born today," and this may mean simply, "This is his birthday." Or it may mean, "Today is the birthday of a new state of being for me, that of being in love with him." Either way, he hopes for a wonderful birthday greeting from her—especially if she says it with feeling (co'l desio).

77

Madonna, udite come
questa vostra dolcissima pietate
    in voi cresca beltate.
Per la pietate in me sorge il desio,
    ch'avviva il foco mio;
dal mio bel foco esce la fiamma, ed ella
splende nel vostro viso, e vi fa bella.

    I'll tell you this:
love makes your beauty grow.
    And how is that?
Your mercy warms my love,
    desire flares up,
the radiance shines on you,
and makes you beautiful.

A kindness from the beloved is so welcome that the lover calls it dolcissima pietate (sweetest mercy). How can he make sure it continues? He can show her that granting love to him makes her more beautiful by increasing his desire, which reflects on her. The madrigal won't win any prizes for logic, but it's inventive and has a ring of assured contentment.

78

Con che soavità, labbra odorate,
*   e vi bacio, e v'ascolto;*
ma se godo un piacer, l'altro m'è tolto.
*   Come i vostri diletti*
s'ancidono fra lor, se dolcemente
vive per ambiduo l'anima mia?
*   Che soave armonia*
fareste, o dolci baci, o cari detti,
*   se foste unitamente*
d'ambedue le dolzezze ambo capaci:
baciando, i detti, e ragionando, i baci.

She's sweet to kiss, and just as sweet
    to listen to;
but I can't manage both at once.
    Why should these joys
cancel each other? Is it too much
to taste the honey of them both?
    What counterpoint
they'd make, those kisses and those words,
    if both at once
could link their notes in harmony,
to speak in kisses, kiss in words!

This madrigal articulates the tension between two functions of the mouth: as the source of speech (talking, reasoning—*ragionando*) and as a site of sensuality (kissing—*baciando*).

A third function of the mouth is singing: composers, performers, and audiences expected from the musical versions of madrigals a conjunction of rhetoric and sensuality. Playing with the poem's theme of contrast between words and kisses and its dynamic of union through harmony and counterpoint, Monteverdi set this madrigal with a rich texture for both voice and instruments.

79

Se per estremo ardore
morir potesse un core,
saria ben arso il mio
fra tanto incendio rio.
Ma come salamandra, nel mio foco
vivo per la mia donna in festa e'n gioco.
E se m'avien talora
che per dolcezza i' mora,
mercé d'Amor risorgo qual fenice
sol per viver ardendo ogn'or felice.

If one could die
from too much love,
this crucible
would melt me down.
But like a salamander, I
thrive in the fire, and play, and sing.
And if someday
love does me in,
I'll die and rise again in love,
a phoenix, happy on my pyre.

The poem evokes two mythical beasts of the Renaissance, the salamander that lives in the heat of the fire (see #40) and the phoenix that dies and is reborn in its fiery nest. It is hot stuff, with an erotic undertone about orgasm and tumescence; but a light touch belies the mythical and sexual subject matter—most of the lines are short, and the tone is calm.

At the center is a wonderful line, *vivo per la mia donna in festa e'n gioco*—literally, "I live through my lady in happiness and play." It reminds me of William Blake's *Songs of Innocence*, in which children sing and dance even while terrible things are happening around them: they're simply not afraid of what terrifies everyone else.

80

T'amo, mia vita, la mia cara vita
dolcemente mi dice, e 'n questa sola
     sì soave parola
par che trasformi lietamente il core,
     per farmene signore.
O, voce di dolcezza, e di diletto,
     prendila tosto Amore;
     stampala nel mio petto;
spiri solo per lei l'anima mia:
T'AMO MIA VITA, la mia vita sia.

"My life, I love you," said my love.
Those simple words transformed my life,
     infusing me
with joy; deliciously, they gave
     me back my heart!
May Love take hold of those sweet words
     and fasten them
     deep in my chest,
so every breath will be of love.
"MY LIFE, I LOVE YOU" will be my life!

The madrigal is focused and resonant. By the lover's own invitation, the words "My life, I love you" are written in his heart. Their fixedness and authority focus his breath, his being, and his soul. So too Guarini uses the phrase both to open and close this prayer for singleness of being, the upper-case typography at the end suggesting that the quotation is now an inscription on a monument.

81

Io veggio pur pietate, ancorche tardi,
     nel indurato core,
ma tarde non fur mai grazie d'Amore.
O dolci meraviglie, il foco mio
     non fu mai sì cocente,
com'or nel refrigerio, né vid'io,

cara mia luce, adorna
voi di tanta bellezza, e sì lucente,
com'ora, che pietà v'accende, ed orna.
  O leggiadra pietate,
che 'n me cresce desire, in voi beltate.

At last, her wintry spirit melts.
   She pities me!
—A miracle: love doesn't run
by calendars! I want her more
      than ever, now
that she returns my love. And now,
   as mercy shines
in her, she grows more beautiful
than she had ever seemed before.
      I bless the change—
more loving, I; and she, more radiant!

Mercy has been a long time coming, but once it comes, it changes the very nature of time. Love is an epiphany that changes even the seasons of freezing and thawing, and the calendar by which we mark those seasons.

And yet, paradoxically, mercy perpetuates the long age of unrequited desire that preceded it, increasing both the beauty that is desired and the desire to possess it. The miracle, then, is that achieving love is both something totally new and, at the same time, an intensification of the life that the lover has led so long.

The third line in the original poem is a quote from Petrarch's *Trionfo dell'Eternità*.

82

O notturno miracolo soave
   né già sognando il veggio.
Al lume della Luna il Sol vagheggio.
   Luna cortese ond'io
godo quel ben, che mi contende il giorno,
   mentre lampeggi intorno
all'amata beltà dell'Idol mio,

portami tu con quel beato raggio,
    che il suo bel viso tocca,
un bacio sol della soave bocca:
    poi ferma il tuo viaggio,
    sì che'l suo non m'invole
l'importuno tuo Sole. Ah potrò mai
stender le braccia, ove stendi i rai?

Surely I dream! A miracle—
    that I can gaze
at her, at last, without restraint!
    O blessed moon,
allowing me this radiance,
    this sight of her
among those swirling galaxies!
O moon, use your transcendent light
    to steal for me
just one sweet kiss from those fair lips;
    then go your way,
    before she sees
what you have done. —Ah, could I kiss
like you, and hold her in my arms!

The madrigal begins in a moment of moonlight bliss, the lover dreaming of his beloved lady. The dream becomes the occasion for a prayer to that most feminine of goddesses, the moon: help me get just one kiss! But, as always, one kiss would never be enough, so the poem ends with a sudden explosion, an anguished longing for more.

83

Udite, amanti, udite
meraviglia dolcissima d'Amore.
    La mia vita, il mio core,
quella Donna già tanto sospirata,
    e tanto in van bramata,
    quella fugace, quella,
che fu già tanto cruda quanto bella,

è fatta amante; ed io
il suo cor, la sua vita, il suo desio.

Hear me, lovers,
as I proclaim love's miracle!
My life, my heart,
she for whom I sighed so long,
so hopelessly,
she who rejected me,
she, cruel as she is beautiful—
she is in love!
And I? her life—her heart—her joy!

Udite (hear!) is emphatic and declamatory, proclaimed twice in the very
first line. Indeed, the whole poem is a proclamation to the community of
lovers, for they will understand this miracle (*meraviglia*, "a wonder"). The
lover gladly announces that the beloved shows mercy, takes him as her heart,
her life. How did this miracle happen? It's a mystery. Guarini gives us simply
this statement in the ambiguous passive voice: *è fatta amante*—she *has been
made* a lover.

84

Volgea l'anima mia soavemente
    quel suo caro, e lucente
sguardo, tutto beltà, tutto desire
verso me scintillando, e parea dire,
dammi il tuo cor, che non altronde i' vivo:
e mentre il cor se 'n vola ove l'invita
    quella beltà infinita,
sospirando gridai misero, e privo
    del cor, chi mi dà vita?
Mi rispos'ella in un' sospir d'Amore,
    io, che sono il tuo core.

My own beloved turned to me
    in all her warmth
and beauty; with sparkling eyes

she looked at me, and seemed to say,
"Give me your heart, so I may live."
My heart immediately obeyed
    that summons.
A sudden pang: "How can I live
    without my heart?"
She answered in a sigh of love,
    "I'll be that heart."

In these madrigals, being loved is no less difficult than loving. The lover repeatedly asks his beloved for her heart, but now, suddenly, *she* demands *his*. He finds that giving his heart away is an overwhelming, fatal experience. He feels like a soul in hell: wretched and deprived (*misero e privo*). In all this pain, he can hardly see how to keep alive. And then she sets him straight: she *is* his heart.

85

Arsi già solo, e non sostenni il foco,
    or che nel vostro avampo,
com'avrò mai da tant'incendio scampo?
Se 'n queste belle vostre amate braccia
ardo de l'ardor vostro, ardo del mio,
    com'è che non mi sfaccia
doppia fiamma d'Amor, doppio desio?
    O meraviglie nate
    da la vostra pietate,
per cui s'accende un sì vitale ardore,
che fiamma cresce, e non consuma il core.

I burned once by myself, and it was hell.
    Now you're on fire too,
and how can I survive *two* fires at once?
If your desire meets mine, and at long last
those lovely arms reach out and hold me tight,
    can I survive the heat,
these doubled and redoubled flames of love?
    It is a miracle!

Because you're merciful,
you've found the secret of that living fire
that kindles flame but never burns the heart.

The sudden, unpredictable nature of fire evokes the miracle of unexpected love. In this poetic riff on fire and doubleness, there is a compressed inventiveness. For example, the fifth line—*ardo de l'ardor vostro, ardo del mio* (I burn with your burning, I burn with mine) uses, in one line, three variants of a single verb, *ardire*. In its resonant language, the poem enacts the very multiplying effect that it relates.

86

Baci soavi e cari,
   cibi della mia vita,
ch'or m'involate or mi rendete il core,
      per voi convien ch'impari
      come un' alma rapita
non senta il duol di mort'e pur si more.
      Quant'ha di dolce amore,
      perché sempr'io vi baci,
      o dolcissime rose,
      in voi tutto ripose;
e s'io potessi ai vostri dolci baci
      la mia vita finire,
      o che dolce morire!

   Kissing you—
      my life's food—
takes me away, brings me back,
      teaches me
      how to die
with no pain, no sorrow.
      Whatever is
      sweet in love
      lingers here
      every time.
I'll kiss my days away

on those lips—
a sweet end!

The "forever" of kissing melds imperceptibly into a "death" that is, nonetheless, part of the pleasure.

This madrigal demonstrates much of why Guarini was beloved by composers: the intermingling of sweetness and sorrow makes it both single-minded and complicated.

87

Tirsi morir volea,
gli occhi mirando di colei ch'adora;
quand'ella, che di lui non meno ardea,
gli disse: Oimè, ben mio,
deh non morir ancora,
che teco bramo di morir anch'io.
Frenò Tirsi il desio
ch'ebbe di pur sua vita al'or finire,
ma sentia morte in non poter morire.
E mentre il guardo pur fiso tenea
ne' begli occhi divini,
e 'l nettar amoroso indi bevea;
la bella Ninfa sua, che già vicini
sentia i messi d'Amore,
disse, con occhi languidi, e tremanti,
mori, ben mio, ch'io moro.
Ed io; rispose subito il pastore,
e teco nel morir mi discoloro.
Così moriro, i fortunati amanti
di morte sì soave, e sì gradita,
che per anco morir tornaro in vita.

He longed to die,
his eyes fixed on the one he loved;
but she, who loved as much as he,
said, "No, my love;
do not die yet;

I want to die along with you."
    So he held back
on his desire to end it all,
but dying still in his delay.
Then, while he gazed his fill, hanging
        on her fair eyes,
drinking the honey of her looks,
she felt his eager messages
        of urgent love,
and, trembling, gasped, "Die now, my love;
        I'm dying too."
"And I," her lover answered her,
"am growing pale, dying with you."
And so these lovers came to die
so blessedly that they returned
to life, happy to die again.

This poem, longer than most of the madrigals, plays two narratives at once: a tragedy of star-crossed love like *Romeo and Juliet* and a barely veiled description of orgasm, which was widely known in the Renaissance as "death."

There are over twenty-five extant vocal settings of this madrigal, including one by Luca Marenzio, whose modern editor, John Steele, notes, "A cause of some scandal, this text was first attributed to Torquato Tasso (1571), but eventually acknowledged by Guarini in his *Rime* (1598)."

In the Italian, this madrigal identifies its male lover (Tirso) as a shepherd and his beloved as a nymph; the name and attributes place the story in the genre of pastoral romance—which is the subject of the next section of this collection.

SECTION 6   Love's Theatrics

If you don't know how much
  I love you, ask;
  the wilderness
will testify

Petrarch's poems are, for the most part, grounded in actual place and time: we travel with him on the River Po, we encounter his friends, and we hear the voice of his beloved Laura. For Petrarch, the emotions of love "in a little room" were congruent with the world outside, whether the world of family, court, politics, thought, or literature. Shakespeare's sonnets, too, show us ample evidence of the everyday life of a young poet in late sixteenth-century London—even the ink that stains the hands of the poet and records his love:

> *Since brass, nor stone, nor earth, nor boundless sea,*
> *But sad mortality o'ersways their power,*
> *How with this rage shall beauty hold a plea,*
> *Whose action is no stronger than a flower?*
> *O how shall summer's honey breath hold out*
> *Against the wrackful siege of batt'ring days,*
> *When rocks impregnable are not so stout,*
> *Nor gates of steel so strong, but Time decays?*
> *O fearful meditation! where, alack,*
> *Shall Time's best jewel from Time's chest lie hid?*
> *Or what strong hand can hold his swift foot back?*
> *Or who his spoil [of] beauty can forbid?*
>   *O none, unless this miracle have might,*
>   *That in black ink my love may still shine bright.*

Like little dramas, Shakespeare's sonnets are theatrical in their insistence on a world of human interaction and complication: beauty, in line 3 above, arguing in a courtroom against rage is not unlike Portia in the trial scene of

The Merchant of Venice, or Isabella pleading with Angelo for the life of her brother in *Measure for Measure*.

Sidney's Astrophil, too, lives in something like a real world. The dramas of *Astrophil and Stella* reflect the intricacies of the Elizabethan court circles in which Sidney lived and loved. Real-world events occur in his poems, certainly recognizable to Sidney's contemporaries. One such event was a joust known to have taken place in 1591, at which Sidney gained acclaim for his horsemanship: "Having this day my horse, my hand, my lance, / Guided so well that I obtained the prize." Theatrically, the poem goes on to record a gabble of gossip from the court: How did Sidney win? Skill? Strength? Dexterity? Luck? Genetics? No, Sidney tells us, all these speculations are wrong:

> How far they shoot awry! *The true cause is,*
> *Stella looked on, and from her heavenly face*
> *Sent forth the beams which made so fair my race.*

With Guarini's madrigals, we are less sure of a world of real people and real interactions. Do these abstract sketches take place in a court, a city, or a country house? We have almost no idea. What do these lovers do when they are not despairing of love? Are they lawyers, soldiers, rulers? Again, we get almost no clue. Occasionally a rose or an almond gives us a tiny bit of everyday life, but for the most part we see nothing of the world, only the brief, heightened emotions of the lover and the beloved.

It is in the madrigals excerpted from the verse drama *Il pastor fido* that Guarini comes closest to this world of human interaction. Shakespeare, working in the world of the public theater, had to keep his writing taut and actable; Guarini, whose audience lived in the richer and more indulgent world of the courtly entertainment, naturally enough wrote at great length and with a grander and more hyperbolic rhetoric of passion. Consequently, *Il pastor fido* is unwieldy: long and complicated, more than a little implausible, and nearly impossible to stage even in its own day. Guarini initiated at least two unsuccessful attempts to stage the play, first in Mantua and then Ferrara, before managing a performance of part of it at a royal wedding in Turin in 1585, but even after that, there were continued difficulties in getting the cumbersome play on stage. In 1590 Guarini published the text, and at long last the play was performed three times in 1598.

Despite its length and overheated rhetoric—or perhaps in part because of them—*Il pastor fido* was immensely popular with readers across Europe, for at least a century and a half. Experienced in short doses, the play presents a memorably romantic world where human struggles with identity and love find powerfully intense expression. The key lay with the composers who saw in the play the theatrical equivalents of the madrigal poems they had found among Guarini's *Rime*: tightly crafted like the madrigals, the speeches of *Il pastor fido* (or portions of them) became viable lyric poems on their own. But unlike those madrigals, these excerpted poems had a known theatrical reality—the world of the play—to give them even more intensity and continuity. As James Chater writes, composers "recognised that the play is composed at least in part of miniature, semi-independent poetical unities . . . which were imbued with the same lyrical qualities as much contemporary poetry."

The play is set in remote Arcadia, where the goddess Diana has demanded that a virgin be sacrificed to her each year. This curse will be averted (so says an oracle) only when two Arcadians descended from the gods marry each other. The prime candidates for marriage are Silvio and Amarilli, so their fathers arrange for their betrothal. But Silvio loves only hunting, not girls, and Amarilli loves a shepherd, Mirtillo, who loves her as well—but is not permitted to marry her. Meanwhile Dorinda is in love with Silvio, but in vain. Through some knavery too complicated to summarize here, Amarilli is condemned to death. Mirtillo offers himself as a substitute to die in place of Amarilli. Just before Mirtillo is to be executed, he is revealed as the long-lost brother of Silvio—and a descendent of the gods. Thus he and Amarilli can marry each other, and Diana's curse will be lifted. In the meantime, however, there is one final near tragedy: Dorinda (in love with Silvio, the hunter) follows him into the forest. She is disguised as a wolf; he mistakes her for a real wolf and shoots her. In remorse, he realizes that he loves her; she recovers, and they too are married.

Accustomed as we are to valuing realism in our narratives, we may think of sprawling Renaissance romances like *Il pastor fido* as hopelessly detached from the world. Nonetheless, Guarini's pastoral world does reflect, theatrically, some of the very real anxieties of Early Modern European courts: arranged marriages, cultural taboos, and sexual politics. The pastoral conventions of the Arcadian setting, as well as the tense and complicated interactions of the plot, gave Guarini the opportunity for lyric poetry that was also theatrical, both resonant and passionate. These were qualities that were not lost on the composers who drew their texts from Guarini's play. This section presents a selection of these, all of which were set by Monteverdi in 1605 in his fifth book of madrigals. The section begins with four madrigals in the voices of Mirtillo and Amarilli, and concludes with five madrigals based on Silvio's wounding of Dorinda in her wolf's clothing.

88

Ch'i' t'ami e t'ami più de la mia vita,
se tu no'l sai crudele,
chiedilo a queste selve,
che te'l diranno, e te'l diran con esse
le fere loro, i duri sterpi, e i sassi
di questi alpestri monti,
ch'i' ho sì spesse volte
inteneriti al suon de' miei lamenti.

If you don't know how much
I love you, ask;
the wilderness
will testify; the rocks
and cliffs, the wild beasts
will tell how they
have heard me weep,
and how they've wept with me.

Mirtillo here declares his love for Amarilli and invokes the natural world as witness to his love. Guarini is drawing on that familiar pastoral trope called the "pathetic fallacy"—the premise that the natural world shares our human feelings, and enters into the theatricality of our human interactions.

89

Cruda Amarilli, che col nome ancora
d'amar; ahi lasso, amaramente insegni
Amarilli del candido ligustro
più candida, e più bella,
ma de l'Aspido sordo
e più sorda, e più fera, e più fugace;
poi che col dir t'offendo
i' mi morrò tacendo.

Harsh Amaryllis, aptly named,
alas, you "mar" me cruelly.
You're far more beautiful
    than daffodils,
      but you're as wild
and heartless as a rattlesnake.
    I'll not mess with you:
    I'll hold my peace and die.

Mirtillo speaks his grief: bitterness marks the beginning, sadness the end, and silence the follow-up. Like other madrigals, this uses a bitter pun on the name of the beloved: *Amaryllis* contains the Italian word *amar*, "bitter."
It was a favorite poem with composers, for its drama, passion, and wit.

90

O Mirtillo, Mirtillo, anima mia
    se vedessi qui dentro
    come sta il cor di questa,
che chiami crudelissima Amarilli,
    so ben che tu di lei
quella pietà, che da lei chiedi, avresti.
O anime in amor troppo infelici:
che giova a te, cor mio l'esser amato?
Che giova a me l'aver sí caro amante?
    Perché crudo destino
ne disunisci tu, s'amor ne stringe?
    E tu perché ne stringi,
se ne parte il destin, perfido Amore?

Mirtillo, you're my only love.
    You call me harsh,
      but if you saw
my heart, you'd know my love for you
    and recognize
the pity that I cannot show.
Love's made it all impossible.
I love, but it's no use to you;
you love, but it's no good to me.

We're joined by love,
but there's no way to make love work;
    fate intervenes,
and love just laughs, and ties the noose.

Amarilli, alone, confesses that she loves Mirtillo, but she cannot respond to his desire. If we know the plot of *Il pastor fido*, we ascribe this inertia to the overly complex dramatic situation. But what if we encounter this poem outside of the plot of the play? *Why* doesn't she respond? We can't know. Her situation takes on a strange resonance with the real world, outlining one of those terrible and mysterious binds in which humans tie themselves up.

91

E tu Mirtillo (anima mia) perdona
a chi t'è cruda sol dove pietosa
esser non può: perdona a questa solo
    nei detti; e nel sembiante
rigida tua nemica, ma nel core
    pietosissima amante?
E se pur hai desio di vendicarti:
deh qual vendetta aver puoi tu maggiore
    del tuo proprio dolore?

Forgive my cruelty.
I'm hard on you because
I have to be. I know,
    I look dead set
against you, but at heart
    I long for you.
Want to get back at me?
Showing that you're in pain
    is your revenge.

Against her own will, Amarilli has to reject Mirtillo (see the plot summary above). Here, confessing her own sorrow over this rejection, she affirms both the sorrow that this causes for Mirtillo and the pain that his sorrow gives her. Perhaps what she really regrets is *his* unhappiness. In a dark situation, it's a tender expression.

92

Che se tu se' il cor mio,
come se' pur, malgrado
del ciel, e de la terra,
qualor piangi, e sospiri
quelle lagrime tue son il mio sangue,
quei sospiri il mio spir'to, e quelle pene,
e quel dolor, che senti
son miei: non tuoi tormenti.

Because you're mine
(you are, despite
heaven and earth),
your sorrow's mine:
your tears my blood, your sighs
my own soul's breath, and all
my suffering—
all mine, not yours.

Amarilli accepts Mirtillo's love, and with it she accepts the blame for what
he has suffered. She accepts him despite what religion and society (*ciel* and
terra) decree. And she does it in a remarkable way: she does not erase the long
history of pain and rejection; rather, she takes it on, as in some strange ritual
of sexual courtship. "I feel your pain," she says, "and it hurts."

But this acceptance is only in soliloquy: Mirtillo does not hear it, and the
stalemate of frustrated desire goes on for the two of them. As it does for Silvio
and Dorinda, in the next sequence of five madrigals.

93

Ecco Silvio colei, che 'n odio hai tanto,
eccola in quella guisa,
che la volevi a punto.
Bramastila ferir, ferita l'hai,
bramastila tua preda, eccola preda,
bramastila al fin morta, eccola a morte.
Che vuoi tu più da lei? che ti può dare
più di questo Dorinda? ah garzon crudo,

ah cor senza pietà: tu non credesti
la piaga, che per te mi fece Amore,
puoi questa or tu negar de la tua mano?
    Non hai credut'il sangue,
    ch'i' versava per gli occhi,
crederai questo che'l mio fianco versa?

You hated me before; now see
    how you have made
    that hatred real.
You hoped to hurt me: see the wound.
You called me beastly: here I am,
your prey. You wanted me to die:
what can I give you, more than this?
What could you want from me, cruel man?
You never pitied, never thought
that I could feel the pains of love.
Now can you say it isn't so?
    My eyes wept blood;
    you saw nothing.
Now look at me: *this* blood is real.

Dorinda, in love with Silvio and rejected by him, disguises herself as a wolf and gets shot by her beloved Silvio. Petrarchan tradition is filled with metaphors of suffering and wounds, but here they become startlingly real. Dorinda's very real wound intensifies and validates the metaphorical wounds of love: "before, you wanted to hurt me; now here I am bleeding from your arrow; do you now understand the hurt I felt earlier?"

Using a woman's suffering as an instrument to make her lover pay attention, the poem enters painful territory. There is a long history of trying to make sweetness out of sexual violence: "Batti, batti" (Beat me!) cries the abused and forgiving Zerlina in *Don Giovanni.*

94

Ma se con la pietà non è in te spenta
gentilezza, e valor, che teco nacque,
    non mi negar, ti prego

(anima cruda sì, ma però bella)
non mi negar a l'ultimo sospiro
un tuo solo sospir. Beata morte,
se l'addolcissi tu con questa sola
    voce cortese, e pia
    va 'n pace anima mia.

If you can't pity me, perhaps
you'll show that generosity
    that's yours from birth.
Cruel and beautiful, you might
show me a little sign of love
in my last hour. I'd welcome death
if you would temper it and say
    in your sweet voice,
    "Rest well, my soul."

The wounded Dorinda acknowledges Silvio's innate gentility and worth. He may not be willing to pity her in that deepest sense of the word—the reciprocity of love—but she hopes that he will soothe her death with courtesy and faith. All this despite the fact that he has just wounded her with his arrow!

95

Dorinda, ah dirò mia, se mia non sei,
se non quando ti perdo? e quando morte
da me ricevi, e mia non fosti allora
    ch'i ti potei dar vita?
    Pur mia dirò, che mia
sarai malgrado di mia dura sorte;
e se mia non sarai con la tua vita,
    sarai con la mia morte.

"Mine"—can I call you mine, when now
I'm losing you? When I have wronged
you so? When I've given you death
    instead of life?

But you *are* mine!
I'll call you mine in spite of all:
you will be mine, not with your life,
    but in my death.

Silvio reacts to Dorinda's imminent death by offering to die. Within the implausible contrivances of the plot, repetition and resonance underline the plausible, tragic possessiveness of these two unfortunates: the word *mia* (my, mine) occurs eight times.

96

Ecco piegando le genocchie a terra
    riverente t'adoro,
e ti cheggio perdon, ma non già vita.
    Ecco li strali, e l'arco,
ma non ferir già tu gli occhi, o le mani,
    colpevoli ministri
d'innocente voler, ferisci il petto,
    ferisci questo mostro
di pietad' e d'Amor aspro nemico,
ferisci questo cor, che ti fu crudo:
    eccoti il petto ignudo.

Look! On my knees, I worship you.
    I beg of you,
forgive my crimes and take my life.
    Here is the bow,
here is the arrow: use them! Don't shoot
    my guilty eyes,
my murdering hands: aim at my chest,
    pierce my cold heart,
so merciless—so cruel to you.
I offer you your enemy—
    my naked breast.

Silvio begs the wounded Dorinda to kill him. It is cast as a fervent plea, but the tone is oddly imperative: "Kill me! Shoot me in the breast! *Just do it!*" Even as he exposes his physical vulnerability—baring his chest—he also controls the action, commanding her to take revenge. The rhetoric, like the whole situation, is deeply ironic: he directs her weapon to that very heart that she has loved. As he draws her to that physical center of his life, he draws her attention to her own emotional center—that is, her love. Desire and repentance are inseparable from manipulation and cruelty.

97

> *Ferir quel petto Silvio?*
> *Non bisognava a gli occhi miei scovrirlo,*
> *s'avevi pur desio, ch'io te'l ferissi.*
>   *O bellissimo scoglio*
>   *già da l'onde, e dal vento*
> *de le lagrime mie, de' miei sospiri*
>   *sì spesso in van percosso.*
>   *È pur ver che tu spiri?*
> *E che senti pietade? o pur m'inganno.*
> *Ma sii tu pure o petto molle, o marmo,*
>   *già non vo', che m'inganni*
> *d'un candido alabastro il bel sembiante,*
>   *come quel d'una fera*
> *oggi ingannato ha 'l tuo signore, e mio.*
> *Ferir io te? te pur ferisca Amore;*
>   *che vendetta maggiore*
> *non so bramar, che di vederti amante,*
> *sia benedetto il dì, che da prim' arsi.*
> *Benedette le lagrime, e i martiri,*
> *di voi lodar, non vendicar mi voglio.*

>   You're telling me
> to shoot you in the breast, but you
> should not have made me look at it.
>   It's like a rock
>   battered for years
> by waves and winds (my tears and sighs),
>   still standing firm.
>   And does it now

feel something new, some hint of love?
Marble or flesh? How can I tell?
   It seems to be
the purest alabaster, but
    who knows? A lamb
in wolf's disguise duped even you.
Should I shoot you there? No, let Love
    wound you—it's Love
who wants revenge on you, not I.
Happy the day I fell in love!
Blessed be my tears! I only want
to love you, not to take revenge.

This unusually long madrigal, the last in the extended sequence of Dorinda's wounding, revels in love's tragic potential. The metaphor of the rock (his breast) is itself as disturbing as the entire dramatic situation. To Dorinda, the waves and winds represent her desire, and the battered rock represents Silvio's resistance to it. He's acted to her like a dangerous rock threatening a seagoing vessel. But that rock is so very beautiful! She *knows* she should distrust his change of heart, but she *feels* differently. She has loved him for years; now that he seems to be in love too, so she wills herself to trust him. Even though he has just shot her.

SECTION 7   Incursions of Distrust

Why do you put on airs and strut about,
  insidious jealousy?
Do you believe you could usurp my joy?

At the core of Petrarch's concept of love is the lover's constant, unwavering attention to his beloved. All else—the weather, the natural world, the court—simply corroborates his steady desire. Petrarch praised the constancy of a "noble heart," by which all material reality becomes a symbol of desire:

As her white foot moves forward through cool grass,
her sweet and quiet walking starts to spread
a power, emanating from her soles,
that acts to open and renew the flowers.

Love only bothers trapping noble hearts
and doesn't try to wield his power elsewhere;
he makes such warmth rain down from her sweet eyes
that I forget about all other bait.

Her words are matched exactly with her gait
and with her gentle glance at things around,
and with her measured, modest, mild gestures.

From four such sparks, though not from them alone,
comes this great fire in which I live and burn,
for I've become a night bird in the sunlight.

Laura's gait represents the fertility of nature (the flowers bloom), the encompassing power of emotion (he can think of nothing else), the graceful rhetoric of poetry (her words are measured like her walk), and the astonishing impact of desire (the lover is transformed into a phoenix by love).

But Petrarch was writing long before Guarini. The later Petrarchans (particularly in the sixteenth century) were obsessed with inconstancy. The beloved flirts with others; the lover gets angry with her; the beloved accuses him of changing his mind . . . Where Petrarch shows us a steadily deepening emotional trajectory, the poets of the sixteenth century revel in the zigzags of uncertainty. As in the world of opera—which to some degree can be said to have evolved from their poetry and the music written for it—jealousy, inattention, and scorn interrupt the figuration of desire. Perhaps this may be ascribed to the increasing circulation of skeptical ideas (Lucretius, Montaigne) or to the increasing sophistication of courtly life, where the hot-blooded young courtiers (and poets) battled for patronage and attention.

The obsessive constancy of Petrarchan love became in later times the butt of comedy. Shakespeare's Touchstone in *As You Like It* mocks the supposed intensity of a lover's attentions:

> I remember when I was in love, I broke my sword upon a stone, and bid him take that for coming a-night to Jane Smile; and I remember the kissing of her batler and the cow's dugs that her pretty chopp'd hands had milk'd; and I remember the wooing of a peascod instead of her, from whom I took two cods, and giving her them again, said with weeping tears, "Wear these for my sake."

In the same play, Rosalind, posing as a boy, tells Orlando how she taught a fictitious suitor about inconstancy and uncertainty:

> He was to imagine me his love, his mistress; and I set him every day to woo me. At which time would I, being but a moonish youth, grieve, be effeminate, changeable, longing and liking, proud, fantastical, apish, shallow, inconstant, full of tears, full of smiles; for every passion something, and for no passion truly any thing, as boys and women are for the most part cattle of this colour; would now like him, now loathe him; then entertain him, then forswear him; now weep for him, then spit at him; that I drave my suitor from his mad humor of love to a living humor of madness, which was, to forswear the full stream of the world, and to live in a nook merely monastic. And thus I cur'd him, and this way will I take upon me to wash your liver as clean as a sound sheep's heart, that there shall not be one spot of love in't.

Orlando survives his re-education at the hands of this "moonish youth," managing to retain his love and win a happy ending for the comedy. By contrast, Guarini's lovers inhabit a world of inconstancy. If the occasional madrigal speaks of tender faith, there are many more that show the breaking of that faith. Distrustful of other men, uncertain of his beloved's attention, a Guarini lover finds himself on a battlefield of doubts. Sometimes he acknowledges jealousy and overcomes it. Occasionally he lets loose his bitterness, turning vindictive and cruel. At other times, the multiplicity of his feelings simply overwhelms him.

98

Perché di gemme t'incoroni, e d'oro,
*   perfida gelosia,*
turbar già non puoi tu la gioia mia.
Non sai, che la mia Donna altro tesoro,
*   che la sua fè non prezza?*
E se fuss'ella pur vaga d'altezza,
*   chi n'ha più del mio core,*
dov'ha il suo regno, e le sue pompe Amore?

Why do you put on airs and strut about,
    insidious jealousy?
Do you believe you could usurp my joy?
My lover treasures her fidelity
    more than all other gifts.
Why would she look for love in other places?
    In me she has it all:
in me, Love lives, and reigns, and holds his court.

A passionate denunciation of the lover's jealousy, and a confident affirmation of the beloved's faithfulness. And yet . . . that specter of jealousy lurks in his mind, a pagan god or petty dynast that struts about, crowns himself like a Byzantine emperor with jewels and gold, and tempts the lover to cloud his mind with doubt.

99

Quest'è pur il mio core;
quest'è pur il mio ben: che più languisco?
Che fa meco il dolor se ne gioisco?

Fuggite Amor amanti: Amore amico
*   o che fiero nemico.*
Alor che vi lusinga, alor che ride,
*   condisce i vostri pianti*
con quel velen, che dolcemente ancide.
*   Non credete ai sembianti:*
che par soave, ed è pungente, e crudo,
e men è disarmato alor chè nudo.

    I know she is my life,
she is my own; then why so sad?
My joy has turned to sorrow . . .
Lovers, stay far away from Love!
    He'll stab you in the back;
he'll lead you on, he'll smile at you,
    then medicate those wounds
with balm that soothes you while it kills.
    Don't trust his easy looks—
"so cute"—"only a laughing boy"—
that's when he is most dangerous!

Jealousy begins when the beloved shows him attention: but the lover, perversely, will not trust her. He blames the distrust on Cupid, deceptive, cruel, and indifferent to pain. And, of course, his blame is really intended for the beloved: Love's not the only one who turns on his friends.

100

*   Un amoroso agone*
è fatta la mia vita. I miei pensieri
*   son tanti alati arcieri,*
tutti di saettar vaghi, e possenti:
*   ciascun mi fa sentire*
*   com'ha strali pungenti;*
ciascun vittoria attende, e ne 'l ferire
*   mostra forza, ed ingegno.*
Il campo loro è questo petto: il segno
*   è 'l cor costante, e forte;*
e 'l pregio di chi vince è la mia morte.

My life's become
love's firefight, and my fantasies
    are F-16s,
gassed up, and armed, and trigger-mad.
    Locked in on me,
    they start to shoot,
proud of their weapons, confident,
    sure of the kill.
They want my heart, but I won't flinch:
    I'm holding firm
even if constancy means death.

The lover's imagination is populated with archers armed with stinging darts. This dogfight takes place in the lover's own body and soul, a skirmish incited by desire and dominated by conflicting impulses of lust and love, of hope and despair, of adoration and hate. The subtext seems to be the lover resisting his own potential for distrust and jealousy.

The militaristic bravado of fighter pilots in movies like *Top Gun* and *Star Wars* is a plausible modern equivalent to Guarini's sixteenth-century images.

101

O dolce anima mia, dunque è pur vero
    che cangiando pensiero,
    per altrui m'abbandoni?
Se cerchi un cor, che più t'adori, ed ami,
    ingiustamente brami;
se cerchi lealtà, mira che fede,
    amar quand'altrui doni
    la mia cara mercede
e la sperata tua dolce pietate.
    Ma se cerchi beltate,
non mirar me, cor mio mira te stessa
in questo volto, in questo core impressa.

So is it true, my sweetest love,
    you've changed, and want
    to play the field?

You want someone who'd love you more?
   —You'll hunt in vain!
You want a more committed love?
   I'm yours, although
   you throw away
the favors that I hope to have.
   Maybe you want
someone more beautiful? Go find
my heart, and view your beauty there.

The rumor mills must have ground continuously in the inbred court circles where Guarini worked. Here, faced with a rumor that his beloved is unfaithful, the poet speculates on what might be behind it: the desire for more love (how could she want more than he gives?) or more loyalty (could anyone be more constant than he is?). So, not those: but maybe she wants a better-looking lover? The poem makes a swerve into false logic as he tells her: "If you want beauty, look in my heart. There you will see yourself."

102

Se 'l vostro cor, Madonna,
   altrui pietoso tanto,
da quel suo degno al mio non degno pianto
   talor' si rivolgesse,
e una stilla al mio languir, ne desse;
   forse nel mio dolore
vedria l'altrui perfidia, e 'l proprio errore:
e voi seco diresti, ah, sapess'io
usar pietà, come pietà desio.

   You show *him* love;
     but if you'd show
mercy to me, even
     to give me just
one drop of tenderness,
     then, in my pain,
you'd see his treachery
and your mistake; you'd know
how much you need my love.

A whole coterie in one small poem: the poet-lover, the scornful beloved, and someone else she is flirting with. If she were to show the poet a tiny bit of the kindness she shows the other man, she would see the difference between the poet's loyalty and the perfidy of the other. As often, the poet obsessively contemplates both his own pain and her cruelty.

103

> *Ardo sì, ma non t'amo*
> *perfida, e dispietata,*
> *indegnamente amata*
> *da sì leal amante:*
> *più non sarà, che del mio duol ti vante,*
> *ch'i' ho già sano il core:*
> *e s'ardo, ardo di sdegno, e non d'Amore.*

> I burn, but not with love!
> You—fickle, merciless,
> unworthy to be loved
> by such a faithful lover—
> you'll laugh no more about my pain,
> for now my heart is healed:
> it's burning, not with love—with scorn!

Composers loved this poem: thirty-five settings of it are listed in Appendix 2, from as early as 1583 to almost a century later. One can see why: the poem is direct and expressive, while throwing in a couple of clever twists. "Burning" has a double-edged meaning: loving and hating. Having burned with love and watched his love wasted on an inconstant beloved, the lover comes to recognize that love is an inflammatory disease. But, in an odd homeopathy, the fire of disdain cures the fire of love. "I'm healthy now!" And yet that "cure" is hardly believable: can the lover really claim to be healthy if he lives in the fires of scorn? That the poem ends with such an obvious logical flaw (surely not unperceived by Guarini!) may have been what led Tasso to write a madrigal in response, which follows (#104).

104

> *Ardi, e gela a tua voglia,*
> *perfido, ed impudico,*
> *or amante, or nemico;*
> *che d'incostante ingegno*
> *poco l'amor io stimo, e men lo sdegno:*
> *e se 'l tuo amor fu vano,*
> *van fia lo sdegno del tuo cor insano.*

> Burn or freeze,
> shameless one,
> you quisling.
> Fickle soul,
> your love is cheap, your scorn is mad.
> Love's useless?
> So's your insufferable disdain!

This is Torquato Tasso's response to the previous poem, printed in the 1598 edition of Guarini's *Rime* and identified there as *Risposta* (response) *del Tasso*. Tasso, the Ferrarese author of the extravagant epic poem *Gerusalemme liberata*, spent several decades in a hospital for the insane. Various legends circulate about why he was there: the Romantic story is that he made love to the sister of Duke Alfonso II of Ferrara, who had him locked up against his will. More likely mental instability had made it necessary for him to be confined.

Guarini's madrigal (#103) is in the voice of a rejected lover who bitterly turns against his beloved. In this poem, Tasso, who knew Guarini well, scorns that scornful lover. The exchange is about love, of course, but it's also about literature: "How can you pretend to be a poet of love when you write such a fierce diatribe against love?" Tasso angrily nails Guarini for the bizarre logic by which he tries to make constancy out of inconstancy.

Someone—probably Guarini—came back with a counter response, the next madrigal (#105).

105

> *Arsi e alsi a mia voglia,*
> *leal non impudico,*

amant'e non nemico;
e s'al tuo lieve ingegno
poco cale l'amor e men lo sdegno,
sdegn'e amor faran vano
l'altiero suon del tuo parlar insano.

I burned and froze
as I had need—
but firm in love.
Disdain *and* love
are meaningless to you:
well, then, I scorn
your sick, bombastic words.

This response to the above two poems (in Italian, *contra risposta*), is variously ascribed to Guarini (by Denis Stevens) and Tasso (by Angelo Solerti, for example). Its negation of the cynicism of the previous poem suggests Guarini rather than Tasso as the author. Did Tasso's critique touch Guarini to the quick, as the tone implies? Or was it all part of a poetic game?

106

Io disleale? Ah cruda,
voi negate la fede,
per non mi dar mercede.
Se non basta il languire
provatemi al morire,
e se ciò ricusate,
perche la fè negate,
che provar non volete?
O provate, o credete.

Disloyal—me?
You call me that
to put me off.
Go all the way:
try me by fire!
If you've lost faith

in me, then be
empirical:
test, or believe.

This madrigal has only lines of seven syllables, lacking the longer eleven-syllable lines that give metrical variety to most of the others. The rhymes in Italian, too, are straightforward: apart from the first nonrhymed line, the poem is constructed simply in couplets. With that clarity of form comes a rhetoric of sincerity: "No, I'm not complicated. I'm simply in love, with you, and you alone. I know you don't believe in love, but just try me."

107

> Stracciami pure il core;
> ben è ragion ingrato,
> che se t'ho troppo amato,
> porti la pena del commesso errore.
> Ma perché strazii fai de la mia fede?
> Che colpa a l'innocente?
> Se la mia fiamma ardente
> non merita mercede,
> ah non la mer'ta il mio fedel servire!
> Ma straccia pur crudele:
> non può morir d'amor alma fedele.
> Surgerà nel morir quasi fenice
> la mia fede più bella, e più felice.

> Batter my heart;
> I've loved so much
> you have the right
> to punish me for it.
> But do not slander me!
> What have I done?
> If my desire
> deserves your blame,
> my loyalty does not!
> Do what you will,
> you can't get rid of me:

I'll die and rise again,
reborn in faithful love.

The action verb here is *stracciare*—"to tear, shred, attack." It's used three times, each time in a different verb form, and each time bringing its harsh sound to express its equally harsh meaning. In translating the opening use of the verb, I've echoed John Donne speaking to God, in order to capture some of the shock value of finding this violence in a love poem.

108

Mentre una gioia miro
ecco gioia apparir, che lo splendore
tolse a quell'altra, ed a me tolse il core.
    Amor fabro gentile
legami questa, ond'ebbi l'altra a vile;
lega nel seno mio questo tesoro,
che 'l desio darà il foco, e la fé l'oro.

    Looking at *one*,
I see *another* diamond
that steals the light, and steals my heart.
    Jeweler Love,
use this one, let the other go.
Set it in me: use my desire
as crucible, my faith as gold.

This poem, which does not appear in the 1598 edition of *Rime* but in an edition from a year later, differs from other *rime* in speaking more frankly of the lover-poet's inconstancy than Guarini usually manages to do. This lover's eye is wandering. The poem is also more than usually constructed around a single concept: the beloved as jewel, and Love as an artisan commissioned to make a beautiful setting for the gem. At the end, the lover claims that faith (*la fé*) is the gold that Love will use to set this new jewel. Given the lover's temptation to wander, we might question the purity of the gold.

109

Io d'altrui? S'i' volessi, i' non potrei,
   ne potendo vorrei.
Se 'l mio cor tutto quanto
   possedete, se tanto
son trasformato in voi, che non son io,
come sarò d'altrui, se non son mio?

Find a new lover? If I could,
   I wouldn't want to:
   I have become
   completely you,
and I am not myself. So . . .
another's? How? I'm not my own.

The moment of doubt at the beginning of the poem with its shift of loyalty—literally, "I, belonging to another?"—allows the poem to explore a shift of identity. The hypothetical circumstance of loving another comes up against the unwavering condition of belonging to the beloved—and thus being transformed into the beloved.

110

Altro non è il mi' Amore,
che con fede immortal mortal dolore:
   ma nel tormento ho vita;
che se m'ancide l'un, l'altra m'aita.
E sì fermo ho 'l desio contra il martire,
   ch'io non temo il morire,
perché la vita, e non la fé si scioglia;
ch'assai peggio di morte è 'l cangiar voglia.

   My life is pain
endured through constancy,
   drowning in sorrows
but kept afloat by faith.
I'm not afraid of death,
   which only hurts

the body; worse than death
is love's apostasy.

The pain of love is presented here as accompanied by a quasi-religious faith in which suffering becomes a necessary condition of martyrdom. Steadiness in love corresponds to unwavering faith in God. The two, suffering and faith, coexist in the experience of courtly lovers as they do in the lives and deaths of the saints.

111

Ch'io non t'ami, cor mio?
ch'io non sia la tua vita, e tu la mia?
Che per novo desio
e per nova speranza, i' t'abbandoni?
Prima che questo sia,
morte non mi perdoni.
Che se tu se' quel core, onde la vita
m'è sì dolce, e gradita,
fonte d'ogni mio ben, d'ogni desire,
come posso lasciarti, e non morire?

Stop loving you?
Let go of living life in you?
Hunt some new hope
of happiness apart from you?
Impossible!
I'd rather die;
you are all that I am,
my only life,
the source of all that I hold dear.
Could I abandon that, and live?

The poem declares constancy by imagining its opposite. The beloved says something harsh—perhaps "You don't love me anymore"—and the lover uses his rebuttal to show what it means to hold love dear: to leave her would be to leave his heart in her, and thus to die, for she is the heart that gives him life.

In the last line, Italian readers might have heard echoes of the most famous line in Dante, *Lasciate ogni speranza, voi ch'entrate*—"Abandon all hope, you who enter here." Like Dante, Guarini imagines a soul that could perversely turn away from life and good. But in this case, that turning is only suggested, and emphatically denied.

112

M'è più dolce il penar per Amarilli
che'l gioir di mill'altre:
e se gioir di lei
mi vieta il mio destino, oggi si moia,
per me pure ogni gioia.
Viver io fortunato
per altra donna mai, per altro amore?
Né volendo il potrei,
né potendo il vorrei:
e s'esser può che 'n alcun tempo mai
ciò voglia il mio volere.
O possa il mio potere,
prego il ciel, ed amor, che tolto pria
ogni voler, ogni poter mi sia.

The pain of loving her exceeds
all thought of bliss;
if I cannot
enjoy her love, all other loves
are meaningless.
Could I live,
loving another being?
I could not, nor
do I want to.
I'm asking only this: if I
ever long for,
ever achieve
another love, then take away
all my intentions, my desires!

This vow of constancy is another excerpt from *Il pastor fido*, spoken by the shepherd Mirtillo to his beloved Amarilli (see section 6). It has that claustrophobic intensity that Petrarchan poetry demands—without the beloved, joy is not joy; longing is despicable; achievement is meaningless.

SECTION 8　　Lovers' Voices

How similar we lovers are—
each in a cage; each one singing.

In the centuries following Petrarch, the poetry drawn from his influence developed an increasing self-consciousness and a heightened awareness of its own artfulness. The frustrations of unrequited desire correspond, poets realized, to the frustrations of poetry. The lover, dependent on crumbs of sympathy from his beloved, is not unlike the poet, scrounging for recognition or patronage. The poet searches for new inventions and new forms to delight the reader just as the lover struggles to express his love in order to pique the curiosity of the beloved.

Sidney's Astrophil, for example, is stuck, both in love and poetry:

Loving in truth, and fain in verse my love to show,
That the dear She might take some pleasure of my pain,
Pleasure might cause her read, reading might make her know,
Knowledge might pity win, and pity grace obtain,
　　I sought fit words to paint the blackest face of woe,
Studying inventions fine, her wits to entertain,
Oft turning others' leaves, to see if thence would flow
Some fresh and fruitful showers upon my sunburned brain.
　　But words came halting forth, wanting Invention's stay;
Invention, Nature's child, fled step-dame Study's blows,
And others' feet still seemed but strangers in my way.
Thus great with child to speak, and helpless in my throes,
　　Biting my truant pen, beating myself for spite,
"Fool," said my Muse to me, "look in thy heart and write."

The Muse asserts that the image of his mistress, which is fixed in his heart, is the best—or only—inspiration for the poet-lover. It was a mistake to look for inspiration in the world of literature ("turning others' leaves"); "inventions fine" and "fit words" derive only from Stella's beauty. Of course, Sidney

135

and all his courtly readers understood the irony: this poem, like every Renaissance poem, is in fact deeply indebted to "others' leaves" and would have no existence without the inspiration of the literary tradition.

In the courts of northern Italy, the Muse might also have told Guarini and his colleagues to find inspiration in music. Music and poetry were inseparable. Poems were constantly being appropriated or commissioned by composers as texts for the vocal pieces that today we call madrigals. It is no surprise, then, that singing features as an explicit inspiration in many of Guarini's lyrics.

The fraught sexual and social negotiations involved with singing in a courtly environment are evident in a number of the madrigals in this section. In contrast, singing in Renaissance art and poetry often implies the supposed innocence of pastoral, in which music is the province of birds and shepherds. The two are not inconsistent: pastoral served the Renaissance as a mode of representing and critiquing court culture without appearing to get uncomfortably close to those who held power in the court.

I've included a couple of pastoral "echo" poems, in which the woods and hills "sing" verbal echoes back to the poet. Birds figure often in Guarini, as well: the ubiquitous nightingale is a "natural" denizen living free from human social constraints, while its domestic counterpart, the caged songbird, lives its life as a musical prisoner. The powerful effect of song in human circumstances comes out in the madrigals that close this section, especially the long description of the singing of "Angioletta" (#122)—the bravura poetic evocation of a bravura singer that I described in the preface to this volume.

113

> *O come se' gentile,*
> *caro augellino: o quanto*
> *è 'l mio stato amoroso al tuo simile.*
> *Tu prigion, io prigion: tu canti, io canto,*
> *tu canti per colei,*
> *che t'ha legato, ed io canto per lei.*
> *Ma in questo è differente*
> *la mia sorte dolente,*
> *che giova pur te l'esser canoro.*
> *Vivi cantando, e io cantando moro.*

How sweet you are,
my little bird!
How similar we lovers are—
each in a cage; each one singing.
You sing for her
who caught you; and so do I.
The difference
is what's at stake:
singing is happiness for you,
you live by song; I only die.

The poet-lover sees his own life in the life of his mistress's pet bird. Both
are caged, and both sing—the bird literally, the poet figuratively in his madrigals. The difference is that the bird's songs bring food and attention; the
lover's poems bring him only pain. And yet, of course, he goes on writing
these beautiful little madrigals!

114

Dolcissimo Usignuolo,
tu chiami la tua cara compagnia,
cantando vieni, vieni anima mia.
A me canto non vale;
e non ho come tu da volar ale.
O felice augelletto:
come nel tuo diletto
ti ricompensa ben l'alma natura;
se ti negò saver, ti diè ventura.

O nightingale,
you call your mate to you,
singing, "Come to me, dear."
But I can't fly,
and songs don't work for me.
Nature gave you
the happiest
of fates: to sing, and love,
and not to know of it.

The nightingale was a standard of Renaissance poetry, representing happy and spontaneous creativity long before Keats. Here the bird's good fortune—and lack of awareness of it—differentiates it from the self-conscious melancholy of human thought. The nightingale's songs are effective in the realm of desire; the poet's are not. The bird lives with its mate in joy, but the lover lives alone in knowledge and sorrow.

115

> *Quell'augellin, che canta*
> *sì dolcemente, e lascivetto vola*
> *or da l'abete al faggio,*
> *ed or dal faggio al mirto,*
> *s'avesse umano spir'to,*
> *direbbe, ardo d'amore, ardo d'amore.*
> *Ma ben arde nel core,*
> *e parla in suo favella;*
> *che gli risponde, ardo d'amore anch'io.*

> This little bird that sings
> so tenderly, and wings its way
> from pine to beech, and then
> from beech to myrtle, would,
> if it were human, say,
> "I burn with love, I burn with love."
> Hear how his heart's desire
> burns in his song; his mate
> sings back, "I also burn with love!"

Drawn from the opening scene of *Il pastor fido*, this pastoral madrigal posits a love as natural as the birds of the forest, free to move from tree to tree. The lover imagines a conversation of unhampered and mutual love and invests it with the warmth of his own desire.

116

> *Or che 'l meriggio ardente*
> *al dolce sonno, e placido richiama*

e gli uomini, e le belve,
destati Ninfa; il tuo fedel ti chiama
tra le segrete chiostre, e 'l fido horrore
di queste ombrose selve,
dov'è sol meco Amore.
Vieni, deh vieni omai; non far dimora,
odi un antro c'invita, e dice or ora.

Now that the sun
oppresses men and beasts
in noontime heat,
awake! Your lover calls
deep in the hidden cave,
in the cool shade
where love is waiting.
Waste no time; come somehow;
the cave calls out, "Come now!"

This madrigal is an echo poem: a human voice cries out in the woods, and is echoed; nature and human desire are linked in mutual song. Since echoes are not exact repetitions, an echo poem plays with the shifting nature of echoic resonance—the final vowel stays constant, but what precedes it is changed in the repetition. Here, for example, the lover calls *non far dimora* (literally, "don't stay home"); the echo version (what the cave returns) changes that to *e dice or ora*—"the cave now says, 'Now!'"

117

Amiam Fillide, amiamo, ah non rispondi:
queste voci amorose,
che tu disperdi a l'aura in fra le frondi,
son da l'aure pietose
e raccolte, e portate
a tal, che mi risponde, e n'ha pietate.
Odi crudel, ch'a questa voce amiamo
un antro, un bosco, mi risponde amo amo.

I call, "Love me, my love!"
    You don't respond.
You toss my words away
    into the air,
      which nurses them
and echoes them with care.
I call, "Let us try love!"
The woods respond, "I love!"

Without a pastoral landscape, there is no way to hear an echo: we need cliffs to send the echo back and stillness to allow us to hear the faint return. In this madrigal, the silence of the beloved (silent because she is unresponsive to the lover's cry) allows the responding echo to be heard with its promises of love. The poem in Italian is self-consciously resonant, self-echoing: the lover cries *amiamo* (let us love); the echo returns a different call, redoubled and now in the first person: *amo amo* (I love, I love). Desire's optative is fulfilled in love's indicative. But ironically the wrong entity responds—the woods, not the beloved.

118

Deh, come in van chiedete
d'udir, bella Sirena, il canto mio,
se sorda sète voi, muto son io.
    Al suon de vostri accenti
perdei la voce, e sol mi suona al core
armonia di sospiri, e di lamenti.
    E se 'l vostro rigore
a voi ne toglie il suon, mirate il pianto;
che le lagrime mie, sono il mio canto.

It is no use
to ask me for a song—
you're deaf, so I am mute.
    Hearing you sing,
I lose my voice, and make
a dissonance of groans.
    If you won't hear

my sighs, look at my face:
my song is in my tears.

A matrix of vocal and aural antitheses: she wants to hear a song from him, but hearing her voice disturbs him so much that he cannot sing. Since she won't hear him when he speaks (of love, of course), she will be unable to hear his singing. At the end, the poem abandons hearing for sight: the tears she sees on his face represent the song he won't sing.

That unsung song, strangely, is this madrigal itself, which Guarini writes but does not actually "sing." With its play on hearing and not hearing, it's not surprising that the poem was set to music by at least eighteen composers, who could hardly refuse the invitation to make music for the deliciously musical phrase *armonia di sospiri, e di lamenti*—"harmony of sighs and groans."

119

Come cantar poss'io
d'amor, se sdegno ne' begli occhi avete?
Deh, se del canto mio sì vaga sète,
mentre accordo la voce e lo 'ntelletto
al suon del vostro detto,
il vostro detto voi, Donna, accordate
con la vostra beltate;
ch'io non posso cantar, cruda, se 'l canto
mi comanda la lingua, e gli occhi il pianto.

Sing what you wrote?
Not when you look at me like that!
If you want this song that much,
I'll have to shape both mind and voice
to what you wrote—
and you will have to soothe your looks
to match your poem.
How can I sing? Your lips invite
my voice; your eyes leave me in tears.

Again, his beloved asks him for a song, specifically, a song that she has written (*vostro detto*). We do not know if Guarini was a singer, but it seems likely: his daughter Anna was famous for her singing, and he was active as a poet in a court where poetry and music were inseparable. Even if this madrigal is not autobiographical, it must derive from what he knew well: that the voice is subject to the passions.

120

Non è questa colei (ben la conosco
  a le belleze conte)
che del canoro mar, de l'arso monte,
  vicini al suo gran nido,
l'altere meraviglie a noi se 'n porta?
Chiudete amanti miseri, chiudete
  l'orecchie al suono infido,
  se morir non volete:
che quella voce è de l'incendio scorta.
  Non vedete vo' sciocchi,
che 'n bocca ha le Sirene, Etna negli occhi?

She, wondrous herself,
  paints in her song
the wonders of the world—
  the ocean's roar,
the sun-drenched mountainside.
There's danger in her song:
  lovers, beware
  the undertow
that pulls you down; she sings
  with fire as hot
as Etna's lava streams.

From its title in the 1598 Venice edition (in which it is the first madrigal), we learn that this madrigal is dedicated to Ignez Argotta, Marchioness of Grana. It is presumably also about her singing. She was the wife of Prospero, Marquis of Carretto, and the mistress of Vincenzo Gonzaga, Duke of Mantua. She was the driving force behind the abortive attempt to stage *Il pastor fido* in Mantua in the early 1590s.

121

> *Vien da l'onde, o dal cielo*
> *questa nostra bellissima Sirena?*
> *Se n'odo il suono, e se ne miro il viso,*
>   *in cui del Paradiso,*
> *non che del ciel, son le sembianze impresse,*
>   *non è cosa terrena.*
> *Celeste la direi, se non vivesse*
> *ne l'angoscioso mar, che fanno i pianti*
>   *degli infelici amanti.*

> Is sky her home,
> or ocean? As I hear her sing
> and as I see her move, I think:
>   she's beyond it all!
> No semblance there of earth or sea,
>   or even sky:
> heaven's her home, I'd say. And yet
> around her crash the anguished waves
>   of lover's tears.

Like the previous madrigal (#120), this one is dedicated to the Marchioness of Grana. Until the final lines, it seems a straightforward compliment: such a beautiful lady and such an expert singer must be a celestial creature! But in the poem's ambivalent world of metaphor, she's also a Siren—a dangerous and otherworldly temptation—and an island in a sea made turbulent (*angosciosco*—"anxious") by the sighs of her rejected lovers.

It is a telling insight into the complex culture of northern Italian courts that such a critique of the "cruelty" of a highly placed patroness could be offered (and accepted, presumably) as praise.

122

> *Mentre vaga Angioletta*
> *ogni anima gentil cantando alletta,*
>   *corre il mio core, e pende*
> *tutto dal suon del suo soave canto;*
>   *e non so come in tanto*

musico spirto prende,
fauci canore, e seco forma, e finge
per non usata via
garrula, e maestrevole armonia.
Tempra d'arguto suon pieghevol voce,
e la volve, e la spinge
con rotti accenti, e con ritorti giri
qui tarda, e là veloce;
e talor' mormorando
in basso, e mobil suono, ed alternando
fughe, e riposi, e placidi respiri,
or la sospende, e libra,
or la preme, or la frange, or la raffrena;
or la saetta, e vibra,
or in giro la mena,
quando con nodi tremuli, e vaganti,
quando fermi, e sonanti.
Così cantando, e ricantando il core,
o miracol d'Amore,
è fatto un'Usignulo,
e spiega già per non star meco il volo.

As Angie sings,
delighting every listener,
    I'm borne aloft,
a glider carried by her song.
    How does she seize
    the music's soul,
her voice making, remaking it,
    summoning such
delicious, fluent harmony?
Her music's both precise and free:
    it slides and thrusts
with broken accents and with turns;
    now slow, now quick;
    now murmuring
in moving bass lines, mixing runs
with rests and cadences;

focused or loose,
weighty, or broken, or subdued;
   it vibrates, turns
   and pierces through;
pulls back; and once again it's firm
   and resonant.
Inventing, reinventing, she
   makes of my heart
   a nightingale,
flying from sorrow into mystery.

Guarini's knowledgeable description of the singing of Angioletta ("little angel") emphasizes the flexibility, spontaneity, variety, and affective power of late sixteenth-century music. Here music is seen as inseparable from desire: as love works on both the singer and the listener, the heart becomes a nightingale, inhabiting an emotional realm of "shadows numberless," in Keats' metaphor.

Monteverdi set this florid poem as a tenor duet in an appropriately flamboyant style. The two singers represent the variety of Angioletta's singing with the full repertoire of vocal fireworks—trills, runs, breaks, tremors—in a baroque richness that culminates in the nightingale's swirling and brilliant flight of sound.

123

   Aura dolce odorata,
che dall'orecchia penetrando al core,
   tacita, e infiammata
raccendesti il già sopito amore.
   O mie dolcezze ascose
   in due labbia amorose,
che giunta insieme, e questa Rosa, e quella,
mi fer d'Amore il gratioso dono,
   con sì placido suono,
di muta, e soavissima favella,
   che parea dir, Amiamo,
   dolce mio cor, ch'io t'amo.

That voice, so sweet,
that through the ear burns to the heart,
    there silently
kindles my long ash-smothered love.
    That melody
    (shaped by her lips,
working in rosy counterpoint),
I dedicate—an offering—
    a gift to Love—
a prayer of wordless reverence
    that seems to say,
    "Love me, my love!"

The lover, after an unexplained hiatus, hears his lady singing. The song penetrates to his heart, where it works the silent, transcendent force of hope. He, now again warmed with the possibility of love, reimagines that song as an offering to the god of love—a purified song without words that nonetheless speaks his deepest wishes and bears witness to Guarini's faith in the power of song.

SECTION 9   The World's Interruptions

But when two loving hearts are forced
to separate, that anguish feels
like death

The world of Guarini's madrigals can seem stiflingly closed off, as if that world consisted only of a man locked in longing for a woman who resists or ignores him. In that figurative enclosed space, the lover's actions seem tiny, and the little we see of his beloved is even more constrained.

That narrow subject matter matches the form of the madrigal: a single moment, a deliberately restricted personal event, and an unwavering commitment to the one topic of love. Perhaps the closest analogies in English are the tiny gems of the seventeenth-century poet Robert Herrick, such as this poem about a primrose:

> *Ask me why I send you here*
> *This sweet Infanta of the year?*
> *Ask me why I send to you*
> *This primrose, thus bepearl'd with dew?*
> *I will whisper to your ears:*
> *The sweets of love are mix'd with tears.*
>
> *Ask me why this flower does show*
> *So yellow-green, and sickly too?*
> *Ask me why the stalk is weak*
> *And bending (yet it doth not break)?*
> *I will answer: These discover*
> *What fainting hopes are in a lover.*

For Herrick, the simple gift of a flower is sufficient cause for a beautiful miniature of a poem, an English madrigal. Like Guarini, Herrick barely moves beyond the lover himself; the primrose, as transient and as barely visible as the dew upon it, circles us right back to the lover.

But occasionally, the Petrarchan lyric moves outward, acknowledging a world beyond the tight courtly dance of suspended desire. These lovers, it turns out, occasionally have other commitments, other places to go. Accordingly, the love poems sometimes deal with the effects of such real-world comings and goings; Shakespeare, for example, acknowledges an enforced absence from his beloved:

> *From you have I been absent in the spring,*
> *When proud-pied April (dress'd in all his trim)*
> *Hath put a spirit of youth in every thing,*
> *That heavy Saturn laugh'd and leapt with him.*
> *Yet nor the lays of birds, nor the sweet smell*
> *Of different flowers in odor and in hue,*
> *Could make me any summer's story tell,*
> *Or from their proud lap pluck them where they grew;*
> *Nor did I wonder at the lily's white,*
> *Nor praise the deep vermilion in the rose,*
> *They were but sweet, but figures of delight,*
> *Drawn after you, you pattern of all those.*
> > *Yet seem'd it winter still, and, you away,*
> > *As with your shadow I with these did play.*

Without the beloved, the lover's world becomes a mere "shadow" of itself. One of the notable achievements of this sonnet is to show how that shadow world—which should be as bleak as winter—is nonetheless also vivid and memorable, as intensely realized as "the deep vermilion of the rose." Evoking absence, the poet reaches beyond love's obsessions to enliven and intensify love.

In "His Sailing from Julia," Herrick writes of how parting on a voyage at sea magnifies the turbulence and dangers of the lovers' relationship (a remora—line 4—is a shipworm, a real threat to wooden sailing vessels):

> *When that day comes, whose evening says I'm gone*
> *Unto that watery desolation,*
> *Devoutly to thy closet-gods then pray*
> *That my wing'd ship may meet no remora.*
> *Those deities which circum-walk the seas,*
> *And look upon our dreadful passages,*

Will from all dangers re-deliver me
For one drink-offering poured out by thee.
Mercy and truth live with thee! and forbear
(In my short absence) to unsluice a tear;
But yet for love's sake, let thy lips do this,
Give my dead picture one engendering kiss:
Work that to life, and let me ever dwell
In thy remembrance, Julia. So farewell.

Petrarch used the image of the sea voyage repeatedly to evoke the "deso-lation" and "dreadful passages" of love. The first stanza of his sestina "Chi è fermato" imagines a voyage that feels real, in the specific details both of this boat, with its tiller and sail, and of the rocks that threaten to destroy it. The voyage is also obviously an allegory, whether of parting from a lover, losing one's way, or leaving one's life:

He who decides to entrust his life
to treacherous waves and close to the rocks,
preserved from death just by a little boat,
cannot be very far from his own end;
he ought then to turn back to find the port
now while the tiller still governs the sail.

Guarini's madrigals of departure, though there are no sea voyages, simi-larly evoke situations that at once seem grounded in a real world of business and at the same time are figures for desire, frustration, hope, and annoyance. He explores the strange and paradoxical mode in which parting intensifies presence and nurtures hope and despair: "Thinking of you gone," as he writes, "is food that poisons me" (#127).

124

Credetel voi, che non sentite amore,
  non si prova morire
    più crudel del partire.
Quando la vita è spenta è seco spento
  anco tutto il tormento;
e l'alma col morir la morte fugge:

ma se da la sua dolce, e cara vita
un amoroso cor parte, si strugge
partendo, e more, e dopo la partita
    rinasce al suo dolore,
e comincia un morir, che mai non more.

All you who are not lovers, hear:
    parting is worse—
    far worse—than death.
In death, all struggles fade away
    and torments cease;
dying, the soul flies free from death.
But when two loving hearts are forced
to separate, that anguish feels
like death—but death that doesn't end:
    reborn in pain,
we live—only to die again.

The rhetoric is intense—hyperbolically declaiming that parting is worse than death itself; grotesquely describing the heart's agonies in parting; painting the gloomy splendors of the heart after parting, reborn to its sorrow; and wrapping up with a Donne-like paradox in the final line. Its Baroque intensity is justified by the opening premise: a warning to all those apostates who deny love's power.

Death appears six times in eleven short lines as Guarini rings grammatical changes on the root word: *morire, morir, morte, more, morir, more.* With such resonance, it is no wonder that composers loved this poem.

125

Ben fu pari tra noi, Donna, il partire,
    ma non fu pari (ahi lasso)
    né 'l dolor né 'l desire,
    ch'i' piansi, e voi gioiste.
Voi col pensier, più che col piè fuggiste;
    io mossi a pena il passo,
e l'alma a seguir voi ratta si volse.
    Deh se tanto a me dolse

quel, che di me portaste,
perché a voi no, quel che di voi lasciaste?

The fact of parting was the same
    for both of us . . .
    but not its effect:
    I wept, you smiled.
You vanished at the speed of light;
    I couldn't move.
I longed only to be with you.
    Why do I grieve
    that you are gone,
when you are glad that I'm still here?

Parting is nominally a symmetrical business: each person loses the company of the other. But in this case there is no symmetry. She leaves, he is left
behind. He grieves at the separation, she—at least so he imagines—is merely
relieved or indifferent. The poem itself is like the lover: stuck at home, mired
in self-pity.

126

Voi pur da me partite, anima dura,
    né vi duole il partire,
    oimè quest'è morire
    crudele, e voi gioite?
Quest'è vicino aver l'ora suprema,
    e voi non la sentite?
O meraviglia di durezza estrema.
    Esser alma d'un core,
e separarsi, e non sentir dolore.

Hard heart, you're leaving—and you feel
    nothing at all!
    It's killing me,
    but you are fine.
I'm drawing my last breath, and you
    could not care less.

How wonderfully tough you are—
    to take my heart—
to rip it out—to feel no shame!

Here, parting is framed as a deathbed scene—the lover at his last hour, when the soul is parting from the body. She possesses his heart, he's dying: how can she *not* feel the pangs of death? In his view, of course, she's a monster and can feel no guilt, no pain.

Is the poem a put-down? In some ways, of course, it is. But, oddly, it's also a poem of wonder and even praise for how amazingly hard-hearted she is. The madrigal begins with insight into her hardness (*anima dura*—"tough spirit") and ends with a heightened rhetoric of amazement (*O meraviglia di durezza estrema*—"Oh, the wonder of such extreme toughness").

127

    Credete voi ch'i' viva
pascendo il cor famelico, e penoso
del pensiero amoroso? Ahi ch'i' ne moro.
    Perché vita, e ristoro
ben ho pensando, anima cara, in voi,
ma quando penso poi, ch'io ne son privo
moro nel cibo onde mi pasco, e vivo.

    You really think
I live on thought alone?
This diet's killing me!
    The thought of you
is all I want to eat;
but thinking of you gone
is food that poisons me.

To a degree, imagination can compensate for deprivation: though the beloved is unattainable, the lover can live by thinking, desiring, and writing, as if thought were nutrition. But under duress, in her absence, metaphor breaks down: the supposed food becomes mere fantasy, or worse.

Sir Philip Sidney's Astrophil knows the limit of imagining: "But 'Ah,'

Desire still cries, 'give me some food!'" And Orlando, in *As You Like It*, corroborates: "I can live no longer by thinking."

128

> *Pur venisti, cor mio,*
> *e pur t'ho qui presente, e pur ti veggio,*
> *e non dormo, e non sogno, e non vaneggio.*
> *Venisti sì, ma fuggi*
> *sì ratto, che mi struggi.*
> *Ahi fuggitiva vista degli amanti:*
> *come sogno se' tu d'occhi vegghianti.*

> You came to me,
> my love, just now; it was no dream,
> no fantasy. I saw you here,
>   but then you fled
>   and I dissolved.
> So was that fleeting sight of you
> a vision, or a waking dream?

This is one of Guarini's most compressed madrigals; it packs a powerful emotional experience into seven lines. Unlike other partings, with their cerebral arguments about constancy, this lays out the pain of a paradoxical reality with heartfelt bluntness. The lover asserts emphatically that he saw his (absent?) beloved in the flesh—not as a dream, not as a vision; but then, overcome by the transience of the vision, he doubts its reality. I have borrowed Keats's summary of his encounter with the nightingale to catch Guarini's questioning of the visionary experience.

In English, it is hard to capture the elusive Italian word *pur*, which opens the poem and recurs twice more in the second line. It might be translated as "so" or "however" or "yet," but none of these quite captures its sense of suspended thought. Here I think *pur* sets up the mood of uncertainty from the beginning, adding conditionality to the assertion of reality: "So . . . I *know* that you came to me . . . *and yet* . . ."

129

Al partir del mio sole
piansi la vista sua, la vita mia,
ch'al suo duro partir da me partia.
Or ch'egli torna, i' canto,
e con la rimembranza di quel giorno
sì pien d'amaro pianto
addolcisco la gioia del ritorno.
O felice partita,
che fai più cara col morir la vita.

She went away—
and I, deprived of her,
grieved for my sun's eclipse.
Now she returns.
I sing; the memory
of all that grief
makes for a sweeter joy.
Parting's a death
that brings more precious life!

Parting and return: mourning and rejoicing. By the end of the madrigal, the lover realizes how life has become dearer (*più cara*) through deprivation. The power of the poem comes not only from the sadness of parting but also from the memory of sorrow, and above all from the poetic imagination that takes grief and uses it to "sweeten"—*addolcire*—his song and his life.

130

Amor, i' parto, e sento nel partire
al penar, al morire
ch'io parto da colei, ch'è la mia vita.
Ma che vita diss'io, s'ella gioisce
quando 'l mio cor languisce?
O durezza incredibile infinita
d'anima, che 'l suo core
può lasciar morto, e non sentir dolore.

I have to go away from you—
   it feels like death:
parting from you, leaving my life.
My life? No life could smile at death
   the way you do.
You'd have to have a soul of steel
   to shred a heart,
to leave it dead, and feel no pain.

The pivot here is *la mia vita*. The poem takes the figurative commonplace—
she's my life—and thinks of it literally: if she is his life, then in leaving her, he
must die. But it's not so simple: if she feels nothing in his dying, how can she
be his life?

131

   Non sa che sia dolore
chi da la Donna sua parte, e non more.
Cari lumi leggiadri, amato volto,
   che 'l mio fero destino,
   sì tosto oggi m'ha tolto;
viver lungi da voi? Tanto vicino
son di mia vita al termine fatale?
Se vivo torno a voi, torno immortale.

   The deepest grief—
to leave your love and realize
you're still alive: so suddenly
   deported from
   those eyes, that face,
to live apart from her. To live?
Barely. If ever I come back,
I'll make it only as a ghost.

The last line is resonant in Italian: *Se vivo torno à voi, torno immortale*—
literally, "If I return to you alive, I return [as an] immortal." In Guarini's day
they spoke more directly about such matters than many of us do today: they
earnestly believed in the soul.

Ghosts can be beautiful and loving too: *Truly, Madly, Deeply.*

132

Quando mia cruda stella
mi fe' da voi partire,
non mi vedeste voi, Donna, morire?
Non mi vedeste no; perché 'l mio core
corse ne lo splendore
de be' vostri occhi, e con la sua partita:
a voi tolse la vista, a me la vita.

When fate sent me
away from you,
you didn't know that I had died.
You couldn't see, because my heart
ran straightaway
to your bright eyes, and blinded you.
It stayed with you, and left me dead.

The obsessive miniaturizing of this madrigal is the kind of intricate sixteenth-century wit (or "conceit," as they called it) that Shakespeare satirizes in the "seven ages of man"—"the lover, / Sighing like furnace, with a woeful ballad / Made to his mistress' eyebrow." But though the idea of the heart running away to the eyes may seem laughable, here the grief of parting is real and serious.

133

Parto, o non parto? ahi come
resto, se parte la corporea salma?
O come parto, se qui resta l'alma?
E se ne l'alma è vita,
come non moro, se di lei son privo?
O come moro, s'a la pena i' vivo?
Ahi fiera dipartita:
come m'insegna la mia dura sorte
che 'l partir degli amanti è viva morte.

So, have I left or not?
My body's gone: can I be here?

My soul's still here, so I must be.
 But soul is life, so why,
deprived of her, am I alive?
Can I be dead, if I feel pain?
    This harsh condition
 is purgatorial; I learn
 that parting is a living death.

The Renaissance postulated a dualistic condition for humans—body and soul, working together during life but separated after death. Neither state describes how the lover feels upon leaving his beloved: his body elsewhere, his soul here with his beloved. His identity, like Hamlet's, is shaken by questions like *Parto, o non parto?* and "To be, or not to be?"

134

Ah dolente partita.
Ah fin de la mia vita.
Da te parto, e non moro? E pur i' provo
la pena de la Morte,
e sento nel partire
un vivace morire,
che dà vita al dolore,
per far che moia immortalmente il core.

   Pulling away,
   my blood runs cold.
I check my pulse . . . yes, still alive . . .
   the walking dead.
   I give myself
   a shot of grief—
   adrenalin!
It brings me back to die again.

This intense poem, drawn from *Il pastor fido*, encapsulates the contradictions that run throughout Guarini's work and the Petrarchan tradition: separation makes love even more acute; the body lives on even while the emotions die; pain is intensely present in the moment but will last forever; "immortality" to the lover means not life after death, but death itself in life.

135

Come sian dolorose
lunge da voi del viver mio le tempre,
chiedetelo al mio cor, chè con voi sempre.
Ma se 'n lingua d'Amor egli favella,
  che voi non intendete
con quella mente di pietà rubella;
  almen l'intenderete
ai sospiri, a le lagrime, al sembiante,
ch'io moro senza voi misero amante.

To learn how sad
I am, living away from you,
interrogate your prisoner;
and if you scorn the way he speaks—
  the "mushy words
of love," as you have labeled them—
  at least take in
his sighs and groans, and understand
his message: "Without you, I'm dead."

How can lovers communicate, if they are separated both by distance and by disposition? The "prisoner," of course, is his heart. Since his heart is in his lady's care, perhaps it can communicate his feelings to her. But then he realizes that his heart would be talking in the romantic diction that she hates to hear. So maybe there is an alternative, some direct communication of pain, from heart to heart. It culminates in a tautology: only if she sees his pain will she see his pain.

136

Donna, voi vi credete
d'avermi tolto il core
col tormi il vostro amore;
vano pensier. Chi non ha core è morto.
  Ed io mi son accorto
d'esser tanto del solito più vivo,
  quanto di voi son privo.

Anzi era morto, e quando vi lasciai
rinacqui sì, ch'io non morrò più mai.

> You think you've ripped
> my heart from me?
> Well, think again.
> If you had taken it from me,
>   I would be dead;
> and yet I'm more alive, the more
>   you cut me out.
> Once I felt dead, but now you're gone,
> I'm born again: I'll stay that way.

In the Italian, the poem begins with a declamatory *Donna*—"Lady!" I have substituted bluntness of address, a kind of rude taunt: "You *think*. . .?" She believes that she's broken his heart; he claims he's better off without her. It's a fierce game: resentment is the order of the day.

137
> *Tu parti a pena giunto*
> *fuggitivo crudel. Fia mai quel giorno*
> *che fine al tuo partir ponga il ritorno?*
>   *O dolcissimo vago,*
> *se tu non fossi di vagar sì vago.*
>   *Almen ferma la fede,*
> *né da me fugga il cor, se fugge il piede.*

> Barely returned,
> you're off again? No chance
> you'd be back home for good!
>   You vagabond,
> if you can't stick around,
>   promise at least
> to leave your heart with me.

This madrigal's title in the 1598 volume—*Querela dell'amata* (the beloved's complaint)—indicates that it is written in the voice of the woman. After so many poems about the lover's aggravation, now we get to hear her side of the story. The poem is brief, so brief that it hardly makes a case that would convince him to change his behavior. Indeed, that's not the point of the poem, which seems more interested in representing an affect than in changing the situation.

The lover gets to respond to this complaint in the next madrigal (#138).

138

> *Con voi sempre son io*
> *agitato, ma fermo;*
> *e se 'l meno v'involo, il più vi lasso.*
> *Son simile al compasso,*
> *ch'un piede in voi quasi mio centro i' fermo,*
> *l'altro patisce di fortuna i giri,*
> *ma non può far, che 'ntorno a voi non giri.*

> A vagabond?
> I travel, yes,
> but I am never gone from you.
> A compass swoops
> around its wide circumference
> by making sure the center holds.
> My steady arc is fixed on you.

This madrigal is a direct response to the previous one (#137)—the title in the 1598 edition is *Risposta dell'amante* (The lover's reply). In the earlier poem, the beloved complains of the lover's constant travel; here he calmly reassures her of his unwavering connection to her.

Readers of English poetry will be reminded of Donne's famous image of love as a draughtsman's compass: one foot wanders, but the other remains in one place, since the relationship between the two is fixed by the nature of the instrument.

Love in Old Age

With one sweet word,
the ancient spark, damped
down so long, revives
and catches fire again.

Petrarch's love poems sketch out a trajectory of time and age. The poet often meditates on his own impending death, by which he would rejoin his beloved Laura:

I seem to hear, each hour, in my ear
the messenger my lady sends to call me,
and thus it is I've changed, inside and out,
and in a few years I have shrunk so much

that I can hardly recognize myself:
all my accustomed life has now been banished.

Time calms the storms of desire and grief and, paradoxically, makes loss even more poignant:

Love helped me sail into a tranquil harbor
after the long, tumultuous times of storm,
into the years of chaste maturity
that rids itself of vice and takes on virtue;

my heart and my great loyalty were clear
and not displeasing to her lovely eyes.
Oh, vicious Death, how quick you are to spoil
the fruit of years in something like an hour!

If she had lived, we were approaching this:
I could have spoken and in those chaste ears
set down my ancient burden of sweet thoughts,

and she'd have answered me, perhaps, in kind,
sighing a little, using holy words,
our hair and faces showing how we'd changed.

The aging Petrarch often adopts a meditative and even religious state of mind; he's never far from a sober Christian reflection on the destiny of the soul. In contrast, Shakespeare wrote Petrarchan poems about *this* world rather than the next. For Shakespeare, time drives an essentially secular world—cruel, erosive, and debilitating. It is a miracle of imagination and love that mere verse can stand up against these fiercely erosive antagonists, time and life. The only hope of permanence is through writing:

Like as the waves make towards the pebbled shore,
So do our minutes hasten to their end,
Each changing place with that which goes before,
In sequent toil all forwards do contend.
Nativity, once in the main of light,
Crawls to maturity, wherewith being crown'd,
Crooked eclipses 'gainst his glory fight,
And Time that gave doth now his gift confound.
Time doth transfix the flourish set on youth,
And delves the parallels in beauty's brow,
Feeds on the rarities of nature's truth,
And nothing stands but for his scythe to mow:
    And yet to times in hope my verse shall stand,
    Praising thy worth, despite his cruel hand.

Like Shakespeare, Guarini writes of the way love keeps hold on our lives even as it ought to be dying out:

And even now,
    in age myself,
I feel the same old pain, and weep
for ancient sorrows with fresh tears.

This final section collects some of Guarini's madrigals that take a longer view of the chronology of love. The lovers in these madrigals seem to have matured. In some poems, the lover sees the possibility of a quieter and more loving life; in others, the passage of time has brought a kind of exhaustion, a forced relaxation of the tensions of love. But even in age and retrospect, the bitterness of love is not fully gone: sorrow, scorn, and revenge still affect the lover.

139

Oimè, l'antica fiamma,
ch'era sopita, a l'aura d'una sola
dolcissima parola
si desta, e nel mio cor arde, e sfavilla.
Lasso che 'ncontra Amore,
quando le prime sue dolcezze stilla
in un tenero core,
né sdegno, né dolore,
né tempo, né ragion, né forza vale.
Chi spegne antico incendio il fa immortale.

With one sweet word,
the ancient spark, damped
down so long, revives
and catches fire again.
When Love ignites
in fresh and tender youth,
nothing puts out
that fire; disdain
and time have no effect.
Love burns eternally.

Love's fire, kindled in a fresh soul, may seem to have been extinguished over time, but in fact it smolders on, and one day, unexpectedly, it bursts into flame.

The last line (also used in #42) sounds like an aphorism or quotation, perhaps from one of the courtly "devices" or emblems that were popular in the courts of the time. Roughly, it seems to mean, "whoever tries to put out an old fire makes it last longer."

140

Ardo non più di sdegno, e nel cor sento
 addolcirsi l'ardore;
e farsi l'ira, e la vendetta amore.
  Se mai sdegnoso affetto
s'avampò nel mio petto, or me ne pento;
e sì del mio sdegnar, meco mi sdegno,
che s'è fatto d'amor esca lo sdegno.

Hatred has died away;
  revenge lies cold,
and scorn is smothered up.
  Now I repent
having fed those flames;
one spark remains—enough
to kindle love again.

The fire of disdain is a bitter one and will be intensely remembered even after it's gone. But the memory of it serves to ignite new love.

The Italian word *sdegno* occurs five times in this poem, in various forms—noun, verb, and adjective. The cognate in English is "disdain," but in Italian the negative prefix *s* is shorter and harsher, giving it a dismissive hiss.

141

Vivo in foco amoroso
 non crudel, non penoso,
ch'arde, e non coce: e tanto alletta, e piace,
 quant'ha salute, e pace.

 Qui di mobile ingegno
 né ferità, né sdegno,
né dubbia fede, o certa gelosia
 turba la gioia mia.

 Ma fermezza, e pietate,
 valor con humiltate,
negletto volto, e coltivata fede
 è del mio amor mercede.

O beltà senza inganni,
poiché de' miei verd'anni
non fosti il primo, or l'ultimo desio
sarai del viver mio.

I'm warmed by love—
a gentle flame
that doesn't sear, but nurtures me
to health and peace.

No restlessness
ruins my bliss,
no doubt, or fear, or jealousy
disturbs my joy.

Here loyalty,
humility,
simplicity, and steadfastness
are love's rewards.

A faithful love—
which in my youth
I never had—now, near the end,
is all I want.

This poem is not technically a madrigal, since it is strophic (that is, built in four stanzas, each adhering to the same pattern of meter and rhyme). Even so, it was printed in the 1598 collection of madrigals, and I include it as a mellow contrast to the turbulent poems that characterize most of Guarini's work.

142

Dolce, amato, leggiadro, unico, e caro,
*   pegno d'Amor, e mio;*
poiché 'l cor vostro, il mio pensier non vede,
*   deh morir potess'io,*
*   per far morendo fede*
ch'ogni mio ben dal voler vostro pende.
*   Ma troppo oimè s'offende*

con la mia morte voi, che 'n me vivete,
        e la mia vita sète.
E se 'l cor m'è pur caro, è perché in vui
egli si vive, e voi vivete in lui.

My dearest one, my joy,
        love's prize, and mine,
you cannot see my heart.
        I'd gladly die
        if that would show
that all my life is yours.
        But no, you are
my life, and so my death
        would injure you:
I'll hold to life, living
in you, as you in me.

This madrigal works in an argumentative and almost pedantic register: if he died, it would show her that he loves, but since he lives in her, his death would diminish her, which would negate the evidence of his love. But this framework of rather chopped logic is not the whole of the poem, which has also an emotional quality evoking the intertwined lives of the two, the way neither of them feels a complete existence without the other.

143

Se vuoi ch'io torni a le tue fiamme, Amore,
        non far idolo il core
        né di fredda vecchiezza,
né d'incostante, e pazza giovanezza.
        Dammi, se puoi, Signore,
cor saggio in bel sembiante,
canuto amore in non canuto amante.

Love, if you want to win me back,
        don't make me fall
        for some old dame,
or for some dizzy teenage girl.

Give me, I pray,
wisdom and beauty both in one—
a new bottle, a well-aged wine.

The lover is free for the moment, but he doesn't expect to remain free. So he respectfully petitions the god of Love to give him a nicer situation this time around. The final metaphor in the translation is mine, not Guarini's.

144

Già comincia a sentire
la bella Donna mia l'ingiurie, e i danni
de l'etate, e degli anni,
né però il mio desire
vien che s'intepidisca, o si rallenti.
O veloci, e possenti
armi del tempo al mio soccorso tarde.
La fiamma incenerisce, e 'l mio cor arde.

As she gets old
she starts to feel the slights
that age deals out,
but my desire
has yet to slow its pace.
Too late for me!
Time does its work on her;
but love still burns in me.

The beloved gets older, and the lover seems to welcome that aging. He hopes that since she's been diminished by time, she will settle down and consider his love. But he knows that it is too late. If he still desires her, and she still rejects him, then he can have no real hopes for a mellow old age.

145

Amor, questa crudele
cangia, come tu vedi, e volto, e spoglie,
né però cangia ancor pensieri, e voglie.

Sì sorda a' miei sospiri,
sì aspra a' miei martiri;
così dopo tant'anni
convien che i primi affanni
pianga canuto amante, e non mi giove
trar d'antico dolor lagrime nove.

She's getting on—
older, and not as beautiful;
and still she keeps her attitude—
   deaf to my words,
    mocking my pain.
    Yet even now,
    in age myself,
I feel the same old pain, and weep
for ancient sorrows with fresh tears.

In time, both beloved and lover get old. Looks change, the body changes, but the tension does not relax: desire remains in a state of suspended animation. Guarini touches on the classical poetic tradition of elegy: the subdued pleasure of remembering and revisiting the past.

Aeneas's famous lament—*sunt lacrimae rerum et mentem mortalia tangunt* (these are tears for what happens, tears that touch the minds of mortals)—may be echoed in Guarini's *lagrime nove*—"new tears."

146

Arsi un tempo, ed amai;
e di che fiamma, e con che fede, Amore,
   tu 'l sai, ch'eri Signore
de la mia vita. Or se l'usato foco
   in me non ha più loco,
perdona al cor tradito, ed innocente;
   che non ha si cocente
   fiamma tutto'l tuo Regno,
che non la spegna il gel d'un giusto sdegno.

Back then, I burned with love—
and with what flames, and with what faithfulness,
    Love only knows, who was
the master of my life. Now, if that flame
    no longer burns in me,
forgive me, Love, for I am not to blame:
    there is no forge so hot
    in all Love's factories
that can endure the chill of constant scorn.

Faith and betrayal: there was a time when the lover was constant in love, but now he has abandoned his faith (or so he asserts—we might wonder). The lover has betrayed his master, Love. At the end, ironically, it is the beloved who is faithful—not in ardor but in disdain (*sdegno*), that steady coldheartedness that extinguishes any fire of love.

147

Deh bella, e cara, e sì soave un tempo
cagion del viver mio mentre a Dio piacque
    volgi una volta, e volgi
    quelle stelle amorose,
come le vidi mai, così tranquille,
e piene di pietà prima ch'i' moia,
    che 'l morir mi sia dolce,
e dritto è ben che se mi furo un tempo
dolci segni di vita, or sien di morte
    que' begli occhi amorosi,
    e quel soave sguardo
    che mi scorse ad amare
    mi scorga anco a morire,
    e chi fu l'alba mia
del mio cadente dì l'Espero or sia.

Once—it was ages past—
your eyes were the sparks
    of life. Turn them
    again to me;

if I could see those stars
shining with love for me,
    I'd die in peace.
There was a time they seemed
the messengers of life;
    now they mean death.
Eyes that lit love
in me should watch
me die; they were
my dawn, and now
my only hope at dusk.

Once, the eyes of the beloved gave the lover joy: they invited his love, a love by which he thrived. Now that there seems no hope, these same eyes declare his death. The mood, however, is so tender that the lover's love is evident, even in death.

148

    Era l'anima mia
    già presso à l'ultim'ore,
e languia come langue alma che more;
quand'anima più bella, e più gradita
volse lo sguardo in sì pietoso giro,
    che mi ritenne in vita.
    Parean dir que' bei lumi,
    deh, perché ti consumi?
Non m'è sì caro il cor ond'io respiro,
    come se' tu, cor mio.
Se mori, oimè, non mori tu, mor'io.

    My final hour
    drew near; my soul
felt the cold hand of death.
And then a blessed one
sent me a look so sweet
    it brought me back.
    She seemed to say,

"How can you die?
I live and breathe through you;
    your death would be
not yours alone, but mine."

Is this a near-death experience? In some ways it seems a brush with physical, concrete death; in other ways, it is simply a conventional metaphor for the "death" of thwarted love. At any rate, it records how some crisis of the soul is averted through a merciful glance.

But death never quite leaves the poem: the beloved's eyes seem to say, "Your heart (*core*) is more dear to me than my own." But *core* rhymes, ominously, with *more*, death. Death sounds three times in the last line; it's softer, without the terror of one's final hour, but still insistently tolling: "If you were to die, alas, you would not die; I would die."

149

Veder il mio bel sole,
    e perderlo in un punto,
parve del ciel quel balenar a punto,
    che la saetta porte:
sì subito disparve, e ferì il core.
    Insidioso Amore,
sì vicina a la vita hai tu la morte?
Come fai l'alba aprir nel occidente,
ed Espero cader nel oriente?

To see the sun
    and then—nothing!
I watched brightness fall from the air,
    an arrow of light.
The darkness left me paralyzed.
    Love inverts all:
the sun rises in the west,
while in the east light fades away
and life undoes itself in death.

This sad madrigal is constructed of contrast: brightness and darkness; sight and blindness; dawn and dusk; hope and despair; life and death. But contrast isn't enough, as these oppositions are packed together in the paradoxical conditions of Love, all linked together, all coexisting. Even the nature of the sun's ecliptic is bizarrely inverted—dawn in the west, sunset in the east.

The courtly rooms of Ferrara, where Guarini must have recited his poems, are filled with swirling frescoes of light, ceilings dizzyingly inhabited by the chariots of Apollo and Phaeton, full of brilliance and danger and uncertainty, life and death linked inseparably.

150

O primavera, gioventù de l'anno,
*   bella madre de' fiori,*
d'erbe novelle e di novelli amori,
*   tu ben, lasso, ritorni,*
*   ma senza i cari giorni*
*   de la speranze mie.*
*   Tu ben sei quella*
ch'eri pur dianzi, sì vezzosa e bella;
ma non son io quel che già un tempo fui,
*   sì caro a gli occhi altrui.*

Sweet spring, full of the year's sweet youth,
    progenitor of flowers,
the force that through each stem drives new desire!
    Now you return; but not
    to me return those days
    of splendor in the grass.
    You are the same as once
you were, graceful and beautiful, but I
will never be again what once I was—
    dear in another's heart.

This beautiful elegy about the gap between natural cycles and human pathos develops, as Tomlinson writes, "the Petrarchan antithesis of serene natural surroundings and the poet's lovesick turmoil." An appropriate ending to this collection of madrigals, it brings the conflicts and uncertainties of the sequence to a quiet close, an understanding of the complex relationship between hope and disappointment.

To match the poem's mood of quiet retrospect, my translation incorporates allusions to elegiac poems by George Herbert, John Milton, William Wordsworth, and Dylan Thomas.

APPENDIX 1

ALPHABETICAL LIST OF FIRST LINES IN ITALIAN

First line	Poem number
A che tanto prezzar porpora, ed oro	18
A un giro sol de' belli occhi lucenti	51
A voi, Donna, volando	26
Ah dolente partita	134
Ahi, come a un vago sol cortese giro	53
Al partir del mio sole	129
Altro non è il mi' amore	110
Ama, ben dice Amore	12
Amiam, Fillide, amiamo, ah non rispondi	117
Amor, i' parto, e sento nel partire	130
Amor, non ha il tuo regno	10
Amor, poiché non giova	5
Amor, questa crudele	145
Anime pellegrine, che bramate	63
Ardemmo insieme, bella Donna, ed io	40
Ardi, e gela a tua voglia	104
Ardo, mia vita, ancor com'io solia	48
Ardo non più di sdegno, e nel cor sento	140
Ardo sì, ma non t'amo	103
Arsi e alsi a mia voglia	105
Arsi già solo, e non sostenni il foco	85
Arsi un tempo, ed amai	146
Aura dolce odorata	123
Baci soavi e cari	86
Baciai, ma che mi valse attender frutto	37
Baciai per aver vita	65
Ben fu pari tra noi, Donna, il partire	125
Che dura legge hai nel tuo regno, Amore	3
Che se tu se' il cor mio	92
Ch'i' t'ami e t'ami più de la mia vita	88
Ch'io non t'ami, cor mio	111
Chi vuol aver felice, e lieto il core	1

First line	Poem number
Come cantar poss'io	119
Come non cangia stile	27
Come sian dolorose	135
Con che soavità, labbra odorate	78
Con voi sempre son io	138
Cor mio, deh, non languire	70
Cor mio, deh non piangete	69
Cor mio tu ti nascondi	28
Credete voi ch'i' viva	127
Credetel voi, che non sentite amore	124
Cruda Amarilli, che col nome ancora	89
Crudel, perch'io non v'ami	57
Cura gelata, e ria	17
Deh bella, e cara, e sì soave un tempo	147
Deh, come in van chiedete	118
Deh dimmi Amor se gli occhi di Camilla	19
Deh ferma, ferma il tuo rubella, Amore	6
Dice la mia bellissima Licori	8
Dolce, amato, leggiadro, unico, e caro	142
Dolce spirto d'Amore	75
Dolcissimo Usignuolo	114
Donna, lasciate i boschi	24
Donna, mentre i' vi miro	49
Donna, voi vi credete	136
Donò Licori a Batto	72
Dorinda, ah dirò mia, se mia non sei	95
Dov'hai tu nido, Amore	4
Dunque vapor mal nato	46
E così a poco a poco	42
E così pur languendo	58
E tu Mirtillo (anima mia) perdona	91
Ecco piegando le genocchie a terra	96
Ecco Silvio, colei che 'n odio hai tanto	93
Era l'anima mia	148
Felice chi vi mira	64
Ferir quel petto Silvio	97
Già comincia a sentire	144
Io d'altrui? S'i' volessi, i' non potrei	109
Io disleale? Ah cruda	106
Io mi sento morir quando non miro	34
Io veggio pur pietate, ancorche tardi	81
Ite amari sospiri	21
La bella man vi stringo	32
La tenera Licori	74

First line	Poem number
Langue al vostro languir l'anima mia	60
Lasso, perché mi fuggi	22
Lauro, oimè, lauro ingrato	16
Lumi miei cari lumi	52
Ma se con la pietà non è in te spenta	94
Ma tu più che mai dura	23
Madonna, udite come	77
M'è più dolce il penar per Amarilli	112
Mentre una gioia miro	108
Mentre vaga Angioletta	122
Morto mi vede la mia Morte in sogno	43
Negatemi pur cruda	50
Non è questa colei (ben la conosco)	120
Non fu senza vendetta	67
Non miri il mio bel sole	71
Non più guerra, pietate	54
Non sa che sia dolore	131
Non sospirar cor mio non sospirare	68
O che soave bacio	66
O come è gran martire	62
O come se' gentile	113
O dolce anima mia, dunque è pur vero	101
O Donna troppo cruda, e troppo bella	33
O Mirtillo, Mirtillo, anima mia	90
O miseria d'amante	2
O notturno miracolo soave	82
O primavera, gioventù de l'anno	150
Occhi, stelle mortali	20
Occhi, un tempo mia vita	35
Oggi nacqui, Ben mio	76
Oimè, l'antica fiamma	139
Oimè, se tanto amate	39
Or che 'l meriggio ardente	116
Parlo, misero, o taccio	29
Parto, o non parto? ahi come	133
Perché di gemme t'incoroni, e d'oro	98
Perfidissimo volto	13
Piangea Donna crudele	30
Poiché non mi credete	15
Punto da un' ape, a cui	9
Può dunque un sogno temerario, e vile	44
Pur venisti, cor mio	128
Quando mia cruda stella	132
Quanto per voi sofferse	47

First line	Poem number
Quell'augellin, che canta	115
Quest'è pur il mio core	99
Rideva (ahi crudo affetto)	45
Se 'l vostro cor, Madonna	102
Se 'n voi pose natura	11
Se per estremo ardore	79
Se vuoi ch'io torni a le tue fiamme, Amore	143
Sì, mi dicesti, e io	61
Sì presso a voi, mio foco	55
Sì voglio, e vorrò sempre	14
Soavissimo ardore	59
Splende la fredda luna	56
Stracciami pure il core	107
T'amo mia vita, la mia cara vita	80
Tirsi morir volea	87
Troppo ben può questo tiranno Amore	7
Tu parti a pena giunto	137
Udite, amanti, udite	83
Udite lagrimosi	25
Un amoroso agone	100
Un bacio solo, a tante pene? Cruda	38
Un cibo di fuor dolce, e dentro amaro	36
Una Farfalla cupida, e vagante	41
Veder il mio bel sole	149
Vien da l'onde, o dal cielo	121
Vivo in foco amoroso	141
Voi, dissi, e sospirando	73
Voi pur da me partite, anima dura	126
Voi volete ch'io mora	31
Volgea l'anima mia soavemente	84

APPENDIX 2

PUBLISHED VOCAL SETTINGS OF GUARINI

This appendix lists published vocal settings of madrigals by Guarini that are included in this volume, up to the year 1700 (as well as two poems perhaps by Tasso—#104 and #105, both responses to Guarini's "Ardo sì, ma non t'amo, #103). The data are derived from Vassalli and Pompilio, "Indice delle rime di Battista Guarini poste in musica," and from Chater, "*Il pastor fido* and Music." Catalog numbers refer to listings in the definitive bibliographies of vocal madrigals: NV = Vogel, Einstein, Lesure, and Sartori, *Bibliografia della musica Italiana vocale profana pubblicata dal 1500 al 1700*; VE = Vogel, *Bibliothek der gedruckten weltlichen Vocalmusik Italiens aus den Jahren 1500–1700*. For each entry, I have added first name(s) of the composer and place of publication from the Vogel bibliographies.

Following the first line, I have given the madrigal's number in this volume in parentheses. Unpublished madrigals found solely in manuscript collections are not included.

Some settings take considerable liberties with the Guarini text, inserting and deleting lines, or changing words, even words in the first lines; such variants are included without comment under the first line as used in this volume. Madrigal settings taken from *Il pastor fido* are especially difficult to keep track of, as composers began and ended their excerpts at different places in the text. To be inclusive, I have conflated settings that overlap on any particular excerpt; I have indicated where the settings begin differently by referencing a line as it is given in this volume, which may differ from the first line in the composer's setting. For example, Chater lists twenty-one published settings that begin at the first line of the popular text "Cruda Amarilli, che col nome ancora" (#89), as well as one text, by the noted composer Phillipo de Monte, that begins with a variant of the fifth line, "Ma de l'Aspido sordo"; that setting is listed here with the others, chronologically, but marked with a note that indicates that it does not begin at the first line.

A un giro sol de' belli occhi lucenti (#51)

1603 Claudio Monteverdi, Venice (NV 1914)

Ah dolente partita (#134)

1593 Girolamo Belli, Venice (NV 314)
1594 Luca Marenzio, Venice (NV 1629)
1595 Jacob de Wert, Venice (NV 2994)
1597 Federico Wynant, Venice (NV 3002)
1598 Antonio Artusini, Venice (NV 172)
1598 Giovanni Antonio Cirullo, Venice (NV 581)
1598 Giulio Cesare Gabussi, Venice (NV 1050)
1599 Ottavio Bargnani, Venice (NV 248)
1600 Giovanni Appolloni, Venice (NV 92)
1600 Filippo de Monte, Venice (NV 806)
1600 Paolo Sartorio, Venice (NV 2559)
1602 Scipione Dentice, Naples (NV 810)
1603 Achille Falcone, Venice (NV 904)
1603 Claudio Monteverdi, Venice (NV 1914)
1604 Alessandro di Costanzo, Naples (NV 817)
1605 Antonio Cifra, Rome (NV 569)
1605 Fattorin da Reggio, Venice (NV 913)
1605 Ruggero Giovannelli, Venice (NV 1210)
1605 Giovanni Domenico Rognoni Taeggio, Venice (NV 2360)
[1605?] Mariano Tantucci, Siena (NV 2698) [begins at "E sento nel partire"]
1608 Giovanni Battista de Bellis, Naples (NV 694)
1608 Vincenzo Liberti, Venice (NV 1511)
1610 Alessandro Scialla, Naples (NV 2592)
1611 Stefano Bernardi, Rome (NV 334)
1612 Antonio Taroni, Venice (NV 2708)
1613 Bertolomeo Cesana, Venice (NV 551)
1614 Salomone Rossi, Venice (NV 2444)
1617 Agostino Agresta, Naples (NV 32)
1617 Girolamo Belli, Venice (NV 310)
1617 Giacomo Fornaci, Venice (NV 1008)
1617 Giovanni Nicolò Mezzogorri, Venice (NV 1840)
1618 Giuseppe Marini, Venice (NV 1721)
1621 Scipione Cerreto, Naples (NV 548)

Ahi, come a un vago sol cortese giro (#53)

1587 Filippo de Monte, Venice (NV 773)
1590 Girolamo dalla Casa, Venice (NV 682)
1592 Giovanni Croce, Venice (NV 668)
1596 Alessandro Striggio, Venice (NV 2670)
1600 Benedetto Pallavicino, Venice (NV 2123)
1605 Claudio Monteverdi, Venice (NV 1922)
1606 Agostino Agazzari, Venice (NV 17)
1609 Vincenzo Liberti, Venice (NV 1512)
1611 Giovanni Francesco Anerio, Venice (NV 73)
1614 Pietro Maria Marsolo, Venice (NV 1733)
1615 Antonio Cifra, Venice (NV 571)
1617 Giuseppe Olivieri, Rome (NV 2051)
1636 Ambrosio Cremonese, Venice (NV 654)
1649 Gaspare Filippi, Venice (NV 986)

Al partir del mio sole (#129)

1600 Guglielmo Arnoni, Venice (NV 169)
1600 Salamone Rossi, Venice (NV 2445)
1601 Francesco Stivori, Venice (NV 2647)
1604 Giovanni Priuli, Venice (NV 2280)
1606 Sigismondo d'India, Venice (NV 823)
1607 Ludovico Bellanda, Venice (NV 292)
1607 Giovan Domenico Montella, Naples (NV 1880)
1608 Giovanni Battista de Bellis, Naples (NV 694)
1611 Giovanni Francesco Anerio, Venice (NV 73)
1612 Francesco Genvino, Naples (NV 1121)
1612 Antonio Taroni, Venice (NV 2708)
1616 Claudio Pari, Palermo (NV 2140)
1616 Filippo Vitali, Venice (NV 2943)
1620 Claudio Saracini, Venice (NV 2556)
1627 Antonio Rinoldi, Venice (NV 2352)
1681 Carlo Grossi, Venice (NV 1290)

Altro non è il mi' amore (#110)

1605 Giovanni del Turco, Venice (NV 1580)
1609 Michelangelo Nantermi, Venice (NV 1995)
1610 Giovan Paolo Costa, Venice (NV 646)

1611 Cornelis Schuyt, Leiden (NV 2590)
1623 Paolo Quagliati, Rome (NV 2295)
1626 Francesco Costa, Venice (NV 639)
1668 Giovanni Battista Mazzaferrata, Bologna (NV 1763)

Ama, ben dice Amore (#12)

1598 Giovanni Battista Galeno, Venice (NV 1053)
1599 Ruggero Giovannelli, Venice (NV 1223)

Amiam, Fillide, amiamo, ah non rispondi (#117)

1607 Crescenzio Salzilli, Naples (NV 2537)
1611 Sigismondo d'India, Venice (NV 826)
1612 Lucrezio Ruffulo, Venice (NV 2496)
1613 Biagio Tomasi, Venice (NV 2728)
1615 Francesco Pasquali, Venice (NV 2143)
1617 Giacomo Fornaci, Venice (NV 1008)

Amor, i' parto, e sento nel partire (#130)

1594 Filippo de Monte, Venice (NV 800)
1597 Allesandro Savioli, Venice (NV 2563)
1599 Geminiano Capilupi, Venice (NV 484)
1600 Benedetto Pallavicino, Venice (NV 2123)
1601 Ottavio Bargnani, Venice (NV 249)
1602 Giulio Caccini, Florence (NV 450)
1608 Vincenzo Liberti, Venice (NV 1511)
1611 Crescenzio Salzilli, Naples (NV 2538)
1612 Tommaso Pecci, Venice (NV 2161)
1615 Nicolo Rubini, Venice (NV 2470)
1621 Giovanni Bernardo Colombi, Venice (NV 596)
1678 Giovanni Maria Bononcini, Bologna (NV 397)

Amor, questa crudele (#145)

1622 Alfonso Montesano, Naples (NV 1896)

Anime pellegrine, che bramate (#63)

1600 Guglielmo Arnoni, Venice (NV 169)
1602 Aurelio Bonelli, Venice (NV 385)

1604 Benedetto Pallavicino, Venice (NV 2126)
1612 Antonio Taroni, Venice (NV 2710)
1615 Francesco Pasquali, Venice (NV 2143)
1620 Claudio Saracini, Venice (NV 2556)
1625 Orazio Modiana, Venice (NV 1868[bis])
1629 Giovanni Rovetta, Venice (NV 2461)

Ardemmo insieme, bella Donna, ed io (#40)

1592 Filippo de Monte, Venice (NV 776)
1596 Flaminio Tresti, Venice (NV 2751)
1597 Francesco Bianciardi, Venice (NV 361)
1600 Guglielmo Arnoni, Venice (NV 169)
1600 Allesandro Savioli, Venice (NV 2564)
1608 Pomponio Nenna, Naples (NV 2027)
1615 Antonio Cifra, Venice (NV 571)
1615 Sigismondo d'India, Venice (NV 827)
1615 Nicolo Rubini, Venice (NV 2470)
1620 Bizzarro Accademico Capriccioso, Venice (NV 371)
1621 Giovanni Ghizzolo, Venice (NV 1190)
1622 Alessandro Grandi, Venice (NV 1277)

Ardi, e gela a tua voglia (#104)

1587 Claudio Monteverdi, Venice (NV 1900)

Ardo, mia vita, ancor com'io solia (#48)

1600 Guglielmo Arnoni, Venice (NV 169)
1601 Francesco Stivori, Venice (NV 2647)
1608 Vincenzo Liberti, Venice (NV 1511)
1609 Johann Grabbe, Venice (NV 1264)
1612 Lucrezio Ruffulo, Venice (NV 2496)
1612 Antonio Taroni, Venice (NV 2708)
1624 Francesco Turini, Venice (NV 2772)
1635 Giovan Giacomo Arrigoni, Venice (NV 170)

Ardo non più di sdegno, e nel cor sento (#140)

1601 Antonio Il Verso, Venice (NV 1336)
1609 Vincenzo Liberti, Venice (NV 1512)
1612 Antonio Taroni, Venice (NV 2708)

Ardo sì, ma non t'amo (#103)

1583 Orazio Vecchi, Venice (NV 2827)
1585 Orazio Angelini, Venice (NV 78)
1585 Fillippo Nicoletti, Venice (NV 2036)
1586 Giulio Eremita, Ferrara (NV 892)
1586 Ruggero Giovannelli, Venice (NV 1211)
1586 Paolo Masnelli, Venice (NV 1743)
1586 Filippo de Monte, Venice (NV 772)
1586 Costanzo Porta, Venice (NV 2246)
1586 Ascanio Trombetti, Venice (NV 2759)
1586 Michele Varotti, Venice (VE 1586[5])
1587 Francesco Farina, Venice (NV 909)
1587 Marc'Antonio Ingegneri, Venice (NV 1347)
1587 Claudio Monteverdi, Venice (NV 1900)
1587 Alfonso Preti, Venice (NV 2266)
1587 Rocco Rodio, Naples (NV 2358)
1587 Ippolito Sabino, Venice (NV 2531)
1588 Tommaso Graziani, Venice (NV 1282)
1588 Giovanni Battista Mosto, Venice (NV 1979)
1591 Serafino Cantone, Venice (NV 479)
1591 Scipione Dentice, Naples (NV 807)
1596 Hans Leo Hassler, Augsburg (NV 1309)
1598 Giulio Cesare Gabussi, Venice (NV 1050)
1598 Giovanni Battista Galeno, Venice (NV 1053)
1600 Paolo Sartorio, Venice (NV 2559)
1600 Allesandro Savioli, Venice (NV 2564)
1601 Antonio Il Verso, Venice (NV 1336)
1608 Adriano Banchieri, Venice (NV 214)
1609 Johann Grabbe, Venice (NV 1264)
1611 Pietro Benedetti, Florence (NV 322)
1612 Antonio Taroni, Venice (NV 2708)
1617 Giacomo Fornaci, Venice (NV 1008)
1620 Carlo Milanuzzi, Venice (NV 1848)
1622 Alessandro Grandi, Venice (NV 1277)
1628 Domenico Crivellati, Rome (NV 655)
1678 Giovanni Maria Bononcini, Bologna (NV 397)

Arsi e alsi a mia voglia (#105)

1587 Claudio Monteverdi, Venice (NV 1900)

Arsi già solo, e non sostenni il foco (#85)

1582 Luzzasco Luzzaschi, Venice (NV 1527)
1600 Filippo de Monte, Venice (NV 806)
1600 Allesandro Savioli, Venice (NV 2564)
1603 Tommaso Pecci, Venice (NV 2153)
1609 Vincenzo Liberti, Venice (NV 1512)

Arsi un tempo, ed amai (#146)

1595 Filippo de Monte, Venice (NV 778)
1600 Salamone Rossi, Venice (NV 2445)
1600 Allesandro Savioli, Venice (NV 2564)
1602 Scipione Dentice, Naples (NV 810)
1604 Giovanni Battista Caletti, Venice (NV 463)
1605 Francesco Genvino, Naples (NV 1120)
1617 Giuseppe Olivieri, Rome (NV 2051)

Aura dolce odorata (#123)

1590 Flaminio Tresti, Venice (NV 2750)
1592 Filippo de Monte, Venice (NV 776)

Baci soavi e cari (#86)

1581 Pietro Vecoli, Turin (NV 2840)
1583 Girolamo Belli, Ferrara (NV 311)
1584 Giovanni Battista Della Gostena, Venice (NV 709)
1585 Vincenzo Dal Pozzo, Venice (NV 687)
1587 Claudio Monteverdi, Venice (NV 1900)
1587 Rocco Rodio, Naples (NV 2358)
1588 Gasparo Costa, Venice (NV 642)
1589 Alessandro Orologio, Dresden (NV 2068)
1590 Francesco Mazza, Venice (NV 1762)
1591 Luca Marenzio, Venice (NV 1665)
1594 Carlo Gesualdo, Ferrara (NV 1153)
1596 Paolo Masnelli, Venice (NV 1744)
1597 Federico Wynant, Venice (NV 3002)
1605 Adriano Banchieri, Venice (NV 211)
1613 Amadio Freddi, Antwerp (VE 1613[1])
1616 Scipione Dentice, Naples (NV 817)
1640 Pietro Andrea Ziani, Venice (NV 3026)

Baciai, ma che mi valse attender frutto (#37)

1592 Filippo de Monte, Venice (NV 776)
1596 Peter Philips, Antwerp (NV 2209)
1597 Federico Wynant, Venice (NV 3002)
1600 Antonio Il Verso, Venice (NV 1332)
1600 Allesandro Savioli, Venice (NV 2564)
1605 Santi Orlandi, Venice (NV 2058)
1605 Enrico Radesca, Milan (NV 2300)
1606 Giuseppe de Puente, Naples (NV 2284)
1607 Ludovico Bellanda, Venice (NV 292)
1609 Giovanni Antonio Cirullo, Venice (NV 583)
1609 Giovanni Ghizzolo, Venice (NV 1192)
1640 Pietro Andrea Ziani, Venice (NV 3026)

Baciai per aver vita (#65)

1592 Filippo de Monte, Venice (NV 776)
1593 Vittoria Aleotti, Venice (NV 46)
1596 Paolo Masnelli, Venice (NV 1744)
1596 Peter Philips, Antwerp (NV 2209)
1596 Bartolomeo Ratti, Venice (NV 2319)
1599 Geminiano Capilupi, Venice (NV 484)
1600 Antonio Il Verso, Venice (NV 1332)
1602 Giovan Giacomo Gastoldi, Venice (NV 1114)
1604 Pietro Francesco Guerini, Venice (NV 463)
1616 Liberale Zanchi, Antwerp (VE 1616[1])

Che dura legge hai nel tuo regno, Amore (#3)

1586 Filippo de Monte, Venice (NV 772)
1590 Girolamo dalla Casa, Venice (NV 682)
1612 Lucrezio Ruffulo, Venice (NV 2496)

Che se tu se' il cor mio (#92)

1594 Luca Marenzio, Venice (NV 1629)
1600 Filippo de Monte, Venice (NV 806)
1603 Claudio Monteverdi, Venice (NV 1914)
1608 Antonio Cifra, Venice (NV 570)
1609 Marsilio Casentini, Venice (NV 498)
1613 Francesco Rognoni Taeggio, Venice (NV 2359)

1614 Giovan Paolo Costa, Venice (NV 647)
1617 Giovanni Nicolò Mezzogorri, Venice (NV 1840)
1618 Giuseppe Marini, Venice 1618 (NV 1721)
1623 Giacinto Merulo, Venice 1623 (NV 1837)

Ch'i' t'ami e t'ami più de la mia vita (#88)

1599 Filippo de Monte, Venice (NV 734)
1605 Antonio Cifra, Rome (NV 569)
1605 Claudio Monteverdi, Venice (NV 1922)
1608 Antonio Cifra, Venice (NV 570)
1609 Marsilio Casentini, Venice (NV 498)
1614 Raffaello Rontani, Florence (NV 2363)
1617 Giovanni Nicolò Mezzogorri, Venice (NV 1840)
1622 Allessandro Costantini, Orvieto (VE 1622[1])

Ch'io non t'ami, cor mio (#111)

1591 Serafino Cantone, Venice (NV 479)
1592 Claudio Monteverdi, Venice (NV 1906)
1593 Vittoria Aleotti, Venice (NV 46)
1594 Antonio Dueto, Venice (NV 877)
1596 Paolo Masnelli, Venice (NV 1744)
1598 Scipione Dentice, Naples (NV 809)
1599 Geminiano Capilupi, Venice (NV 484)
1599 Giovanni Cavaccio, Venice (NV 519)
1600 Benedetto Pallavicino, Venice (NV 2123)
1601 Giuseppe Guami, Venice (NV 1301)
1601 Luzzasco Luzzaschi, Rome (NV 1524)
1604 Giovanni Priuli, Venice (NV 2280)
1605 Giovan Domenico Montella, Naples (NV 1887)
1606 Agostino Agazzari, Venice (NV 17)
1606 Sigismondo d'India, Venice (NV 823)
1606 Hans Nielsen, Venice (NV 2041)
1607 Pomponio Nenna, Naples (NV 2023
1607 Crescenzio Salzilli, Naples (NV 2537)
1608 Antonio Cifra, Venice (NV 570)
1608 Paolo Quagliati, Venice (NV 2294)
1609 Johann Grabbe, Venice (NV 1264)
1610 Giovanni Ghizzolo, Milan (NV 1187)
1610 Enrico Radesca, Venice (NV 2306)

1611 Marsilio Casentini, Venice (NV 499)
1614 Giulio Caccini, Florence (NV 454)
1615 Francesco Pasquali, Venice (NV 2143)
1617 Filippo Vitali, Florence (NV 2946)
1629 Pietro Francesco Garzi, Venice (NV 1059)
1633 Giovanni Battista Camarella, Venice (NV 466)
1656 Pompeo Natali, Rome (NV 2010)

Chi vuol aver felice, e lieto il core (#1)

1602 Scipione Dentice, Naples (NV 810)
1612 Giovanni Priuli, Venice (NV 2282)
1614 Francesco Genvino, Naples (NV 1122)
1615 Sigismondo d'India, Venice (NV 827)
1617 Giovanni Francesco Anerio, Rome (NV 69)
1617 Giovanni Battista Bartoli, Florence (NV 253)
1620 Giuseppe Palazzotto-Tagliavia, Palermo (NV 2088)
1621 Giovanni Ghizzolo, Venice (NV 1190)
1621 Pietro Maria Lamoretti, Venice (NV 1375)
1621 Francesco Turini, Venice (NV 2769)
1626 Francesco Costa, Venice (NV 639)
1629 Giovanni Rovetta, Venice (NV 2461)
1638 Claudio Monteverdi, Venice (NV 1941)
1640 Pietro Andrea Ziani, Venice (NV 3026)
1653 Giuseppe Tricario, Rome (VE 1653[1])

Come cantar poss'io (#119)

1604 Benedetto Pallavicino, Venice (NV 2126)
1608 Vincenzo Liberti, Venice (NV 1511)
1608 Paolo Quagliati, Venice (NV 2294)

Come non cangia stile (#27)

1612 Lucrezio Ruffulo, Venice (NV 2496)

Come sian dolorose (#135)

1607 Crescenzio Salzilli, Naples (NV 2537)
1617 Filippo Vitali, Florence (NV 2946)
1623 Antonio Cifra, Rome (NV 574)

1634 Giacinto Mattei, Naples (NV 1757)
1640 Giovanni Maria Costa, Venice (NV 644)

Con che soavità, labbra odorate (#78)

1586 Filippo de Monte, Venice (NV 772)
1588 Benedetto Pallavicino, Venice (NV 2114)
1590 Girolamo dalla Casa, Venice (NV 682)
1604 Giovan Giacomo Gastoldi, Venice (NV 1109)
1609 Giovanni Antonio Cirullo, Venice (NV 583)
1613 Francesco Rognoni Taeggio, Venice (NV 2359)
1619 Antonio Marastoni, Venice (NV 1571)
1619 Claudio Monteverdi, Venice (NV 1936)
1629 Francesco Turini, Venice (NV 2773)
1633 Orazio Tarditi, Venice (NV 2706)

Con voi sempre son io (#138)

1593 Orazio Scaletta, Venice (NV 2573)
1600 Paolo Sartorio, Venice (NV 2559)
1608 Giovanni Francesco Anerio, Venice (NV 72)

Cor mio, deh, non languire (#70)

1597 Allesandro Savioli, Venice (NV 2563)
1599 Geminiano Capilupi, Venice (NV 484)
1600 Benedetto Pallavicino, Venice (NV 2123)
1600 Salamone Rossi, Venice (NV 2445)
1601 Luzzasco Luzzaschi, Rome (NV 1524)
1601 Francesco Stivori, Venice (NV 2647)
1602 Giulio Caccini, Florence (NV 450)
1602 Leone Leoni, Venice (NV 1508)
1604 Alessandro di Costanzo, Naples (NV 817)
1604 Giovanni Priuli, Venice (NV 2280)
1605 Santi Orlandi, Venice (NV 2058)
1606 Sigismondo d'India, Venice (NV 823)
1606 Giuseppe de Puente, Naples (NV 2284)
1609 Giovanni Ghizzolo, Venice (NV 1193)
1609 Johann Grabbe, Venice (NV 1264)
1609 Michelangelo Nantermi, Venice (NV 1995)
1610 Alessandro Scialla, Naples (NV 2592)

1612 Pietro Pace, Venice (NV 2081)
1612 Antonio Taroni, Venice (NV 2710)
1613 Benedetto Magni, Venice (NV 1550)
1615 Enrico Radesca, Venice (NV 2309)
1617 Girolamo Belli, Venice (NV 310)
1617 Giuseppe Palazzotto-Tagliavia, Naples (NV 2087)
1619 Francesco Gonzaga, Venice (NV 1260)
1619 Antonio Marastoni, Venice (NV 1571)
1620 Claudio Saracini, Venice (NV 2555)
1621 Giacomo Tropea, Naples (NV 2765)
1626 Adriano Banchieri, Venice (NV 216)
1626 Giovanni Pasta, Venice (NV 2148)
1640 Francesco Colombini, Antwerp (NV 597)
1656 Pompeo Natali, Rome (NV 2010)
1668 Giovanni Battista Mazzaferrata, Bologna (NV 1763)
1678 Giovanni Maria Bononcini, Bologna (NV 397)

Cor mio, deh non piangete (#69)

1596 Carlo Gesualdo, Ferrara (NV 1168)
1599 Ruggero Giovannelli, Venice (NV 1223)
1602 Domenico Maria Melli, Venice (NV 1796)
1603 Tommaso Pecci, Venice (NV 2153)
1605 Giovanni Righi, Venice (NV 2348)
1606 Hans Nielsen, Venice (NV 2041)
1608 Marco Antonio Negri, Venice (NV 2014)
1609 Scipione Cerreto, Naples (VE 1609[1])
1609 Giovanni Ghizzolo, Venice (NV 1192)
1612 Francesco Genvino, Naples (NV 1121)
1612 Antonio Taroni, Venice (NV 2708)
1613 Pietro Benedetti, Venice (NV 323)
1613 Benedetto Magni, Venice (NV 1550)
1617 Girolamo Belli, Venice (NV 310)
1617 Giovanni Francesco Capello, Venice (NV 483)
1619 Francesco Gonzaga, Venice (NV 1260)
1619 Antonio Marastoni, Venice (NV 1571)
1620 Claudio Saracini, Venice (NV 2555)
1621 Pietro Maria Lamoretti, Venice (NV 1375)
1668 Giovanni Battista Mazzaferrata, Bologna (NV 1763)

Cor mio tu ti nascondi (#28)

1621 Martino Pesenti, Venice (NV 2192)
1633 Benedetto Ferrari, Venice (NV 935)
1640 Pietro Andrea Ziani, Venice (NV 3026)

Credete voi ch'i' viva (#127)

1599 Luca Marenzio, Venice (NV 1639)
1604 Alessandro di Costanzo, Naples (NV 817)
1607 Scipione Dentice, Naples (NV 811)
1609 Giovanni Antonio Cirullo, Venice (NV 583)
1611 Crescenzio Salzilli, Naples (NV 2538)
1612 Antonio Taroni, Venice (NV 2708)
1614 Giovanni del Turco, Florence (NV 729)
1615 Vincenzo Ugolini, Venice (NV 2777)
1617 Giuseppe Marini, Venice (NV 1720)

Credetel voi, che non sentite amore (#124)

1586 Giovanni Maria Nanino, Venice (NV 1992)
1590 Filippo de Monte, Venice (NV 775)
1607 Crescenzio Salzilli, Naples (NV 2537)
1616 Davide Civita, Venice (NV 584)
1629 Giovanni Rovetta, Venice (NV 2461)
1634 Biagio Marini, Venice (NV 1716)
1640 Pietro Andrea Ziani, Venice (NV 3026)

Cruda Amarilli, che col nome ancora (#89)

1590 Filippo de Monte, Venice (NV 775) [begins at "Ma de l'aspida sorda"]
1595 Luca Marenzio, Venice (NV 1633)
1595 Jacob de Wert, Venice (NV 2994)
1600 Benedetto Pallavicino, Venice (NV 2123)
1605 Antonio Cifra, Rome (NV 569)
1605 Ruggero Giovannelli, Venice (NV 1210)
1605 Claudio Monteverdi, Venice (NV 1922)
1606 Sigismondo d'India, Venice (NV 823)
1608 Giovanni Battista de Bellis, Naples (NV 694)
1609 Marsilio Casentini, Venice (NV 498)

1609 Sigismondo d'India, Milan (NV 832)
1610 Raffaello Rontani, Florence (NV 2362)
1612 Vincenzo Dal Pozzo, Venice (NV 688)
1614 Giovanni Ghizzolo, Venice (NV 1189)
1614 Claudio Saracini, Venice (NV 2554)
1616 Claudio Pari, Palermo (NV 2140)
1616 Domenico Visconti, Venice (NV 2934)
1617 Giovanni Nicolò Mezzogorri, Venice (NV 1840)
1621 Scipione Cerreto, Naples (NV 548)
1622 Allessandro Costantini, Orvieto (VE 1622[1])
1623 Johann Nauwach, Dresden (NV 2012)
1626 Giovan Pietro Biandrà, Venice (NV 363)

Crudel, perch'io non v'ami (#57)

1595 Paolo Masnelli, Venice (VE 1595[1])
1602 Giovanni del Turco, Florence (NV 728)
1612 Lucrezio Ruffulo, Venice (NV 2496)
1614 Giovan Paolo Costa, Venice (NV 647)

Cura gelata, e ria (#17)

1592 Filippo de Monte, Venice (NV 776)
1611 Orazio Brognonico, Venice (NV 430)
1616 Sigismondo d'India, Venice (NV 829)
1617 Andrea Anglesio, Venice (NV 82)
1622 Alfonso Montesano, Naples (NV 1896)

Deh bella, e cara, e sì soave un tempo (#147)

1602 Giovan Giacomo Gastoldi, Venice (NV 1114)
1605 Claudio Monteverdi, Venice (NV 1922)
1609 Marsilio Casentini, Venice (NV 498)
1617 Giovanni Nicolò Mezzogorri, Venice (NV 1840)

Deh, come in van chiedete (#118)

1600 Salamone Rossi, Venice (NV 2445)
1602 Scipione Dentice, Naples (NV 810)
1602 Santi Orlandi, Venice (NV 2057)
1603 Francesco Stivori, Venice (NV 2650)
1609 Vincenzo Liberti, Venice (NV 1512)

1610 Raffaello Rontani, Florence (NV 2362)
1610 Alessandro Scialla, Naples (NV 2592)
1612 Benedetto Pallavicino, Venice (NV 2130)
1613 Gregorio Francia, Venice (NV 1012)
1614 Pietro Maria Marsolo, Venice (NV 1733)
1614 Claudio Saracini, Venice (NV 2554)
1615 Vicenzo Ugolini, Venice (NV 2776)
1615 Sisto Visconte, Venice (NV 2933)
1616 Camillo Orlandi, Venice (NV 2056)
1617 Annibale Gregori, Venice (NV 1283)
1619 Raffaello Rontani, Rome (NV 2367)
1623 Giovanni Battista de Bellis, Naples (NV 696)
1623 Pellegrino Possenti, Venice (NV 2260)

Deh dimmi Amor se gli occhi di Camilla (#19)

1607 Ludovico Bellanda, Venice (NV 292)
1612 Lucrezio Ruffulo, Venice (NV 2496)
1618 Giovanni Boschetto Boschetti, Venice (NV 413)

Deh ferma, ferma il tuo rubella, Amore (#6)

1603 Peter Philips, Antwerp (NV 2211)

Dice la mia bellissima Licori (#8)

1587 Filippo de Monte, Venice (NV 773)
1587 Luca Marenzio, Venice (NV 1660)
1589 Orazio Vecchi, Venice (NV 2826)
1590 Girolamo dalla Casa, Venice (NV 682)
1590 Domenico Lauro, Venice (NV 1484)
1591 Jean de Castro, Venice (NV 511)
1607 Giovan Domenico Montella, Naples (NV 1880)
1617 Dattilo Roccia, Naples (NV 2357)
1619 Claudio Monteverdi, Venice (NV 1936)
1689 Angelo Berardi, Bologna (NV 327)

Dolce spirto d'Amore (#75)

1595 Carlo Gesualdo, Ferrara (NV 1163)
1600 Benedetto Pallavicino, Venice (NV 2123)
1605 Giovanni Domenico Rognoni Taeggio, Venice (NV 2360)

1607 Giovan Domenico Montella, Naples (NV 1880)
1608 Dattilo Roccia, Naples (NV 2355)
1609 Johann Grabbe, Venice (NV 1264)
1612 Antonio Taroni, Venice (NV 2708)
1615 Antonio Cifra, Venice (NV 571)
1616 Allesandro Capece, Rome (NV 480)
1619 Francesco Gonzaga, Venice (NV 1260)
1620 Richard Dering, Antwerp (NV 815)
1628 Domenico Crivellati, Rome (NV 655)

Dolcissimo Usignuolo (#114)

1600 Giuseppe Biffi, Naples (NV 368)
1604 Giovan Giacomo Gastoldi, Venice (NV 1109)
1604 Giovanni Priuli, Venice (NV 2280)
1607 Giovan Domenico Montella, Naples (NV 1880)
1610 Alessandro Scialla, Naples (NV 2592)
1619 Antonio Marastoni, Venice (NV 1571)
1638 Claudio Monteverdi, Venice (NV 1941)

Donna, mentre i' vi miro (#49)

1586 Pasquale Tristabocca, Venice (NV 2752)
1589 Paolo Isnardi, Venice (NV 1354)
1589 Andrea Rota, Venice (NV 2460)
1590 Domenico Lauro, Venice (NV 1484)
1598 Antonio Artusini, Venice (NV 172)
1602 Pompeo Signorucci, Venice (NV 2618)
1603 Claudio Monteverdi, Venice (NV 1914)
1608 Mogens Pedersoen, Venice (NV 2169)
1608 Francesco Rasi, Venice (NV 2316)
1609 Sigismondo d'India, Milan (NV 832)
1610 Giovanni Ghizzolo, Milan (NV 1187)
1611 Giovanni Francesco Anerio, Venice (NV 73)
1611 Stefano Bernardi, Rome (NV 334)
1611 Biagio Tomasi, Venice (NV 2727)
1613 Antonio Cifra, Rome (NV 563)
1613 Francesco Rognoni Taeggio, Venice (NV 2359)
1614 Salomone Rossi, Venice (NV 2444)
1619 Francesco Gonzaga, Venice (NV 1260)
1621 Alessandro Constantini, Orvieto (VE 1621[1])

Donna, voi vi credete (#136)

[1597?] Camillo Sarachi, [n.p.] (NV 2553bis)
1588 Jacob de Wert, Venice (NV 2992)
1593 Ruggero Giovannelli, Venice (NV 1218)
1596 Flaminio Tresti, Venice (NV 2751)
1600 Benedetto Pallavicino, Venice (NV 2123)
1606 Enrico Radesca, Milan (NV 2303)
1607 Scipione Dentice, Naples (NV 811)
1607 Giovan Domenico Montella, Naples (NV 1880)
1608 Vincenzo Liberti, Venice (NV 1511)
1609 Camillo Lambardi, Naples (NV 1369)
1611 Giovanni Francesco Anerio, Venice (NV 73)
1611 Marco Antonio Negri, Venice (NV 2015)
1612 Antonio Taroni, Venice (NV 2710)
1628 Domenico Crivellati, Rome (NV 655)
1634 Marco Scacchi, Venice (NV 2570)

Donò Licori a Batto (#72)

1585 Luca Marenzio, Venice (NV 1656)
1586 Ruggero Giovannelli, Venice (NV 1211)
1587 Filippo de Monte, Venice (NV 773)
1590 Domenico Lauro, Venice (NV 1484)
1590 Camillo Zanotti, Nuremberg (NV 3014)
1603 Giovanni Bernardo Colombi, Venice (NV 595)
1614 Claudio Saracini, Venice (NV 2554)
1629 Dionisio Bellante, Venice (NV 294)
1640 Franceso Vignali, Venice (NV 2903)

Dorinda, ah dirò mia, se mia non sei (#95)

1598 Luca Marenzio, Venice (NV 1637)
1605 Claudio Monteverdi, Venice (NV 1922)
1624 Sigismondo d'India, Rome (NV 831)

Dov'hai tu nido, Amore (#4)

1584 Pietro Vinci, Venice (NV 2923)
1585 Lelio Bertani, Venice (NV 347)
1586 Paolo Masnelli, Venice (NV 1743)
1586 Lodovico Spontoni, Venice (NV 2640)

1587 Flaminio Tresti, Venice (NV 2748)
1592 Filippo de Monte, Venice (NV 776)
1596 Rodiano Barera, Venice (NV 246)
1596 Scipione Dentice, Venice (NV 808)
1600 Giuseppe Biffi, Naples (NV 368)
1601 Antonio Il Verso, Venice (NV 1336)
1602 Ludovico Bellanda, Venice (NV 291)
1604 Alessandro di Costanzo, Naples (NV 817)
1607 Giovan Domenico Montella, Naples (NV 1880)
1613 Francesco Costa, Venice (NV 645)
1617 Antonio Cifra, Rome (NV 572)
1621 Pietro Maria Lamoretti, Venice (NV 1375)
1626 Giovan Pietro Biandrà, Venice (NV 363)
1628 Giovanni Ferrari, Venice (NV 938)
1678 Giovanni Maria Bononcini, Bologna (NV 397)

E così a poco a poco (#42)

1592 Filippo de Monte, Venice (NV 776)
1605 Claudio Monteverdi, Venice (NV 1922)
1609 Giovanni Antonio Cirullo, Venice (NV 583)
1609 Vincenzo Liberti, Venice (NV 1512)
1614 Amadio Freddi, Venice (NV 1018)
1649 Gaspare Filippi, Venice (NV 986)

E così pur languendo (#58)

1602 Salomone Rossi, Venice (NV 2450)
1622 Alessandro Grandi, Venice (NV 1277)
1653 Anton Francesco Tenaglia, Rome (VE 1653[1])

Ecco piegando le genocchie a terra (#96)

1605 Claudio Monteverdi, Venice (NV 1922)
1617 Giovanni Battista Bartoli, Florence (NV 253) [begins at "Ecco li strale"]
1678 Domenico del Pane, Rome (NV 685) [begins at "Ecco li strale"]

Ecco Silvio, colei che 'n odio hai tanto (#93)

1605 Claudio Monteverdi, Venice (NV 1922)
1612 Orazio Brognonico, Venice (NV 427)
1633 Giovanni Battista Camarella, Venice (NV 466)

Era l'anima mia (#148)

1600 Benedetto Pallavicino, Venice (NV 2123)
1604 Alfonso Fontanelli, Venice (NV 1002)
1604 Orazio Vecchi, Venice (NV 2833)
1605 Claudio Monteverdi, Venice (NV 1922)
1608 Antonio Cifra, Venice (NV 570)
1608 Vincenzo Liberti, Venice (NV 1511)
1612 Tommaso Pecci, Venice (NV 2161)
1613 Gregorio Francia, Venice (NV 1012)
1615 Nicolo Rubini, Venice (NV 2470)
1616 Claudio Pari, Palermo (NV 2140)
1616 Enrico Radesca, Venice (NV 2305)
1617 Pietro Benedetti, Florence (NV 324)
1617 Annibale Gregori, Venice (NV 1283)
1622 Girolamo Frescobaldi, Orvieto (VE 1622[1])
1634 Marco Scacchi, Venice (NV 2570)

E tu, Mirtillo (anima mia) perdona (#91)

1594 Luca Marenzio, Venice (NV 1629)
1600 Giovanni Appolloni, Venice (NV 92)
1600 Filippo de Monte, Venice (NV 806)
1603 Claudio Monteverdi, Venice (NV 1914)
1608 Antonio Cifra, Venice (NV 570)
1609 Marsilio Casentini, Venice (NV 498)
1613 Francesco Rognoni Taeggio, Venice (NV 2359)
1614 Giovan Paolo Costa, Venice (NV 647)
1617 Giovanni Nicolò Mezzogorri, Venice (NV 1840)
1618 Giuseppe Marini, Venice (NV 1721)
1621 Scipione Cerreto, Naples (NV 548)
1621 Scipione Cerreto, Naples (NV 548) [begins at "E, se pur hai desio di vendicarti"]
1623 Giacinto Merulo, Venice (NV 1837)

Felice chi vi mira (#64)

1595 Paolo Bellasio, Verona (NV 298)
1599 Mariano Tantucci, Venice (NV 2164)
1600 Salamone Rossi, Venice (NV 2445)
1602 Leone Leoni, Venice (NV 1508)
1602 Giovanni Piccioni, Venice (NV 2226)

1604 Benedetto Pallavicino, Venice (NV 2126)
1606 Bartolomeo Barbarino, Venice (NV 240)
1606 Orindio Bartolini, Venice (NV 255)
1606 Sigismondo d'India, Venice (NV 823)
1606 Hans Nielsen, Venice (NV 2041)
1608 Adriano Banchieri, Venice (NV 214)
1608 Sigismondo d'India, Naples (NV 838)
1608 Paolo Quagliati, Venice (NV 2294)
1609 Giovanni Ghizzolo, Venice (NV 1193)
1611 Giovanni Francesco Anerio, Venice (NV 73)
1611 Stefano Bernardi, Rome (NV 334)
1611 Nunzio Ciccarello, Naples (NV 560)
1611 Crescenzio Salzilli, Naples (NV 2538)
1612 Antonio Il Verso, Venice (NV 1339)
1612 Lucrezio Ruffulo, Venice (NV 2496)
1613 Francesco Rognoni Taeggio, Venice (NV 2359)
1614 Pietro Maria Marsolo, Venice (NV 1733)
1617 Andrea Anglesio, Venice (NV 82)
1617 Antonio Cifra, Rome (NV 567)
1617 Antonio Cifra, Rome (NV 572)
1617 Amante Franzoni, Venice (NV 1014)
1618 Orazio Giaccio, Naples (NV 1197)
1619 Francesco Robbiano, Milan (NV 2353)
1619 Giovanni Domenico Rognoni Taeggio, Milan (NV 2361)
1623 Paolo Quagliati, Rome (NV 2295)
1636 Giovanni Antonio Rigatti, Venice (NV 2345)

Ferir quel petto Silvio (#97)

1598 Luca Marenzio, Venice (NV 1637)
1605 Claudio Monteverdi, Venice (NV 1922)
1624 Sigismondo d'India, Rome (NV 831)

Io d'altrui? S'i' volessi, I' non potrei (#109)

1582 Luzzasco Luzzaschi, Venice (NV 1527)
1604 Giovanni Battista Caletti, Venice (NV 463)
1610 Giovan Paolo Costa, Venice (NV 646)
1612 Antonio Taroni, Venice (NV 2710)
1615 Alessandro Grandi, Venice (NV 1271)

1615 Vincenzo Ugolini, Venice (NV 2777)
1616 Marcello Albano, Naples (NV 36)
1616 Enrico Radesca, Venice (NV 2305)
1617 Paolo Quagliati, Rome (NV 2290)
1619 Giulio Medici, Venice (NV 1787)

Io disleale? Ah cruda (#106)

1595 Leone Leoni, Venice (NV 1505)
1596 Paolo Masnelli, Venice (NV 1744)
1597 Francesco Bianciardi, Venice (NV 361)
1600 Benedetto Pallavicino, Venice (NV 2123)
1602 Tommaso Pecci, Venice (NV 2157)
1605 Adriano Banchieri, Venice (NV 211)
1605 Amadio Freddi, Venice (NV 1019)
1605 Enrico Radesca, Milan (NV 2300)
[1605?] Mariano Tantucci, Siena (NV 2698)
1608 Giovanni Ghizzolo, Venice (NV 1194)
1609 Giovanni Antonio Cirullo, Venice (NV 583)
1611 Stefano Bernardi, Rome (NV 334)
1613 Gregorio Francia, Venice (NV 1012)
1614 Giovanni del Turco, Florence (NV 729)
1615 Domenico Visconti, Florence (NV 2935)
1617 Giacomo Fornaci, Venice (NV 1008)
1625 Léonard de Hodemont, Antwerp (NV 1317)
1627 Giovanni Ceresini, Venice (NV 547)
1629 Filippo Vitali, Venice (NV 2945)
1656 Pompeo Natali, Rome (NV 2010)
1675 Giovanni Battista Bianchi, Bologna (NV 357)

Io mi sento morir quando non miro (#34)

1587 Andrea Gabrieli, Venice (NV 1046)
1599 Geminiano Capilupi, Venice (NV 484)
1600 Guglielmo Arnoni, Venice (NV 169)
1606 Agostino Agresta, Naples (NV 822)
1607 Ludovico Bellanda, Venice (NV 292)
1607 Scipione Dentice, Naples (NV 811)
1607 Giovanni Priuli, Venice (NV 2281)
1610 Nicolo Rubini, Venice (NV 2471)

1611 Pietro Benedetti, Florence (NV 322)
1612 Giovanni Bernardino Nanino, Rome (NV 1986)
1614 Giovan Paolo Costa, Venice (NV 647)
1614 Raffaello Rontani, Florence (NV 2363)
1616 Sigismondo d'India, Venice (NV 829)
1616 Ortensio Gentile, Venice (NV 1119)
1617 Antonio Cifra, Rome (NV 572)
1617 Giuseppe Palazzotto-Tagliavia, Naples (NV 2087)
1620 Richard Dering, Antwerp (NV 814)
1621 Pietro Maria Lamoretti, Venice (NV 1375)
1622 Alessandro Grandi, Venice (NV 1277)
1627 Simplicio Todeschi, Venice (NV 2725)
1629 Giovanni Rovetta, Venice (NV 2461)

Io veggio pur pietate, anchorche tardi (#81)

1594 Luzzasco Luzzaschi, Ferrara (NV 1528)
1604 Giovan Giacomo Gastoldi, Venice (NV 1109)
1609 Vincenzo Liberti, Venice (NV 1512)
1618 Sigismondo d'India, Milan (NV 834)

Ite amari sospiri (#21)

1598 Luca Marenzio, Venice (NV 1637)
1600 Guglielmo Arnoni, Venice (NV 169)
1602 Flaminio Comanedo, Milan (NV 603)
1603 Tommaso Pecci, Venice (NV 2153)
1604 Giovanni Battista Caletti, Venice (NV 463)
1606 Hans Nielsen, Venice (NV 2041)
1611 Paolo Quagliati, Rome (NV 2293)
1612 Antonio Taroni, Venice (NV 2710)
1613 Benedetto Magni, Venice (NV 1550)
1614 Giovan Paolo Costa, Venice (NV 647)
1615 Antonio Cifra, Rome (NV 565)
1616 Allesandro Capece, Rome (NV 480)
1619 Giulio Medici, Venice (NV 1787)
1620 Richard Dering, Antwerp (NV 815)
1620 Scipione Lacorcia, Naples (NV 1366)
1620 Claudio Saracini, Venice (NV 2555)
1640 Pietro Andrea Ziani, Venice (NV 3026)

La bella man vi stringo (#32)

1590 Domenico Lauro, Venice (NV 1484)
1593 Filippo de Monte, Venice (NV 777)
1599 Luca Marenzio, Venice (NV 1639)
1600 Antonio Il Verso, Venice (NV 1332)
1601 Valerio Bona, Venice (NV 378)
1601 Nicolo de Grecis, Venice (NV 731)
1608 Vincenzo Liberti, Venice (NV 1511)
1613 Pietro Benedetti, Venice (NV 323)
1614 Giulio Caccini, Florence (NV 454)
1614 Giovanni Battista de Bellis, Naples (NV 695)
1616 Francesco Ugoni, Milan (NV 2778)
1617 Antonio Cifra, Rome (NV 572)
1620 Biagio Marini, Venice (NV 1713)
1627 Galeazzo Sabbatini, Venice (NV 2505)

La tenera Licori (#74)

1617 Girolamo Belli, Venice (NV 310)

Langue al vostro languir l'anima mia (#60)

1586 Filippo de Monte, Venice (NV 772)
1590 Girolamo dalla Casa, Venice (NV 682)
1592 Giovanni Croce, Venice (NV 668)
1609 Giovanni Antonio Cirullo, Venice (NV 583)
1611 Marsilio Casentini, Venice (NV 499)
1613 Crescenzio Salzilli, Naples (NV 2541)
1615 Sigismondo d'India, Venice (NV 833)
1617 Girolamo Belli, Venice (NV 310)
1621 Giovanni Ghizzolo, Venice (NV 1190)
1624 Claudio Saracini, Venice (NV 2557)
1625 Alessandro Capece, Rome (NV 481)
1631 Antonio Guelfi, Florence (NV 1307)
1634 Giacinto Mattei, Naples (NV 1757)

Lasso, perché mi fuggi (#22)

1585 Arcangelo Gherardini, Ferrara (NV 1179)
1586 Pasquale Tristabocca, Venice (NV 2752)

1587 Luca Marenzio, Venice (NV 1660)
1587 Benedetto Pallavicino, Venice (NV 2131)
1588 Annibale Coma, Venice (NV 598)
1588 Giovanni Battista Mosto, Antwerp (NV 1976)
1590 Claudio Monteverdi, Venice (NV 1903)
1591 Pier Andrea Bonini, Venice (NV 388)
1601 Valerio Bona, Venice (NV 378)
1602 Salomone Rossi, Venice (NV 2450)
1605 Adriano Banchieri, Venice (NV 211)
1605 Ruggero Giovannelli, Venice (NV 1210)
1607 Giovanni Ceresini, Venice (NV 546)
1607 Scipione Dentice, Naples (NV 811)
1609 Johann Grabbe, Venice (NV 1264)
1609 Vincenzo Liberti, Venice (NV 1512)
1611 Giovanni Francesco Anerio, Venice (NV 73)
1611 Stefano Bernardi, Rome (NV 334)
1611 Sigismondo d'India, Venice (NV 826)
1614 Giovanni del Turco, Florence (NV 729)
1617 Pietro Benedetti, Florence (NV 324)
1617 Antonio Il Verso, Palermo (NV 1329)
1619 Giulio Medici, Venice (NV 1787)
1620 Claudio Saracini, Venice (NV 2555)
1622 Pietro Paolo Torre, Venice (NV 2736)
1625 Orazio Modiana, Venice (NV 1868bis)
1627 Simplicio Todeschi, Venice (NV 2725)
1629 Pietro Francesco Garzi, Venice (NV 1059)
1629 Filippo Vitali, Venice (NV 2941)
1640 Francesco Colombini, Antwerp (NV 597)
1675 Giovanni Battista Bianchi, Bologna (NV 357)

Lauro, oimè, lauro ingrato (#16)

1582 Giovanni Bardi, Ferrara (VE 1582[1])
1590 Marcello Tosone, Genoa (NV 2742)
1602 Santi Orlandi, Venice (NV 2057)
1610 Raffaello Rontani, Florence (NV 2362)
1615 Francesco Pasquali, Venice (NV 2143)

Lumi miei cari lumi (#52)

1592 Filippo de Monte, Venice (NV 776)
1592 Claudio Monteverdi, Venice (NV 1906)

1597 Francesco Bianciardi, Venice (NV 361)
1597 Allesandro Savioli, Venice (NV 2563)
1602 Salomone Rossi, Venice (NV 2450)
1606 Marco da Gagliano, Venice (NV 1581)
1609 Pomponio Nenna, Venice (NV 2020)
1610 Giovanni Ghizzolo, Milan (NV 1187)
1616 Gio. Pietro Flaccomio, Antwerp (VE 1616[1])
1617 Giuseppe Olivieri, Rome (NV 2051)
1619 Giovanni Domenico Rognoni Taeggio, Milan (NV 2361)
1656 Pompeo Natali, Rome (NV 2010)

M'è più dolce il penar per Amarilli (#112)

1596 Rodiano Barera, Venice (NV 246) [begins at "Viver io fortunato"]
1597 Pietro Pace, Venice (NV 2080) [begins at "Viver io fortunato"]
1597 Allesandro Savioli, Venice (NV 2563) [begins at "Viver io fortunato"]
1598 Giovan Giacomo Gastoldi, Venice (NV 1113)
1600 Filippo de Monte, Venice (NV 806) [begins at "Viver io fortunato"]
1600 Benedetto Pallavicino, Venice (NV 2123) [begins at "Viver io fortunato"]
1602 Domenico Maria Melli, Venice (NV 1796) [begins at "Viver io fortunato"]
1605 Claudio Monteverdi, Venice (NV 1922)
1607 Bartolomeo Barbarino, Venice (NV 242)
1617 Giovanni Francesco Capello, Venice (NV 483)
1620 Richard Dering, Antwerp (NV 815) [begins at "Viver io fortunato"]
1620 Richard Dering, Antwerp (NV 815) [begins at "E s'esser puo"]
1621 Scipione Cerreto, Naples (NV 548)
1621 Scipione Cerreto, Naples (NV 548) [begins at "Viver io fortunato"]
1622 Pietro Paolo Torre, Venice (NV 2736)
1625 Allegro Porto, Venice (NV 2257)
1626 Francesco Costa, Venice (NV 639)

Ma se con la pietà non è in te spenta (#94)

1594 Luca Marenzio, Venice (NV 1629) [begins at "(Anima cruda si, ma pero
    bella)"]
1605 Claudio Monteverdi, Venice (NV 1922)
1619 Francesco Robbiano, Milan (NV 2353) [begins at "(Anima cruda si, ma pero
    bella)"]
1624 Sigismondo d'India, Rome (NV 831)
1678 Domenico del Pane, Rome (NV 685) [begins at "(Anima cruda si, ma pero
    bella)"]

Ma tu più che mai dura (#23)

1602 Giovan Giacomo Gastoldi, Venice (NV 1114)
1605 Claudio Monteverdi, Venice (NV 1922)
1609 Marsilio Casentini, Venice (NV 498) [begins at "A chi parlo infelice"]
1613 Francesco Rognoni Taeggio, Venice (NV 2359)

Madonna, udite come (#77)

1603 Peter Philips, Antwerp (NV 2211)
1607 Giovan Domenico Montella, Naples (NV 1880)
1609 Vincenzo Liberti, Venice (NV 1512)
1616 Marcello Albano, Naples (NV 36)
1616 Sigismondo d'India, Venice (NV 829)
1653 Anton Francesco Tenaglia, Rome (VE 1653[1])

Mentre una gioia miro (#108)

1611 Giovan Piero Flaccomio, Venice (NV 992)

Mentre vaga Angioletta (#122)

1589 Giorgio Florio, Venice (NV 994)
1604 Giovanni Battista Caletti, Venice (NV 463)
1604 Tiburzio Massaino, Venice (NV 1751)
1612 Johannes Hieronymus Kapsperger, Rome (NV 1357)
1629 Francesco Turini, Venice (NV 2773)
1638 Claudio Monteverdi, Venice (NV 1941)

Morto mi vede la mia Morte in sogno (#43)

1591 Filippo de Monte, Venice (NV 797)
1614 Giovanni del Turco, Florence (NV 729)

Negatemi pur cruda (#50)

1607 Crescenzio Salzilli, Naples (NV 2537)
1610 Johannes Hieronymus Kapsperger, Rome (NV 1361)
1612 Benedetto Pallavicino, Venice (NV 2130)
1614 Pietro Maria Marsolo, Venice (NV 1733)
1617 Giovanni Francesco Capello, Venice (NV 483)

1617 Antonio Cifra, Rome (NV 572)
1619 Francesco Gonzaga, Venice (NV 1260)
1620 Carlo Milanuzzi, Venice (NV 1848)
1621 Pietro Maria Lamoretti, Venice (NV 1375)
1622 Alessandro Grandi, Venice (NV 1277)
1631 Gregorio Veneri, Florence (NV 2849)

Non fu senza vendetta (#67)

1575 Giovanni Agostino Veggio, Parma (NV 2846)
1576 Luzzasco Luzzaschi, Venice (NV 1526)
1581 Giovan Pietro Cottone, Turin (NV 650)
1585 Annibale Coma, Venice (NV 600)
1586 Costanzo Porta, Venice (NV 2246)
1593 Filippo de Monte, Venice (NV 777)
1595 Antonio Il Verso, Palermo (NV 1331)
1597 Pietro Pace, Venice (NV 2080)
1598 Giulio Cesare Gabussi, Venice (NV 1050)
1600 Allesandro Savioli, Venice (NV 2564)
1610 Giovan Paolo Costa, Venice (NV 646)
1616 Davide Civita, Venice (NV 584)
1619 Allegro Porto, Venice (NV 2258)
1630 Michele Delipari, Venice (NV 702)

Non miri il mio bel sole (#71)

1585 Arcangelo Gherardini, Ferrara (NV 1179)
1615 Enrico Radesca, Venice (NV 2309)
1607 Giovanni Croce, Venice (NV 669)
1608 Maffeo Cagnazzi, Venice (NV 457)
1610 Giovan Paolo Costa, Venice (NV 646)
1615 Vicenzo Ugolini, Venice (NV 2776)
1621 Martino Pesenti, Venice (NV 2192)

Non più guerra, pietate (#54)

1586 Filippo de Monte, Venice (NV 772)
1590 Girolamo dalla Casa, Venice (NV 682)
1594 Simone Balsamino, Venice (NV 209)
1598 Peter Phillips, Antwerp (NV 2213)
1599 Geminiano Capilupi, Venice (NV 484)

1602 Giulio Caccini, Florence (NV 450)
1603 Claudio Monteverdi, Venice (NV 1914)
1621 Giovanni Valentini, Venice (NV 2785)
1626 Alesandro Della Chiaia, Rome (NV 2152)
1627 Simplicio Todeschi, Venice (NV 2725)
1656 Pompeo Natali, Rome (NV 2010)
1678 Giovanni Maria Bononcini, Bologna (NV 397)

Non sa che sia dolore (#131)

1600 Giuseppe Biffi, Naples (NV 368)
1601 Luzzasco Luzzaschi, Rome (NV 1524)
1604 Giovan Domenico Montella, Naples (NV 1890)
1615 Alessandro Grandi, Venice (NV 1271)
1617 Girolamo Belli, Venice (NV 310)
1618 Giuseppe Marini, Venice (NV 1721)
1640 Francesco Colombini, Antwerp (NV 597)

Non sospirar cor mio non sospirare (#68)

1588 Annibale Coma, Venice (NV 598)
1603 Claudio Monteverdi, Venice (NV 1914)

O che soave bacio (#66)

1587 Luca Marenzio, Venice (NV 1660)
1597 Allesandro Savioli, Venice (NV 2563)
1604 Benedetto Pallavicino, Venice (NV 2126)
1607 Ludovico Bellanda, Venice (NV 292)
1607 Giovan Domenico Montella, Naples (NV 1880)
1608 Mogens Pedersoen, Venice (NV 2169)
1608 Dattilo Roccia, Naples (NV 2355)
1610 Antonio Savetta, Venice (NV 2561)
1610 Alessandro Scialla, Naples (NV 2592)
1615 Antonio Cifra, Rome (NV 565)
1615 Enrico Radesca, Venice (NV 2309)
1616 Allesandro Capece, Rome (NV 480)
1617 Antonio Cifra, Rome (NV 572)
1617 Giacomo Fornaci, Venice (NV 1008)
1617 Giuseppe Marini, Venice (NV 1720)
1619 Francesco Gonzaga, Venice (NV 1260)

1622 Pietro Paolo Torre, Venice (NV 2736)
1634 Marco Scacchi, Venice (NV 2570)

O come è gran martire (#62)

1582 Luzzasco Luzzaschi, Venice (NV 1527)
1586 Giulio Eremita, Ferrara (NV 892)
1587 Flaminio Tresti, Venice (NV 2748)
1590 Paolo Masnelli, Venice (VE 1590[3a])
1590 Cornelio Verdonch, Antwerp (VE 1590[10])
1591 Andrea Pevernage, Antwerp (VE 1591[1])
1592 Claudio Monteverdi, Venice (NV 1906)
1594 Carlo Gesualdo, Ferrara (NV 1157)
1597 Pietro Pace, Venice (NV 2080)
1599 Francesco Maria Borelli, Venice (NV 401)
1600 Salamone Rossi, Venice (NV 2445)
1603 Tommaso Pecci, Venice (NV 2153)
1605 Amadio Freddi, Venice (NV 1019)
1605 Santi Orlandi, Venice (NV 2058)
1609 Bernardino Bertolotti, Venice (NV 354)
1610 Enrico Radesca, Venice (NV 2306)
1616 Davide Civita, Venice (NV 584)
1617 Agostino Agresta, Naples (NV 32)
1617 Antonio Cifra, Rome (NV 572)
1617 Giuseppe Olivieri, Rome (NV 2051)
1618 Giuseppe Marini, Venice (NV 1721)
1619 Allegro Porto, Venice (NV 2258)
1620 Richard Dering, Antwerp (NV 815)
1621 Giovanni Bernardo Colombi, Venice (NV 596)
1622 Alessandro Grandi, Venice (NV 1277)

O come se' gentile (#113)

1601 Antonio Il Verso, Venice (NV 1336)
1601 Francesco Stivori, Venice (NV 2647)
1602 Tommaso Pecci, Venice (NV 2157)
1604 Tiburzio Massaino, Venice (NV 1751)
1605 Santi Orlandi, Venice (NV 2058)
1606 Bartolomeo Barbarino, Venice (NV 240)
1606 Giuseppe de Puente, Naples (NV 2284)
1610 Alessandro Scialla, Naples (NV 2592)

1611 Paolo Quagliati, Rome (NV 2293)
1613 Bertolomeo Cesana, Venice (NV 551)
1613 Gregorio Francia, Venice (NV 1012)
1614 Pietro Maria Marsolo, Venice (NV 1733)
1617 Giuseppe Marini, Venice (NV 1720)
1618 Raffaello Rontani, Florence (NV 2365)
1619 Claudio Monteverdi, Venice (NV 1936)
1626 Adriano Banchieri, Venice (NV 216)
1634 Marco Scacchi, Venice (NV 2570)
1646 Michelangelo Grancino, Milan (NV 1266)

O dolce anima mia, dunque é pur vero (#101)

1582 Luca Marenzio, Venice (NV 1613)
1592 Claudio Monteverdi, Venice (NV 1906)
1593 Vittoria Aleotti, Venice (NV 46)
1596 Paolo Masnelli, Venice (NV 1744)
1599 Giovanni Cavaccio, Venice (NV 519)
1600 Salamone Rossi, Venice (NV 2445)
1608 Giovanni Ghizzolo, Venice (NV 1194)
1609 Jacopo Peri, Florence (NV 2181)
1613 Pietro Benedetti, Venice (NV 323)
1614 Marco da Gagliano, Florence (NV 729)
1614 Pietro Maria Marsolo, Venice (NV 1733)
1617 Andrea Anglesio, Venice (NV 82)
1629 Pietro Francesco Garzi, Venice (NV 1059)
1656 Pompeo Natali, Rome (NV 2010)

O Donna troppo cruda, e troppo bella (#33)

1599 Geminiano Capilupi, Venice (NV 484)
1600 Salamone Rossi, Venice (NV 2445)
1602 Tommaso Pecci, Venice (NV 2157)
1609 Johann Grabbe, Venice (NV 1264)
1609 Pomponio Nenna, Venice (NV 2020)
1611 Paolo Quagliati, Rome (NV 2293)
1614 Amadio Freddi, Venice (NV 1018)
1615 Giovan Lorenzo Missino, Venice (NV 1868)
1618 Giuseppe Marini, Venice (NV 1721)
1622 Alessandro Grandi, Venice (NV 1277)
1623 Mutio Effrem, Florence (NV 2944)
1627 Simplicio Todeschi, Venice (NV 2725)

O Mirtillo, Mirtillo, anima mia (#90)

1595 Luca Marenzio, Venice (NV 1633)
1600 Giovanni Appolloni, Venice (NV 92)
1600 Filippo de Monte, Venice (NV 806)
1605 Ruggero Giovannelli, Venice (NV 1210)
1605 Claudio Monteverdi, Venice (NV 1922)
1606 Orindio Bartolini, Venice (NV 255)
1606 Arcangelo Crivelli, Venice (NV 656) [begins at "Che giova a te"]
1607 Giovanni Croce, Venice (NV 669)
1609 Marsilio Casentini, Venice (NV 498)
1612 Antonio Taroni, Venice (NV 2708)
1613 Giovanni Boschetto Boschetti, Rome (NV 412)
1613 Giovanni Ghizzolo, Milan (NV 1188)
1614 Amadio Freddi, Venice (NV 1018)
1614 Salomone Rossi, Venice (NV 2444)
1616 Claudio Pari, Palermo (NV 2140)
1617 Antonio Il Verso, Palermo (NV 1329)
1617 Antonio Il Verso, Palermo (NV 1329) [begins at "Che giova a te"]
1617 Giovanni Nicolò Mezzogorri, Venice (NV 1840)
1618 Giovanni Boschetto Boschetti, Venice (NV 413)
1618 Giuseppe Marini, Venice (NV 1721)
1619 Giulio Medici, Venice (NV 1787)
1621 Scipione Cerreto, Naples (NV 548)
1626 Adriano Banchieri, Venice (NV 216)

O miseria d'amante (#2)

1620 Scipione Lacorcia, Naples (NV 1366)
1621 Giovanni Francesco Anerio, Rome (NV 70)

O notturno miracolo soave (#82)

1587 Filippo de Monte, Venice (NV 773)
1598 Giovan Giacomo Gastoldi, Venice (NV 1113)
1604 Francesco Spongia, Venice (NV 2779)

O primavera, gioventù de l'anno (#150)

1592 Claudio Monteverdi, Venice (NV 1906)
1595 Jacob de Wert, Venice (NV 2994)
1598 Giovanni Francesco Anerio, Venice (NV 60)

1598 Giuseppe Biffi, Milan (NV 367)
1599 Filippo de Monte, Venice (NV 734)
1599 Filippo de Monte, Venice (NV 734) [begins at "Tu ben, lasso, ritorni"]
1601 Luzzasco Luzzaschi, Rome (NV 1524)
1608 Paolo Quagliati, Venice (NV 2294)
1609 Sigismondo d'India, Milan (NV 832)
1611 Stefano Bernardi, Rome (NV 334)
1611 Stefano Bernardi, Rome (NV 334) [begins at "Tu ben sei quella"]
1611 Heinrich Schütz, Venice (NV 2589)
1614 Giovanni Ghizzolo, Venice (NV 1189)
1614 Raffaello Rontani, Florence (NV 2363)
1614 Raffaello Rontani, Florence (NV 2363) [begins at "Tu ben, lasso, ritorni"]
1614 Raffaello Rontani, Florence (NV 2363) [begins at "Tu ben sei quella"]
1615–16 Stefano Bernardi, Venice (NV 338)
1616 Domenico Visconti, Venice (NV 2934)
1617 Giovanni Battista Bartoli, Florence (NV 253)
1617 Giovanni Battista Bartoli, Florence (NV 253) [begins at "Tu ben, lasso, ritorni"]
1617 Giovanni Battista Bartoli, Florence (NV 253) [begins at "Tu ben sei quella"]
1617 Girolamo Belli, Venice (NV 310)
1617 Giovanni Bettini, Venice (NV 462)
1617 Giovanni Nicolò Mezzogorri, Venice (NV 1840)
1617 Giuseppe Olivieri, Rome (NV 2051)
1623 Antonio Cifra, Rome (NV 574)
1623 Paolo Quagliati, Rome (NV 2295)

Occhi stelle mortali (#20)

1596 Bartolomeo Ratti, Venice (NV 2319)
1599 Ottavio Bargnani, Venice (NV 248)
1600 Camillo Lambardi, Naples (NV 1368)
1603 Giovan Domenico Montella, Naples (NV 1885)
1609 Vincenzo Liberti, Venice (NV 1512)
1617 Giovanni Francesco Anerio, Rome (NV 69)
1617 Giacomo Fornaci, Venice (NV 1008)

Occhi, un tempo mia vita (#35)

1588 Benedetto Pallavicino, Venice (NV 2114)
1590 Giovanni Croce, Venice (NV 670)
1592 Claudio Monteverdi, Venice (NV 1906)
1594 Luca Bati, Venice (NV 286)

1599 Filippo de Monte, Venice (NV 734)
1599 Mariano Tantucci, Venice (NV 2164)
1601 Ottavio Bargnani, Venice (NV 249)
1603 Francesco Stivori, Venice (NV 2650)
1604 Francesco Spongia, Venice (NV 2779)
1605 Amadio Freddi, Venice (NV 1019)
1605 Giovanni Domenico Rognoni Taeggio, Venice (NV 2360)
1606 Bartolomeo Barbarino, Venice (NV 240)
1606 Marco da Gagliano, Venice (NV 1581)
1607 Salustio Palmiero, Venice (NV 2134)
1610 Raffaello Rontani, Florence (NV 2362)
1611 Carlo Gesualdo, [Venice] (NV 1172)
1612 Francesco Genvino, Naples (NV 1121)
1612 Antonio Il Verso, Venice (NV 1339)
1613 Antonio Cifra, Rome (NV 564)
1613 Angelo Notari, London (NV 2043)
1614 Pietro Maria Marsolo, Venice (NV 1733)
1617 Vincenzo Calestani, Venice (NV 462)
1615 Antonio Cifra, Venice (NV 571)
1619 Francesco Gonzaga, Venice (NV 1260)
1620 Hettore della Marra, Naples (NV 1366)
1622 Giovanni Priuli, Venice (NV 2283)
1640 Francesco Colombini, Antwerp (NV 597)
1668 Giovanni Battista Mazzaferrata, Bologna (NV 1763)

Oggi nacqui, Ben mio (#76)

1600 Benedetto Pallavicino, Venice (NV 2123)
1604 Luzzasco Luzzaschi, Venice (NV 1531
1604 Giovanni Priuli, Venice (NV 2280)
1605 Adriano Banchieri, Venice (NV 211)
1608 Paolo Quagliati, Venice (NV 2294)
1608 Dattilo Roccia, Naples (NV 2355)
1616 Sigismondo d'India, Venice (NV 829)
1617 Andrea Anglesio, Venice (NV 82)
1619 Giulio Medici, Venice (NV 1787)
1621 Pietro Maria Lamoretti, Venice (NV 1375)

Oimè, se tanto amate (#39)

1582 Luca Marenzio, Venice (NV 1613)
1600 Benedetto Pallavicino, Venice (NV 2123)

1600 Salamone Rossi, Venice (NV 2445)
1603 Claudio Monteverdi, Venice (NV 1914)
1604 Giovanni Battista Caletti, Venice (NV 463)
1605 Giovanni Domenico Rognoni Taeggio, Venice (NV 2360)
1606 Giuseppe de Puente, Naples (NV 2284)
1606 Enrico Radesca, Milan (NV 2303)
1609 Giovanni Ghizzolo, Venice (NV 1193)
1611 Stefano Bernardi, Rome (NV 334)
1616 Giacomo Bonzanini, Venice (NV 399)
1619 Andrea Falconieri, Venice (NV 905)
1621 Martino Pesenti, Venice (NV 2192)
1622 Giovanni Priuli, Venice (NV 2283)
1622 Pietro Paolo Torre, Venice (NV 2736)
1625 Orazio Modiana, Venice (NV 1868bis)

Oimè, l'antica fiamma (#139)

1584 Paolo Virchi, Venice (NV 2929)
1585 Luca Marenzio, Venice (NV 1622)
1589 Francesco Soriano, Venice (VE 1589[5])
1609 Giovanni Antonio Cirullo, Venice (NV 583)
1609 Vincenzo Liberti, Venice (NV 1512)
1619 Giovanni Domenico Rognoni Taeggio, Milan (NV 2361)
1621 Giovanni Francesco Anerio, Rome (NV 70)
1622 Alessandro Grandi, Venice (NV 1277)
1630 Michele Delipari, Venice (NV 702)
1649 Gaspare Filippi, Venice (NV 986)

Or che 'l meriggio ardente (#116)

1636 Alessandro Della Ciaia, Venice (NV 703)

Parlo, misero, o taccio (#29)

1600 Salamone Rossi, Venice (NV 2445)
1601 Francesco Stivori, Venice (NV 2647)
1602 Giovanni del Turco, Florence (NV 728)
1602 Santi Orlandi, Venice (NV 2057)
1602 Tommaso Pecci, Venice (NV 2157)
1604 Giovanni Battista Caletti, Venice (NV 463)

1604 Gerolamo Ghisuaglio, Venice (NV 1186)
1604 Benedetto Pallavicino, Venice (NV 2126)
1604 Francesco Spongia, Venice (NV 2779)
1605 Enrico Radesca, Milan (NV 2300)
1606 Orindio Bartolini, Venice (NV 255)
1606 Arcangelo Crivelli, Venice (NV 656)
1606 Sigismondo d'India, Venice (NV 823)
1606 Gio. Paolo Nodari, Copenhagen (VE 1606[2])
1606 Giuseppe de Puente, Naples (NV 2284)
1607 Scipione Dentice, Naples (NV 811)
1608 Geminiano Capilupi, Venice (NV 485)
1608 Antonio Cifra, Venice (NV 570)
1608 Vincenzo Liberti, Venice (NV 1511)
1608 Marco Antonio Negri, Venice (NV 2014)
1609 Severo Bonini, Florence (NV 393)
1609 Marsilio Casentini, Venice (NV 498)
1609 Giovanni Antonio Cirullo, Venice (NV 583)
1609 Ettore de la Marra, Naples (VE 1609[1])
1613 Francesco Rognoni Taeggio, Venice (NV 2359)
1614 Pietro Maria Marsolo, Venice (NV 1733)
1619 Claudio Monteverdi, Venice (NV 1936)
1619 Allegro Porto, Venice (NV 2258)
1621 Giovanni Francesco Anerio, Rome (NV 70)
1626 Carlo Gesualdo, Naples (NV 1178)
1634 Marco Scacchi, Venice (NV 2570)
1640 Francesco Colombini, Antwerp (NV 597)

Parto, o non parto? ahi come (#133)

1599 Luca Marenzio, Venice (NV 1639)
1601 Valerio Bona, Venice (NV 378)
1608 Giovanni Ghizzolo, Venice (NV 1194)
1614 Claudio Saracini, Venice (NV 2554)
1625 Orazio Modiana, Venice (NV 1868[bis])
1626 Francesco Costa, Venice (NV 639)

Perche di gemme t'incoroni, e d'oro (#98)

1585 Dominico Lauro, Venice (NV 2649)
1590 Francesco Mazza, Venice (NV 1762)

Perfidissimo volto (#13)

1586 Filippo de Monte, Venice (NV 772)
1592 Claudio Monteverdi, Venice (NV 1906)
1601 Valerio Bona, Venice (NV 378)
1602 Giulio Caccini, Florence (NV 450)
1602 Scipione Dentice, Naples (NV 810)
1602 Tommaso Pecci, Venice (NV 2157)
1603 Antonio Il Verso, Venice (NV 1333)
1605 Santi Orlandi, Venice (NV 2058)
1606 Marco da Gagliano, Venice (NV 1581)
1608 Geminiano Capilupi, Venice (NV 485)
1608 Giovanni Battista de Bellis, Naples (NV 694)
1610 Raffaello Rontani, Florence (NV 2362)
1611 Pietro Benedetti, Florence (NV 322)
1614 Giovanni Ghizzolo, Venice (NV 1189)
1617 Giuseppe Olivieri, Rome (NV 2051)
1623 Antonio Cifra, Rome (NV 574)

Piangea Donna crudele (#30)

1602 Santi Orlandi, Venice (NV 2057)
1629 Giovanni Rovetta, Venice (NV 2461)

Poiché non mi credete (#15)

1609 Santi Orlandi, Venice (NV 2060)
1612 Pietro Pace, Venice (NV 2081)
1613 Biagio Tomasi, Venice (NV 2728)
1614 Giovanni del Turco, Florence (NV 729)
1616 Enrico Radesca, Venice (NV 2305)
1625 Orazio Modiana, Venice (NV 1868bis)

Punto da un' ape, a cui (#9)

1600 Giuseppe Biffi, Naples (NV 368)

Pur venisti, cor mio (#128)

[1597?] Camillo Sarachi, [n.p.] (NV 2553bis)
1598 Luca Marenzio, Venice (NV 1637)
1600 Salamone Rossi, Venice (NV 2445)

1604 Gerolamo Ghisuaglio, Venice (NV 1186)
1606 Sigismondo d'India, Venice (NV 823)
1607 Giovan Domenico Montella, Naples (NV 1880)
1611 Stefano Bernardi, Rome (NV 334)
1611 Crescenzio Salzilli, Naples (NV 2538)
1612 Lucrezio Ruffulo, Venice (NV 2496)
1613 Pietro Pace, Venice (NV 2079)
1615 Lodovico Arrighetti, Venice (NV 1585)
1619 Allegro Porto, Venice (NV 2258)
1622 Giovanni Priuli, Venice (NV 2283)
1625 Orazio Modiana, Venice (NV 1868bis)

Quando mia cruda stella (#132)

1615 Francesco Pasquali, Venice (NV 2143)
1616 Sigismondo d'India, Venice (NV 829)
1616 Carlo Fiorillo, Rome (NV 987)
1618 Pomponio Nenna, Rome (NV 2032)
1623 Filippo Vitali, Florence (NV 2944)

Quanto per voi sofferse (#47)

1600 Guglielmo Arnoni, Venice (NV 169)
1601 Antonio Il Verso, Venice (NV 1336)

Quell'augellin, che canta (#115)

1591 Leone Leoni, Venice (NV 1503)
1595 Luca Marenzio, Venice (NV 1633)
1598 Giovanni Domenico Carrozza, Venice (NV 495)
1598 Giovanni Domenico Carrozza, Venice (NV 495) [begins at "Ma ben arde nel
   core"]
1598 Francesco Stivori, Venice (NV 2651)
1599 Filippo de Monte, Venice (NV 734)
1599 Filippo de Monte, Venice (NV 734) [begins at "Ma ben arde nel core"]
1603 Claudio Monteverdi, Venice (NV 1914)
1606 Nicolo Gistou, Copenhagen (VE 1606²)
1606 Nicolo Gistou, Copenhagen (VE 1606²) [begins at "Ma ben arde nel core"]
1607 Marc'Antonio Ingegneri, Venice (NV 1348)
1610 Alessandro Scialla, Naples (NV 2592)
1610 Alessandro Scialla, Naples (NV 2592) [begins at "Ma ben arde nel core"]
1611 Stefano Bernardi, Rome (NV 334)

1615 Sigismondo d'India, Venice (NV 827)
1616 Domenico Visconti, Venice (NV 2934)
1619 Giovanni Valentini, Venice (NV 2784)

Quest'è pur il mio core (#99)

1597 Geminiano Capilupi, Venice (NV 2835)
1600 Guglielmo Arnoni, Venice (NV 169)
1601 Luzzasco Luzzaschi, Rome (NV 1524)
1602 Scipione Dentice, Naples (NV 810)
1607 Giovanni Priuli, Venice (NV 2281)
1615 Flaminio Comanedo, Venice (NV 604)
1615 Marco da Gagliano, Venice (NV 1585)
1627 Giovan Pietro Bucchianti, Venice (NV 438)
1635 Giovan Giacomo Arrigoni, Venice (NV 170)

Rideva (ahi crudo affetto) (#45)

1608 Giovanni Battista de Bellis, Naples (NV 694)
1608 Giovanni Ghizzolo, Venice (NV 1194)
1610 Antonio Savetta, Venice (NV 2561)
1616 Claudio Pari, Palermo (NV 2140)

Se 'l vostro cor, Madonna (#102)

1614 Francesco Dognazzi, Venice (NV 843)
1619 Claudio Monteverdi, Venice (NV 1936)

Se per estremo ardore (#79)

1592 Claudio Monteverdi, Venice (NV 1906)

Se vuoi ch'io torni a le tue fiamme, Amore (#143)

1589 Camillo Zanotti, Venice (NV 3012)

Si, mi dicesti, e io (#61)

1588 Benedetto Pallavicino, Venice (NV 2114)
1590 Flaminio Tresti, Venice (NV 2750)
1591 Paolo Isnardi, Venice (VE 1591[5])
1593 Francesco Guami, Venice (NV 1299)

1594 Filippo de Monte, Venice (NV 800)
1596 Peter Philips, Antwerp (NV 2209)
1602 Luzio Billi, Venice (NV 370)
1603 Giuseppe Colaianni, Venice (NV 592)
1616 Enrico Radesca, Venice (NV 2305)
1619 Giulio Medici, Venice (NV 1787)
1629 Giovanni Rovetta, Venice (NV 2461)
1634 Marco Scacchi, Venice (NV 2570)

Sì presso a voi, mio foco (#55)

1582 Luca Marenzio, Venice (NV 1613)
1615 Antonio Cifra, Rome (NV 565)
1619 Giovanni Domenico Rognoni Taeggio, Milan (NV 2361)

Sì voglio, e vorrò sempre (#14)

1607 Scipione Dentice, Naples (NV 811)
1612 Orazio Brognonico, Venice (NV 427)
1619 Antonio Marastoni, Venice (NV 1571)
1622 Giovanni Priuli, Venice (NV 2283)
1626 Giovanni Battista Crivelli, Venice (NV 657)
1634 Marco Scacchi, Venice (NV 2570)

Soavissimo ardore (#59)

1586 Paolo Masnelli, Venice (NV 1743)
1592 Filippo de Monte, Venice (NV 776)
1598 Francesco Stivori, Venice (NV 2651)
1603–4 Adriano Banchieri, Milan (NV 237)
1605 Santi Orlandi, Venice (NV 2058)
1608 Dattilo Roccia, Naples (NV 2355)
1609 Giovanni Ghizzolo, Venice (NV 1193)
1615 Nicolo Rubini, Venice (NV 2470)
1617 Giuseppe Marini, Venice (NV 1720)
1619 Giovanni Domenico Rognoni Taeggio, Milan (NV 2361)

Splende la fredda luna (#56)

1586 Filippo de Monte, Venice (NV 772)
1600 Antonio Il Verso, Venice (NV 1332)

Stracciami pure il core (#107)

1590 Flaminio Tresti, Venice (NV 2750)
1592 Claudio Monteverdi, Venice (NV 1906)
1596 Paolo Masnelli, Venice (NV 1744)

T'amo mia vita, la mia cara vita (#80)

1591 Vincenzo Isnardi, Venice (VE 1591[5])
1593 Vittoria Aleotti, Venice (NV 46)
1593 Benedetto Pallavicino, Venice (NV 2118)
1594 Filippo de Monte, Venice (NV 800)
1597 Allesandro Savioli, Venice (NV 2563)
1599 Ruggero Giovannelli, Venice (NV 1223)
1601 Luzzasco Luzzaschi, Rome (NV 1524)
1604 Giovan Giacomo Gastoldi, Venice (NV 1109)
1605 Antonio Cifra, Rome (NV 569)
1605 Claudio Monteverdi, Venice (NV 1922)
1606 Domenico Brunetti, Venice (NV 436)
1606 Hans Nielsen, Venice (NV 2041)
1608 Mogens Pedersoen, Venice (NV 2169)
1609 Giovanni Antonio Cirullo, Venice (NV 583)
1614 Francesco Genvino, Naples (NV 1122)
1616 Enrico Radesca, Venice (NV 2305)
1617 Filippo Vitali, Florence (NV 2946)
1619 Allegro Porto, Venice (NV 2258)
1620 Biagio Marini, Venice (NV 1713)
1622 Giovanni Priuli, Venice (NV 2283)

Tirsi morir volea (#87)

1578 Leenard Meldert, Venice (NV 1791)
1580 Giulio Cesare Gabussi, Venice (NV 1049)
1580 Luca Marenzio, Venice (NV 1597)
1580 Giovanni Piccioni, Venice (NV 2220)
1581 Benedetto Pallavicino, Venice (NV 2105)
1581 Jacob de Wert, Venice (NV 2988)
1582 Democrito Vicomanni, Perugia (NV 2902)
1584 Cristofano Malvezzi, Venice (NV 1558)
1584 Alesandro Milleville, Ferrara (NV 1859)
1585 Giuseppe Caimo, Venice (NV 460)
1585 Vincenzo Dal Pozzo, Venice (NV 687)

1585 Fillippo Nicoletti, Venice (NV 2036)
1586 Filippo de Monte, Venice (NV 772)
1586 Giulio Eremita, Ferrara (NV 892)
1586 Ascanio Trombetti, Venice (NV 2759)
1587 Andrea Gabrieli, Venice (NV 1046)
1587 Camillo Zanotti, Venice (NV 3011)
1588 Jean de Castro, Antwerp (NV 509)
1588 Giovanni Battista Gabella, Venice (NV 1025)
1588 Filippo Maria Perabovi, Venice (NV 2177)
1590 Giovanni Croce, Venice (NV 670)
1594 Carlo Gesualdo, Ferrara (NV 1153)
1602 Luzio Billi, Venice (NV 370)
1604 Luzzasco Luzzaschi, Venice (NV 1531)
1613 Biagio Tomasi, Venice (NV 2728)
1617 Giacomo Fornaci, Venice (NV 1008)
1633 Giovanni Felice Sances, Venice (NV 2546)

Troppo ben può questo tiranno Amore (#7)

1587 Filippo de Monte, Venice (NV 773)
1601 Luzzasco Luzzaschi, Rome (NV 1524)
1601 Francesco Stivori, Venice (NV 2647)
1603 Tommaso Pecci, Venice (NV 2153)
1605 Claudio Monteverdi, Venice (NV 1922)
1606 Agostino Agazzari, Venice (NV 17)
1606 Marco da Gagliano, Venice (NV 1581)
1608 Antonio Cifra, Venice (NV 570)
1609 Vincenzo Liberti, Venice (NV 1512)
1610 Raffaello Rontani, Florence (NV 2362)
1610 Salomone Rossi, Venice (NV 2454)
1614 Amadio Freddi, Venice (NV 1018)
1615 Lorenzo Ratti, Venice (NV 2320)
1617 Giuseppe Palazzotto-Tagliavia, Naples (NV 2087)
1621 Martino Pesenti, Venice (NV 2192)
1624 Innocenzo Vivarino, Venice (NV 2953)
1630 Michele Delipari, Venice (NV 702)
1689 Angelo Berardi, Bologna (NV 327)

Tu parti a pena giunto (#137)

1593 Orazio Scaletta, Venice (NV 2573)
1600 Paolo Sartorio, Venice (NV 2559)

1604 Benedetto Pallavicino, Venice (NV 2126)
1608 Giovanni Francesco Anerio, Venice (NV 72)
1609 Giovanni Antonio Cirullo, Venice (NV 583)
1609 Santi Orlandi, Venice (NV 2060)
1611 Stefano Bernardi, Rome (NV 334)
1613 Pietro Pace, Venice (NV 2079)
1614 Francesco Genvino, Naples (NV 1122)
1614 Salomone Rossi, Venice (NV 2444)
1615 Antonio Cifra, Venice (NV 571)
1617 Giacomo Fornaci, Venice (NV 1008)
1620 Claudio Saracini, Venice (NV 2555)
1622 Alessandro Grandi, Venice (NV 1277)
1623 Filippo Vitali, Florence (NV 2944)
1626 Giovanni Pasta, Venice (NV 2148)
1626 Cristofano Piochi, Venice (NV 2230)
1627 Giovan Pietro Bucchianti, Venice (NV 438)

Udite, amanti, udite (#83)

1600 Guglielmo Arnoni, Venice (NV 169)
1600 Filippo de Monte, Venice (NV 806)
1604 Giovan Giacomo Gastoldi, Venice (NV 1109)
1606 Hans Nielsen, Venice (NV 2041)
1607 Ludovico Bellanda, Venice (NV 292)
1607 Giovan Domenico Montella, Naples (NV 1880)
1607 Giovanni Priuli, Venice (NV 2281)
1608 Paolo Quagliati, Venice (NV 2294)
1609 Vincenzo Liberti, Venice (NV 1512)
1613 Benedetto Magni, Venice (NV 1550)
1621 Pietro Maria Lamoretti, Venice (NV 1375)
1623 Giacinto Merulo, Venice (NV 1837)
1629 Giovanni Rovetta, Venice (NV 2461)
1634 Marco Scacchi, Venice (NV 2570)

Udite lagrimosi (#25)

1594 Luca Marenzio, Venice (NV 1629)
1595 Jacob de Wert, Venice (NV 2994)
1595 Jacob de Wert, Venice (NV 2994) [begins at "La mia Donna crudel piu de l'inferno"]

1600 Filippo de Monte, Venice (NV 806)

1600 Filippo de Monte, Venice (NV 806) [begins at "La mia Donna crudel piu de l'inferno"]

1600 Salamone Rossi, Venice (NV 2445)

1602 Giovanni Piccioni, Venice (NV 2226)

1605 Antonio Cifra, Rome (NV 569)

1606 Domenico Brunetti, Venice (NV 436)

1608 Giovanni Ghizzolo, Venice (NV 1194)

1611 Stefano Bernardi, Rome (NV 334)

1611 Lucia Quinciani, Venice (NV 2015)

1615 Alessandro Grandi, Venice (NV 1271)

1617 Bartolomeo Barbarino, Venice (NV 239)

1617 Giovanni Nicolò Mezzogorri, Venice (NV 1840)

1619 Lelio Basile, Venice (NV 262)

1619 Lelio Basile, Venice (NV 262) [begins at "La mia Donna crudel piu de l'inferno"]

1619 Giulio Medici, Venice (NV 1787)

1620 Claudio Saracini, Venice (NV 2555)

1624 Sigismondo d'India, Rome (NV 830)

1652 Domenico Dal Pane, Rome (NV 684)

Un amoroso agone (#100)

1675 Carlo Grossi, Venice (NV 1289)

Un bacio solo, a tante pene? Cruda (#38)

1588 Jacob de Wert, Venice (NV 2992)

1607 Ludovico Bellanda, Venice (NV 292)

1608 Giovanni Ghizzolo, Venice (NV 1194)

1616 Scipione Lacorcia, Naples (NV 1365)

1616 Enrico Radesca, Venice (NV 2305)

1618 Francesco Pasquali, Venice (NV 2144)

1620 Bizzarro Accademico Capriccioso, Venice (NV 371)

1628 Giovanni Battista Locatello, Venice (NV 1516)

Un cibo di fuor dolce, e dentro amaro (#36)

1609 Giovanni Antonio Cirullo, Venice (NV 583)

Una Farfalla cupida, e vagante (#41)

16ѹ Giuseppe Biffi, Naples (NV 368)
1604 Giovan Giacomo Gastoldi, Venice (NV 1109)
1604 Benedetto Pallavicino, Venice (NV 2126)
1607 Marc'Antonio Ingegneri, Venice (NV 1348)
1618 Ubaldino Malevolti, Venice (NV 2144)
1626 Giovan Pietro Biandrà, Venice (NV 363)
1635 Giovan Giacomo Arrigoni, Venice (NV 170)

Veder il mio bel sole (#149)

1602 Stefano Felis, Venice (NV 926)
1604 Giovanni Priuli, Venice (NV 2280)

Vivo in foco amoroso (#141)

1590 Orazio Vecchi, Venice (NV 2815)
1600 Simone Molinara, Venice (NV 1873)
1629 Giovanni Rovetta, Venice (NV 2461)
1636 Giovanni Antonio Rigatti, Venice (NV 2345)

Voi, dissi, e sospirando (#73)

1594 Giulio Ferro, Venice (NV 968)
1608 Dattilo Roccia, Naples (NV 2355)
1614 Abbondio Antonelli, Rome (NV 91)
1616 Sigismondo d'India, Venice (NV 829)

Voi pur da me partite, anima dura (#126)

1592 Filippo de Monte, Venice (NV 776)
1598 Francesco Stivori, Venice (NV 2651)
1599 Tommaso Pecci, Venice (NV 2164)
1601 Ottavio Bargnani, Venice (NV 249)
1603 Giuseppe Colaianni, Venice (NV 592)
1603 Claudio Monteverdi, Venice (NV 1914)
1606 Giuseppe de Puente, Naples (NV 2284)
1607 Crescenzio Salzilli, Naples (NV 2537)
1608 Francesco Rasi, Venice (NV 2316)
1609 Bernardino Bertolotti, Venice (NV 354)

1611 Pietro Benedetti, Florence (NV 322)
1612 Antonio Il Verso, Venice (NV 1339)
1616 Marcello Albano, Naples (NV 36)
1616 Domenico Belli, Venice (NV 304)
1616 Carlo Fiorillo, Rome (NV 987)
1616 Claudio Pari, Palermo (NV 2140)
1617 Amante Franzoni, Venice (NV 1014)
1620 Bizzarro Accademico Capriccioso, Venice (NV 371)
1622 Pietro Paolo Torre, Venice (NV 2736)
1622 Giacomo Tropea, Naples (NV 2764)
1623 Antonio Cifra, Rome (NV 574)
1623 Francesco Spongia, Venice (NV 2780)
1626 Giovanni Pasta, Venice (NV 2148)
1627 Simplicio Todeschi, Venice (NV 2725)

Voi volete ch'io mora (#31)

1591 Pietro Philipi [Philips], Antwerp (VE 1591[1])
1595 Carlo Gesualdo, Ferrara (NV 1163)
1603 Tommaso Pecci, Venice (NV 2153)
1606 Orindio Bartolini, Venice (NV 254)
1620 Richard Dering, Antwerp (NV 814)
1621 Martino Pesenti, Venice (NV 2192)
1634 Marco Scacchi, Venice (NV 2570)

Volgea l'anima mia soavemente (#84)

1600 Guglielmo Arnoni, Venice (NV 169)
1603 Claudio Monteverdi, Venice (NV 1914)
1609 Giovanni Ghizzolo, Venice (NV 1193)
1610 Giovan Paolo Costa, Venice (NV 646)
1613 Antonio Cifra, Rome (NV 563)

NOTES

Quotations from Shakespeare are from *The Riverside Shakespeare*. Unless otherwise noted, quotations from other English poets are from Greenblatt, *The Norton Anthology of English Literature*. Quotations from Petrarch are from *The Poetry of Petrarch*, translated by David Young.

Abbreviations used in the notes:

1587: *Rime di diversi celebri poeti dell'età nostra*, 1587.
1590: *Nova scelta di rime di diversi eccellenti scrittori dell'età nostra*, 1590.
1591: Guarini, *Il pastor fido: Tragicomedia pastorale*, 1591.
1598: Guarini, *Rime del molto illustre signor cavaliere Battista Guarini*, 1598.
1737: Guarini, *Delle opere del cavalier Battista Guarini*, 1737.
1999: Stevens, *Claudio Monteverdi: Songs and Madrigals*, [1999].

Acknowledgments

"cara mia luce": Guarini, *Io veggio pur pietate, anchorche tardi*, #81 in this volume.

Preface

Mentre vaga Angioletta: #122 in this volume • "a very accomplished singer": a description of a concert that parallels Guarini's is quoted in Durante and Martellotti, "Genesi e sviluppo dei madrigali di Battista Guarini," 156–57 • "precise and free": "Tempra d'arguto suon pieghevol voce"—literally, "she strengthens her flexible voice with intelligence and wit" • "My life's become": #100 in this volume • "Cruel and beautiful": #33 in this volume • "To speak": #29 in this volume • "but then you fled": #128 in this volume • "verbal icons": William K. Wimsatt, *The Verbal Icon: Studies in the Meaning of Poetry* ([Lexington]: University of Kentucky Press, [1954]).

Introduction

"an important Ferrarese musical family": see Hartmann, "Battista Guarini and '*Il pastor fido*,'" for a review of Guarini's life at court, in particular in relationship to music • "revising his madrigals": see Ossi, "Between *Madrigale* and *Altro genere di canto*" and Tomlinson ("Guarini and the Epigrammatic Style") • "begun in the early 1580s": Chater, "'Un Pasticcio di Madrigaletti'?", 141 • "one of Italy's two most celebrated living poets": Tomlinson, "Guarini and the Epigrammatic Style," 73 • "I never saw the sun": Petrarch, *Canzoniere* 144 • "the poetry of ceaseless self-qualification": Took, "Petrarch," 92 • "the viewless wings of Poesy": Keats, "Ode to a Nightingale" • "If it's not love": Petrarch, *Canzoniere* 132 • "Song of Troilus": Chaucer, *Troilus and Criseyde*, 1.400–420 • "Not marble": Shakespeare, sonnet 55 • "My mistress' eyes": Shakespeare, sonnet 130 • "Diana's form": Petrarch, *Canzoniere* 52 • "the significant in the apparently insignificant": Oldcorn, "Lyric Poetry," 259 • "Se mai cortese fusti": Oldcorn, "Lyric Poetry," 259, indented to mark the difference of short and long lines; the literal translation is Oldcorn's, lineated and slightly changed to correspond with the lines in the original Italian • Ciotti: see Nuovo, *The Book Trade in the Italian Renaissance* and Martinelli, "La formazione del libro delle *Rime* di Battista Guarini" • "Most humane readers": 1598, "A benigni lettori" (to the gentle readers), n.p.; my translation • "sprezzatura": Baldesar Castiglione, *The Book of the Courtier*, translated by Sir Thomas Hoby (1561), edited by Walter Raleigh (Renascence Editions online, 1997) • "data": Lorenzo Bianconi, *Music in the Seventeenth Century*, 2 • "More than nineteen hundred settings": Vassalli and Pompilio, "Indice delle rime di Battista Guarini poste in musica" and Chater, "*Il pastor fido* and Music" • "only one line": Tim Shephard, "Voice, Decorum and Seduction in Florigerio's 'Music Lesson'" • "new rules": *L'Artusi, overo delle imperfettioni della moderna musica* (Venice, Giacomo Vincenti, 1600), in Fabbri, *Monteverdi*, 35 • "Another report": Vincenzo Giustiniani, *Discorso sopra la musica de' suoi tempi* (ca. 1625), in Fabbri, *Monteverdi*, 46.

Section 1

Introduction: "All you who want a quiet life": Guarini, *Chi vuol haver felice*, #1 in this volume • "One day as I unwarily did gaze": Spenser, *Amoretti*, sonnet 16, in *Edmund Spenser's 'Amoretti' and 'Epithalamion': A Critical Edition*, ed. Kenneth J. Larsen, Medieval and Renaissance Texts & Studies, vol. 146 (Tempe, AZ: Medieval and Renaissance Texts and Studies, 1977), available at the Internet Archive, https://archive.org/; spelling and punctuation modernized • "knavish lad": *A Midsummer Night's Dream*, 3.2.

1   *1598*, CVII. *Fuggasi Amore* (run away from love).

2   *1598*, XLVIIII. *Incontinenza amorosa* (restlessness in love). "Altro" in line 9 is corrected from *1737*, p. 94 (*1598* reads "alto").

3   *1598*, XVI. *O godere, o non bramare* (to enjoy or not to desire).

4   *1598*, IIII. *Stanza d'Amore* (love's room).

5   *1598*, CV. *Amorosa querela* (complaint in love).

6   *1587*, p. 194.

7   *1598*, CVIII. *Fuga restia* (unwilling flight). In *1587* there is a longer version of the poem, but this version from *1598* is more succinct and balanced; Guarini presumably revised it for that edition.

8   *1598*, LXXVIII. *Lo spiritello* (the sprite).

9   *1598*, LXXIII. *Baciate labra* (kiss the lips).

10   *1598*, XXII. *Donna costante* (faithful lady).

Section 2

Introduction: "Only your cruel heart": Guarini, *Se'n voi pose*, #11 in this volume • "male gaze": see Laura Mulvey, "Visual Pleasure and Narrative Cinema," *Screen* 16.3 (Autumn 1975): 6–18 • "What, have I thus betray'd": Sidney, *Astrophil and Stella*, sonnet 47.

11   *1598*, III. *Bellezza ingrata* (ungrateful beauty).

12   *1587*, p. 194.

13   *1598*, XCVIII. *Bellezza disleale* (unfaithful beauty). A longer version exists in *1587*.

14   *1598*, CIIII. *O tutto o nulla* (all or nothing).

15   *1598*, CXV. *Fè non creduta* (faithfulness untrusted).

16   *1598*, XCVIIII. *Laura perfida* (unfaithful laurel).

17   *1598*, XXXV. *Mortal gelosia* (deadly jealousy).

18   *1598*, LXXIIII. *Bellezza ambiziosa* (ambitious beauty).

19   *1598*, CXVIII. *Camilla Bella. Dialogo. Amante & Amore* (beautiful Camilla—a dialogue of lover and Love).

20   *1598*, XII. *Sogno della sua donna* (his lady's dream).

21   *1598*, XLIII. *Donna dura poco dura* (the cruel lady, too cruel).

22   *1598*, VII. *Fierezza vana* (vain rashness).

23   *1591*, 3.3, p. 87; I follow Monteverdi's omission of three lines from the original, between lines 9 and 10, here (see *1999*, 48, 50).

24   *1598*, XVII. *La bella Cacciatrice* (the beautiful huntress).

25   *1591*, 3.6, pp. 102–3. This popular text from *Il pastor fido* was set as a separate madrigal by many contemporary composers. It does not appear in *1587* or *1598*.

Section 3

Introduction: "In that fierce heat": Guarini, *A voi, Donna*, #26 in this volume • "I find no peace": Petrarch, *Canzoniere* 134; Franz Liszt based the second of his *Sonnets of Petrarch* for piano solo on this poem ("Pace non trovo"; Liszt knew it as sonnet 104) • "At last his sail-broad vans": Milton, *Paradise Lost*, 2.927–38.

26 *1598*, XIIII. *Cor volante* (longing for you). Ellipsis in line 9 supplied from *1737*, 63 (*destino*).

27 *1598*, LVII. *Amante invitto* (the undefeated lover). Ellipses in lines 2 and 4 supplied from *1737*, p. 76 (*destino, fortuna*).

28 *1598*, XXXIII. *Amante timido* (the fearful lover). Ellipsis in line 10 supplied from *1737*, p. 69 (*fato*). "To screw my courage": *Macbeth*, 1.7.

29 *1598*, LIIII. *Amante poco ardito* (the lukewarm lover). Frost, "The Oven Bird," in *The Norton Anthology of Modern and Contemporary Poetry*, edited by Jahan Ramazani, Richard Ellmann, and Robert O'Clair, 3rd ed. (W.W. Norton, New York, 2003), 1. 211.

30 *1598*, XLIIII. *Core in augello* (the heart in a little bird). Ellipsis in line 3 supplied from *1737*, p. 72 (*destino*).

31 *1598*, XXIII. *O vita, o morte* (either life or death). "To be or not to be": *Hamlet* 3.1; "unkindest cut": *Julius Caesar*, 3.2.

32 *1598*, LXI. *Mano stretta* (the hand squeezed).

33 *1598*, XLI. *Poter di Donna amata* (the power of the beloved lady). Ellipsis in line 2 supplied from *1737*, p. 71 (*stella*).

34 *1598*, LV. *Mirar mortale* (deadly glance).

35 *1598*, XXIIII. *Cangiati sguardi* (changed looks). "my play's last scene": Donne, *Holy Sonnets*.

36 *1598*, XVIII. *Mandorla inzuccherata* (sugared almond). "O taste and see": Psalm 34.

37 *1598*, LXXV. *Bacio penoso* (the painful kiss).

38 *1598*, LXXVI. *Un bacio e poco* (one kiss is not much).

39 *1598*, XXXI. *Oimè gradita* ("alas" welcomed).

Section 4

Introduction: "I thought her blazing eyes": Guarini, *Ardemmo insieme*, #40 in this volume • "I burn and turn to ice": Petrarch, *Canzoniere 134* • "In this strange labyrinth": Lady Mary Wroth, sonnet 1, in "A Crown of Sonnets Dedicated to Love" in *Pamphilia to Amphilanthus*, Renascence Editions, http://www.luminarium.org/renascence-editions/ (spelling and punctuation modernized).

40 *1598*, XXV. *Incontro d'occhi* (a meeting of eyes). "Seeming": *Hamlet*, 1.2.

41 *1598*, XXXVII. *Core in Farfalla* (the heart in a moth). "Seeking for light": *Love's Labor's Lost*, 1.1.

42 *1598*, CXII. *Recidiva d'amore* (love's relapse).

43 *1598*, X. *Sogno della sua Donna* (his lady's dream). Ellipsis in line 6 supplied from *1737*, p. 61 (*fato*). Keats: "La Belle Dame sans Merci."

44 *1598*, XI. *Sogno della sua Donna* (his lady's dream). "The lunatic": *A Midsummer Night's Dream*, 5.1.

45   *1598*, L. *Pianto di riso* (tears from laughter).

46   *1598*, XV. *Fumoso pianto* (smoky tears).

47   *1598*, XXI. *Pietoso sguardo* (a look of mercy). Francesca: Dante, *Inferno*, canto 5; Petrarch: *Canzonieri* 241.

48   *1598*, CXIIII. *Pietà se non amore* (mercy, if not love).

49   *1598*, XXVIII. *Beltà possente* (powerful beauty).

50   *1598*, XLII. *O negar, o attendere* (either deny or be patient).

51   *1737*, pp. 131–32.

52   *1737*, pp. 127–28.

53   *1598*, CX. *Recidiva d'amore* (love's relapse).

54   *1587*, p. 195.

55   *1598*, VIIII. *Febre amorosa* (loving fever).

56   *1598*, LI. *Fredda bellezza* (cold beauty). Ellipsis in line 4 supplied from *1737* (*fatal*).

57   *1598*, V. *Amor inevitabile* (inevitable love).

58   *1598*, VI. *Amante infermo* (the sick lover).

59   *1598*, LVIIII. *Viso avampato* (flushed face).

60   *1598*, LVI. *Madonna inferma* (the sick lady). Ellipsis in line 4 supplied from *1737* (*stella*).

61   *1598*, CVI. *Sì, e no* (yes and no).

62   *1598*, LXXXII. *Amor non creduto* (love not believed).

Section 5

Introduction: "Remake your double selves as one": Guarini, *Anime pellegrine*, #63 in this volume • Romeo: *Romeo and Juliet*, 2.2 • "lust in action": sonnet 129 • Wyatt: "They flee from me" • "Now welcome night": Spenser, "Epithalamion" (spelling modernized) • "Love, let us pause": Petrarch, *Canzoniere* 192.

63   *1598*, XIII. *Leggi amorose* (laws of love). "Our two souls": Donne, "A Valediction: Forbidding Mourning."

64   *1598*, LIII. *Beltà felicitante* (pleasurable beauty). *"Mein ist dein herz!"*: Franz Schubert, "Mein!" in *Die Schöne Müllerin*.

65   *1587*, p. 201.

66   *1598*, LXXII. *Bacio rubato* (stolen kiss). Chater concludes that Guarini wrote a longer version first (set to music by Luca Marenzio) and later shortened it to the version used here ("'Un Pasticcio di Madrigaletti'?" 144–45).

67   *1598*, LXXI. *Bacio rubato* (stolen kiss).

68   *1591*, 1.2, p. 19, with an additional line added by Annibale Coma (*Il secondo libro di madrigali* [Venice, *1588*]).

69   *1598*, LXXXI. *Pietà crudele* (cruel mercy).

70   *1598*, LXXXIII. *Pietà dolente* (sad mercy). The Consort of Musicke has a recording of twenty-one settings of this one madrigal: *Cor mio, deh non languire: 21 Settings from Guarini* (Musica Oscura, 1995).

71   *1598*, XXXIIII. *Pretensione d'amor leggitima* (hope for real love).

72   *1598*, LXXVIIII. *Rosa donata* (a rose given).

73   *1598*, LX. *Opportuna risposta* (opportune reply).

74   *1598*, LXXX. *Amoroso furore di Teocrito* (loving frenzy, from Theocritus).

75   *1598*, XXX. *Sospiro di Madonna* (the lady's sigh).

76   *1598*, XXVIIII. *Natale dell'amante* (the lover's birthday).

77   *1598*, LXII. *Pietà fa bella* (mercy makes [her] beautiful).

78   *1598*, LXXVII. *Parole, e baci* (words and kisses).

79   *1999*, p. 184. Set by Monteverdi, *Il terza libro di madrigali*, 1592. Both Stevens (*Claudio Monteverdi: Songs and Madrigals*) and Tomlinson ("Guarini and the Epigrammatic Style") ascribe the text to Guarini, but I have not found it in *1587*, *1598*, or *1737*. Blake's children: "The Chimney Sweeper" (*Songs of Innocence*, 1789) is one example.

80   *1598*, LXX. *Parola di donna amante* (the speech of the lady in love).

81   *1598*, LXIV. *Donna pietosa* (merciful lady).

82   *1737*, p. 126.

83   *1598*, LXIII. *Donna pietosa* (merciful lady).

84   *1598*, LXVI. *Pietà di Donna* (the lady's mercy).

85   *1598*, LXV. *Donna pietosa* (merciful lady).

86   *1999*, p. 34, from Monteverdi, *Madrigali*, 1587. This madrigal does not appear in editions of Guarini (*1587*, *1598*, *1737*) but is ascribed to Guarini by Vassalli and Pompilio ("Indice delle rime di Battista Guarini poste in musica") and a number of other sources (e.g., Solerti, *Le rime di Torquato Tasso*, 1.94).

87   *1598*, CXLVIII. *Concorso d'occhi amorosi* (contest of loving eyes). "A cause of some scandal": Steele, *Luca Marenzio*, 221.

Section 6

Introduction: "If you don't know": Guarini, *Ch'i' t'ami*, #88 in this volume • "Since brass, nor stone": Shakespeare, sonnet 65 • joust: annotation in Greenblatt, *Norton Anthology of English Literature* • "Having this day": Sidney, *Astrophil and Stella*, 41 • "unsuccessful attempts to stage the play": Fenlon, "Music and Spectacle at the Gonzaga Court," 92–93 • Chater: "'Un pasticcio di madrigaletti'?" 141.

88   *1591*, 3.3, p. 85.

89   *1591*, 1.2, p. 10.

90   *1591*, 3.4, pp. 92–93.

91   *1591*, 3.4, p. 93.

92   *1591*, 3.4, p. 94.
93   *1591*, 4.9, p. 165. *"Batti, batti"*: *Don Giovanni*, 1.4.
94   *1591*, 4.9, p. 165–66.
95   *1591*, 4.9, p. 166.
96   *1591*, 4.9, p. 166.
97   *1591*, 4.9, p. 167.

Section 7

Introduction: "Why do you put on airs": Guarini, *Perche di gemme*, #98 in this
volume • "As her white foot": Petrarch, *Canzoniere* 165 • "I remember": *As
You Like It*, 2.4 • "He was to imagine": *As You Like It*, 3.2.
98   *1598*, XXXVI. *Gelosia non temuta* (not afraid of jealousy).
99   *1598*, LXVIII. *Amor penoso* (painful love).
100   *1598*, XLVIII. *Amoroso berzaglio* (love's target).
101   *1737*, p. 130.
102   *1598*, XLV. *Pietà male usata* (mercy badly managed).
103   *1598*, CI. *Foco di sdegno* (fire of scorn).
104   *1598*, unnumbered madrigal following CI. *Risposta del Tasso* (Tasso's
response).
105   *1999*, p. 30; ascribed to Guarini by Stevens, *1999*, p. 30; ascribed to Tasso by
Solerti, *Le rime di Torquato Tasso*, 2.454.
106   *1598*, XL. *Fede giustificata* (loyalty justified).
107   *1737*, p. 129. "Donne speaking to God": for example, *Holy Sonnet* 14: "Batter
my heart, three-personed God."
108   *1737*, p. 94.
109   *1598*, XXXII. *Possesso del cor perduto* (possession of the lost heart).
110   *1598*, VIII. *Amor costante* (constant love).
111   *1598*, LXXXIIII. *Amor costante* (constant love). *Lasciate ogni speranza*:
Dante, *Inferno*, canto 3.
112   *1591*, 3.6, pp. 106–7.

Section 8

Introduction: " How similar we lovers are": Guarini, *O come se' gentile*, #113 in
this volume • "Loving in truth": Sidney, *Astrophil and Stella*, 1.
113   *1598*, LII. *Avventuroso augello* (lucky little bird). Ellipsis in line 8 in *1598*
supplied from *1737*, p. 75 (*sorte*).
114   *1598*, XVIIII. *Felicità d'Usignuolo* (the nightingale's happiness). Nightingale:
Keats, "Ode to a Nightingale."
115   *1591*, 1.1, p. 7, with three lines omitted to follow Monteverdi's use in *Il
quatro libro di madrigali*, 1603 (see *1999*, p. 174).

116   *1598*, XXVII. *Eco amorosa* (loving echo).

117   *1598*, XXVI. *Eco amorosa* (loving echo).

118   *1598*, XLVII. *Canta dicea Madonna* (my lady tells me to sing).

119   *1598*, XLVI. *Canta dicea Madonna* (my lady tells me to sing). Court: see, for example, Newcomb, *The Madrigal at Ferrara*.

120   *1598*, I. *Per D[onna] Ignes Marchesa di Grana* (for Lady Ignes, Marchioness of Grana). Ignez Argotta: Fenlon, "Music and Spectacle at the Gonzaga Court," 92.

121   *1598*, II. *Per D[onna] Ignes Marchesa di Grana* (for Lady Ignes, Marchioness of Grana).

122   *1598*, CXLV. *Gorga da cantatrice* (the singer's throat). "shadows number-less": Keats, "Ode to a Nightingale."

123   *1737*, p. 125.

Section 9

Introduction: "But when two loving hearts": Guarini, *Credetel voi*, #124 in this volume • "Ask me why": Herrick, "The Primrose," in *Hesperides*, from *The Works of Robert Herrick*, ed. Alfred Pollard, www.luminarium.org • "From you I have been absent": Shakespeare, sonnet 98 • "When that day comes": Herrick, "His Sailing from Julia," in *Hesperides*, from *The Works of Robert Herrick*, ed. Alfred Pollard, www.luminarium.org • "He who decides": Petrarch, *Canzoniere* 80.

124   *1598*, LXXXV. *Morte della partenza* (death in parting). "Donne-like para-dox": for example, Holy Sonnet 10: "Death, thou shalt die."

125   *1598*, LXXXVI. *Madonna parte* (my lady goes away).

126   *1598*, LXXXVIIII. *Partita della amata* (the beloved's departure).

127   *1598*, XCII. *Dipartenza mortale* (fatal departure). "But 'Ah,' Desire still cries": Sidney, *Astrophil and Stella*, 71. Orlando: *As You Like It*, 5.2.

128   *1598*, XCVII. *Arrivo dell'amante* (the lover's arrival). "a vision, or a waking dream": Keats, "Ode to a Nightingale."

129   *1598*, XX. *Al tornar di Madonna* (at the return of my lady).

130   *1598*, LXXXVIII. *Partita dell'amante* (the lover's departure).

131   *1598*, XCI. *Partita dolorosa* (sad parting). Ellipses in lines 4 and 7 supplied from *1737*, p. 87 (*destino, fatale*). *Truly, Madly, Deeply*: a film with Juliet Stevenson and Alan Rickman (1990, dir. Anthony Minghella).

132   *1598*, XCIIII. *Lontananza mortale* (fatal distance). Ellipsis in line 1 supplied from *1737*, p. 88 (*stella*). "the lover, / Sighing like furnace": *As You Like It*, 2.7.

133   *1598*, XC. *Dipartenza restia* (reluctant departure). Ellipsis in line 8 supplied from *1737*, p. 87 (*sorte*).

134   *1591*, 3.3, p. 92.

135   *1598*, XCIII. *Lontananza dolente* (sad distance).

136   *1598*, CII. *Amoroso risentimento* (loving animosity).

137   *1598*, XCV. *Querela dell'amata* (the beloved's complaint).

138   *1598*, XCVI. *Risposta dell'amante* (the lover's reply). Ellipsis in line 6 supplied from *1737*, p. 155 (*fortuna*). "compass": Donne, "A Valediction: Forbidding Mourning."

Section 10

Introduction: "With one sweet word": Guarini, *Oimè, l'antica fiamma*, #139 in this volume • "I seem to hear": Petrarch, *Canzoniere* 349 • "Love helped me sail": Petrarch, *Canzoniere* 317 • "Like as the waves": Shakespeare, sonnet 60 • "So, even now": Guarini, *Amor, questa crudele*, #145 in this volume.

139   *1598*, CXI. *Recidiva d'amore* (love's relapse).

140   *1598*, CXIII. *Sdegno cangiata* (disdain transformed).

141   *1598*, CXLIII. *Amor gradito* (love welcomed); stanza breaks added.

142   *1598*, LXVII. *Argomento d'amore* (love's proof).

143   *1598*, CVIIII. *Donna accorta* (clever lady).

144   *1598*, XXXVIIII. *Donna che'nvecchia* (the lady who gets older).

145   *1598*, XXXVIII. *Fierezza non invecchiata* (pride doesn't age). Aeneas: Virgil, *The Aeneid*, book 1; my translation.

146   *1598*, C. *Sdegno amoroso* (love's disdain).

147   *1591*, 3.3, pp. 86–87.

148   *1598*, LXVIIII. *Morte soccorsa* (saved from death).

149   *1598*, LXXXVII. *Partita subita* (sudden departure). "brightness fall[s]": Thomas Nashe, "In Time of Pestilence."

150   *1999*, p. 148, as adapted by Monteverdi, *Il terzo libro di madrigali*, 1592, from *Il pastor fido* (1591, 3.1, p. 75); "the Petrarchan antithesis"; Tomlinson, "Guarini and the Epigrammatic Style," 78. "Sweet spring": Herbert, "Virtue," from *The Temple*; "the force": Thomas, "The force that through the green fuse drives the flower"; "not / to me return": Milton: *Paradise Lost*, book 3; "splendor in the grass": Wordsworth: *Ode: Intimations of Immortality from Recollections of Early Childhood*. Tomlinson ("Guarini and the Epigrammatic Style," 78, note 5) discusses the textual difference of this madrigal from *Il pastor fido*.

BIBLIOGRAPHY

Editions of Guarini and Other Works Containing Guarini Texts

Guarini, Giovanni Battista. *Il pastor fido: Tragicomedia pastorale*. London: Giovanni Volfeo, 1591.

Guarini, Giovanni Battista. *Rime del molto illustre signor cavaliere Battista Guarini*. Venice: Gio[vanni] Battista Ciotti, 1598.

Guarini, Giovanni Battista. *Delle opere del cavalier Battista Guarini*. Vol. 2. Verona: Giovanni Alberto Tumermani, 1737.

Guarini, Giovanni Battista. *Opere*. Edited by Luigi Fassò. Turin: Unione tipografico-editrice torinese, 1950.

Guarini, Giovanni Battista. *Opere*. Edited by Marziano Guglielminetti. [Torino]: Unione tipografico-editrice torinese, [1971].

Guarini, Giovanni Battista. *Il pastor fido = The Faithfull Shepherd*; translated by Richard Fanshawe, 1647. Edited with introduction by J. H. Whitfield. Austin: University of Texas Press, 1976.

Nova scelta di rime di diversi eccellenti scrittori dell'età nostra. Benedetto Varoli, Casalmaggiore, 1590.

Rime di diversi celebri poeti dell'età nostra. Bergamo: Comino Ventura, 1587.

Solerti, Angelo, ed. *Le rime di Torquato Tasso*. 4 vols. Bologna: Romagnoli–dall'Acqua, 1898–1902.

Steele, John, ed. *Luca Marenzio: Le opere complete*. Vol. 7. New York: Éditions Renaissantes, 1975.

Stevens, Denis, ed. and trans. *Claudio Monteverdi: Songs and Madrigals*. Lanham, MD: Scarecrow Press, [1999].

Other Works

Bianconi, Lorenzo. *Music in the Seventeenth Century*. Translated by David Bryant. Cambridge: Cambridge University Press, 1987.

Carter, Tim. "New Songs for Old? Guarini and the Monody." In *Guarini, la musica, i musicisti*, edited by Angelo Pompilio, 61–75. Lucca: Libreria musicale italiana, 1997.

Chater, James. "*Il pastor fido* and Music: A Bibliography." In *Guarini, la musica, i musicisti*, edited by Angelo Pompilio, 157–83. Lucca: Libreria musicale italiana, 1997.

Chater, James. "'Un Pasticcio di Madrigaletti'? The Early Musical Fortune of *Il pastor fido.*" In *Guarini, la musica, i musicisti,* edited by Angelo Pompilio, 139–55. Lucca: Libreria musicale italiana, 1997.

Daniele, Antonio. "Torquato Tasso e Battista Guarini." In *Rime e lettere di Battista Guarini: Atti del convegno di studi Padova 5–6 Dicembre 2003,* edited by Bianca Maria Da Rif, 5–24. Allesandria: Edizioni dell'Orso, 2008.

Durante, Elio and Anna Martellotti. "Genesi e sviluppo dei madrigali di Battista Guarini dalla commissione ducale del 1581 alla stampa del 1598." In *Rime e lettere di Battista Guarini: Atti del convegno di studi Padova 5–6 Dicembre 2003,* edited by Bianca Maria Da Rif, 141–72. Allesandria: Edizioni dell'Orso, 2008.

Fabbri, Paolo. *Monteverdi.* Translated by Tim Carter. Cambridge: Cambridge University Press, 1994.

Fenlon, Iain. "Music and Spectacle at the Gonzaga Court, c. 1580–1600." *Proceedings of the Royal Musical Association* 103 (1976–77): 90–105.

Fenlon, Iain. "Preparations for a Princess: Florence 1588–1589." In *Music and Culture in Late Renaissance Italy,* 205–28. Oxford: Oxford University Press, 2002.

Greenblatt, Stephen, ed. *The Norton Anthology of English Literature.* 9th ed. New York: W. W. Norton, 2012.

Haar, James. *Essays on Italian Poetry and Music in the Renaissance, 1350–1600.* Berkeley: University of California Press, 1986.

Hammond, Susan Lewis. *The Madrigal: A Research and Information Guide.* New York: Routledge, 2011.

Hanning, Barbara Russano. "Guarini, (Giovanni) Battista." *Grove Music Online.*

Hartmann, Arnold, Jr. "Battista Guarini and '*Il pastor fido.*'" *Musical Quarterly* 39 (1953): 415–25.

Italian Madrigal Resource Center. ItalianMadrigal.com

Martinelli, Chiara. "La formazione del libro delle *Rime* di Battista Guarini." In *Rime e lettere di Battista Guarini: Atti del convegno di studi Padova 5–6 Dicembre 2003,* edited by Bianca Maria Da Rif, 111–26. Allesandria: Edizioni dell'Orso, 2008.

McClary, Susan. *Desire and Pleasure in Seventeenth-Century Music.* Berkeley: University of California Press, 2012.

Newcomb, Anthony. *The Madrigal at Ferrara, 1579–1597.* 2 vols. Princeton: Princeton University Press, 1980.

Nuovo, Angela. *The Book Trade in the Italian Renaissance.* Translated by Lydia G. Cochran. Leiden: Brill, 2013.

Oldcorn, Anthony. "Lyric Poetry." In *The Cambridge History of Italian Literature,* edited by Peter Brand and Lino Pertile, 251–76. Cambridge: Cambridge University Press, 1997.

Ossi, Massimo. "Between *Madrigale* and *Altro genere di canto*: Elements of Ambiguity in Claudio Monteverdi's Setting of Battista Guarini's *Con che soavità.*" In *Guarini, la musica, i musicisti,* edited by Angelo Pompilio, 12–29. Lucca: Libreria musicale italiana, 1997.

Ossi, Massimo. "Monteverdi, Marenzio, and Batttista Guarini's 'Cruda Amarilli.'" *Music & Letters* 89, no. 3 (2008): 311–36.

[Petrarca, Francesco.] *The Poetry of Petrarch*. Translated by David Young. New York: Farrar, Straus and Giroux, 2004.

Rhodes, Dennis E. "Guarini e l'editore Giovanni Battista Ciotti." In *Rime e lettere di Battista Guarini: Atti del convegno di studi Padova 5–6 Dicembre 2003*, edited by Bianca Maria Da Rif, 337–44. Allesandria: Edizioni dell'Orso, 2008.

Roche, Jerome. *The Madrigal*. London: Hutchinson University Library, 1972.

Rossi, Vittorio. *Battista Guarini ed Il pastor fido*. Torino: Ermanno Loescher, 1886.

Schuetze, George C., ed. "Settings of 'Ardo sì' and Its Related Texts." In *Recent Researches in the Music of the Renaissance*, vols. 78–79, 80–81. Madison: A-R Editions, 1989.

Shakespeare, William. *The Riverside Shakespeare*. Edited by G. Blakemore Evans. Boston: Houghton Mifflin, 1974.

Shephard, Tim. "Voice, Decorum and Seduction in Florigerio's 'Music Lesson.'" *Early Music* 38, no. 3 (August 2010): 361–67.

Tarling, Judy. *The Weapons of Rhetoric: A Guide for Musicians and Audiences*. St. Albans: Corda Music, 2004.

Tomlinson, Gary. "Guarini and the Epigrammatic Style: Books III and IV." In *Monteverdi and the End of the Renaissance*, 73–113. Oxford: Clarendon Press, 1987.

Tomlinson, Gary. "Guarini, Rinuccini, and the Ideal of Musical Speech." In *Monteverdi and the End of the Renaissance*, 114–47. Oxford: Clarendon Press, 1987.

Took, John. "Petrarch." In *The Cambridge History of Italian Literature*, edited by Peter Brand and Lino Pertile, 89–107. Cambridge: Cambridge University Press, 2008.

Trollope, Frances Eleanor, and T. Adolphus Trollope. "Guarini." In *Homes and Haunts of the Italian Poets*, 2.47–98. London: Chapman and Hall, 1881.

Vassalli, Antonio. "Appunti per una storia della scrittura Guariniana: Le rime a stampa prima del 1598." In *Guarini, la musica, i musicisti*, edited by Angelo Pompilio, 3–12. Lucca: Libreria musicale italiana, 1997.

Vassalli, Antonio, and Angelo Pompilio. "Indice delle rime di Battista Guarini poste in musica." In *Guarini, la musica, i musicisti*, edited by Angelo Pompilio, 185–225. Lucca: Libreria musicale italiana, 1997.

Vogel, Emil, ed. *Bibliothek der gedruckten weltlichen Vocalmusik Italiens aus den Jahren 1500–1700*. Hildesheim: G. Olms, 1962.

Vogel, Emil, Alfred Einstein, François Lesure, and Claudio Sartori, eds. *Bibliografia della musica Italiana vocale profana pubblicata dal 1500 al 1700*. Pomezia: Minkoff, 1977.

SUBJECT INDEX

Note: This index covers the discussion given in this book's Introduction and the commentary sections, by page numbers. See also the Thematic Index, which presents topical entries in the translations by madrigal number.

THEMATIC INDEX